TEA ON THE GREAT WALL

An American Girl in War-Torn China

A Memoir

Patricia Luce Chapman

Tea On The Great Wall
By Patricia Luce Chapman

ISBN-13: 978-988-82730-0-3

Editor: Carole Dawson, Richard Marek
Consultant in Chinese Language: H. Christopher Luce
Cover Design: Coco Huang

First printing January 2015

Published by Earnshaw Books Ltd. (Hong Kong)

DEDICATION

To

William McGill Botond

Henry Booker Botond

Thomas Scott Botond

Glenis Marie Adkins Luce

My beloved grandchildren, who inherit an interesting past, and with God's help will each enjoy an eventful and delightful future;

and to the people of China who cared for me, who taught me right from wrong and who shaped me over my first years. With this book, with these tears in my heart, I thank you.

Zhia zhia noong
謝謝儂
xiexie nin
謝謝您

ALSO BY
PATRICIA LUCE CHAPMAN

Honey Come Dance With Me

Survivor's Guide to Grief: be like a starfish

To Bernard Berenson with Love

It is a terrible thing for a people when an enemy settles over the land.
Edna Lee Booker, 1940

China will be a great force for Good or for Evil. Let us pray that the Good prevails.
Elizabeth Root Luce, 1948

Acknowledgments

ALL OF MY CHILDREN have encouraged and have helped me to write this book. I thank my younger daughter, Tina—Krisztina Lee Botond, who year after year pushed and cajoled me to write about my childhood in China for my children and later my grand-children. She also polished much of the text with her editorial skills.

Lila Frances Livingston Luce, my older daughter, spent precious hours reading and editing the draft manuscript, applying her logical and creative mind to the structure of a complex subject, and helping me in other countless ways.

My older son Kit—Henry Christopher Luce--with his wife Tina emailed replies pithy with content in reply to my questions; I shamelessly drew on his profound knowledge of the Mandarin language and Chinese arts and on her Shanghainese. In addition, Kit has been an exceptional line and content editor. Most recently he entered the Chinese and English inserts in the Glossary.

My youngest, Sandy, Andrew István Botond, with his wife Lucina provided the indispensable motivation: their sons, at that time my only grandchildren, the future of my family. I checked with them for their good sense and their judgment throughout the writing.

Then there's my brother John Stauffer Potter, who appears in and out of the story. In my writing of this book and he of his *My First Nine Lives*, we recaptured a large part of the essence of our lives in China, laughing all the way. I miss him; he died on

January 4th just after taking the final draft of his new book, *On the Track of the HMS Monmouth's Galleon.... and Sunken Treasure,* to the printer.

I have drawn freely from observations and writings by my mother, Edna Lee Booker Potter, as well as on her sense of fun, and from my father John Stauffer Potter's carefully collected family scrapbooks and writings.

My joy in having found, through Kit, my beloved friend/ governess in Shanghai, Erika Resek Meier, living in California can't be imagined. Her daughter Pat Meier-Johnson, Pat's husband Russ Johnson, and Erika's son Bob Meier, all have been very helpful; but none more so than Bob's son Ryan Meier, who loved his "Oma," grandmother Erika, as I loved her. I have drawn from his lovely written testament to her as well as on Erika's own memoir. Her photograph is by Russ.

Marlys Calcina remained a dear friend who confirmed details about our daily lives in Shanghai. Her brain was active until her death at 101 in 2007.

Some true friends have come into my life during the writing of this book, most notably my warm, witty and astute editor Richard Marek in New York who keeps up my self-confidence and gives me moments of laughing out loud by myself here at my desk. My publisher-editor Graham Earnshaw in Shanghai amazes me with his gifts as a singer-songwriter. He also has a supremely professional past in the news world with Reuters, and is now publishing quality books. Austin's Carole Dawson taught me to write pop-up rather than flat reportage. New York's Susan Schulman courageously read and guided me through four drafts of this book.

The Rockport Writers Group has collectively and individually given me courage, support, and constructive critique throughout the writing. Also in Rockport I want to mention Reanna Zuniga whose keen eye saved me from many a typo. Conferences held by the Texas Writers League in Austin have provided me with hard information on the business.

Invaluable help has come from Shanghai: Tina Kanagaratnam, CEO of AsiaMedia (and unbelievably my daughter Tina's classmate in Washington, DC;) Tess Johnston and her Old China Hand Research Service; the Shanghai Historic House Association's Wm. Patrick Cranley, also Managing Director of AsiaMedia; Bill Savadove, from a notable old China Hand family and important journalist himself. These led me to Diana Hutchins Angulo, an American, one of Shanghai's great beauties in the 1930's; Diana and we were in Wei Hai Wei at the same time in 1940 and she has been able to provide me with some details of our lives there. They also led me to Desmond Power, a British Canadian who was interned along with my father in the Poo Tung (Pudong) camp, but then also Lunghua (Longhua) and finally Weihsien (Weixian) Japanese prison camps.

I thank brilliant Lance Morrow for his encouragement and constructive suggestions: "The book is good, but could be better." So work, work, work.

At the same time, I thank God for the peace and freedom that I have found in Texas, for the quality of its people, and for the jumping mullets and playing dolphins in the canal in a few steps away in Rockport. Here too the great white egrets and great blue herons squabble over fishing rights.

It is wondrous to live in a place where the birds have the right of way.

Patricia Luce Chapman

Texas

December 2014

NOTES

USAGE

For simplicity and clarity, I refer to place names with the Westernized name current when I grew up. For some, I give the current spelling according to the Pinyin Chinese system, and I have included a glossary of almost all Chinese words listing the Chinese character equivalents.

I retain the rough and tumble Shanghainese for Chinese words used in Shanghai when I was there. For the Chinese words used in North China – Shanhaiguan, Wei Hai Wei, Beijing, I use Mandarin, the language of that region and the official language of China.

"Pidgin English" is the language created, first for business communication and in my time in China also for general communication, between people who don't speak the same languages. It blends English, Chinese, Portuguese, Malay and Indian words into one curious mix. The word "pidgin" itself means "business", and is said to originate from a Chinese word for business.

SHANGHAI'S FOREIGN SECTORS

Treaties between China and Great Britain, then with the United States and eventually a wide spectrum of other nations, created the International Settlement, a semi-autonomous area governed by the "Shanghai Municipal Council." A similar treaty with the French led to the French Concession, south of and adjoining the International Settlement. These areas maintained their own volunteer army corps and police forces. Other Western countries also enjoyed these arrangements. The International Settlement was protected until Pearl Harbor. The French Concession came under the Nazi and Japanese authorities after the Germans conquered Paris.

TREATY PORTS

Several nations established "Treaty Ports" at many of China's prime harbors to enable trade arrangements profitable to all parties. In some cases, these ports became equivalent to colonies. This was so with Wei Hai Wei, where the British Royal Navy summered, and Tsing Tao (Qingdao) and Tientsin (Tianjin), where the Far Eastern Squadron of the Imperial German Navy in China was based until World War One. A map of concession territories in that city shows, on the Eastern bank of the Hai River: Austria-Hungary, Italy, Russia (two separated areas,) and Belgium. On the Western bank: Japan, France, United Kingdom, and Germany. The United States claimed bits of land on both sides. Even after the ports had been ceded back to China in the early 20th century, foreigners continued to enjoy some privileges and protection.

THE UNEQUAL TREATIES

In the 1840s, the issue of China's refusal to open itself to trade with the West came to a head. The West was buying large quantities of goods from China, particularly tea, but China would basically only take silver in return, leading to a severe global shortage of silver. Western traders, particularly the English, found that there was a ready market in China for opium, produced cheaply in their new colonies in India, and so smuggling of opium was ramped up to balance off the tea exports, leading to confrontations and then the first of what was known as the Opium Wars in 1842. China lost both this war and a return match in 1858-60, largely due to the superior military technology and tactics of the British, who then imposed on China the "Unequal Treaties" that forced the country open to foreign traders and missionaries on terms that led to a century and more of anger, frustration and further wars. The foreigners were granted special privileges, including "Extraterritoriality", under which foreign citizens could not be tried by Chinese courts for criminal or civil cases in China, but only by a court of their own nationality. These treaties remained in force until 1943, when they were unilaterally rescinded by the foreign powers, except for Japan, which at that time was occupying most of China, to be defeated only as a result of the atomic bomb attacks by the United States on Hiroshima and Nagasaki in 1945.

THE BOXER REBELLION AND PROTOCOL 1900-1901

The so-called Boxers, who called themselves "The Righteous and Harmonious Fists," were peasants who passionately wanted to drive all foreigners and foreign ideas out of China. They attacked foreigners and particularly Christian missionaries and Chinese Christians, and many thousands of them were killed by the fanatic Boxers across northern China. Among the missionaries forced to escape to save their lives were two of my children's great-grandparents, the Henry Winters Luces, with their baby Harry, my future father-in-law. They fled from their home in Weihsien in Shandong, to sail across the sea to Korea for safety. The Boxers besieged the foreign legation area of Beijing for nearly two months and an army was formed to relieve those trapped. This 'Eight Power Alliance' included five European nations — Britain, France, Italy, Austria-Hungary, and Germany, plus America, Japan, and Russia. About 20,000 Alliance troops poured into China through Shanhaiguan and Tientsin, then marched to Beijing, looting and killing as they went. The Chinese court capitulated, the Empress Dowager escaped to Xi'an and many of the Boxers were executed.

The Boxer Protocol, signed in September, 1901 ended the Rebellion and required the Chinese to make huge reparation payments. Looting by the occupying foreign troops throughout Beijing was rampant. Thus China was, at the beginning of the 20th century, bankrupt, humiliated, and angry.

ACCURACY AND HISTORY

Many records have been misplaced or destroyed during wars, displacement, and destruction since the 1930's in China. It has been hard to find reliable information, and sometimes not possible to find source material. I have chosen, where there are unresolved conflicts, to select what seems to be the most logical. In some cases I have sharpened fuzzy memories. I apologize for any errors.

Dialogue: of course I don't remember exactly what I or anyone else said decades ago. I know from my writings that I was articulate very young, exposed to adult discussions, and was shaped by the discipline of the German school. I have tried to convey the gist of what other people and I were thinking and saying at that time.

PERSONAL.

My life in China was sweet and interesting, despite the daily horror shows of dying bodies lying like trash on the streets, the smells and sounds of war a few miles away, Japanese and Nazi bullies, the abiding sorrow of bidding farewell to people I loved. Not even the memory of the Japanese who grabbed me could daunt my optimism.

OUR HOUSEHOLD

Each one of our servants was important to me, as I believe I was to each of them. It may seem that there was a superfluity of them—but each one was necessary to maintain the lives of the

Shanghailanders. To the Chinese, with their sense of dignity and "face," my parents could not do otherwise. In this environment Father could not mow the grass or stir the soup, as he did later in America; Mother could not set the table or swat the mosquitoes as she did in America. And, we supported many families through our servants' salaries and bonuses. The "face" went two ways. They looked out for us; we looked out for them. There was a protectiveness that flowed back and forth between us.

The key Shanghai servants who moved in and out of the story of my young life include:

Chiao Kwei (巧貴). Amah (阿媽): She was the person dearest to all of us. Together with the Number One Boy, she ran the household. She was cozy and huggable, but would not put up with my naughtiness. She had been with Mother since she arrived in China in 1918. Chiao Kuei traveled to Europe and America to look after us children and learned enough French to parade her linguistic skills to the staff.

Ah Kung (阿公): Number One Boy. He was the equivalent of butler and major domo. Tall, dignified, supremely disciplined and conscious of behavior appropriate to rank, the household would have fallen apart without him. He could have run a Duke's domain.

Ah Ching (阿清): The Chauffeur. A fun-loving, jolly young man, he played with us, carrying us around on his shoulders. He was good at getting other cars, people, camels, buffalos, chickens, out of his way when he was driving us. He also knew how to get things done.

Lin Sing: (林興): Number Two Boy. Young and brash, he answered to lordly Number One. He answered the phone, assisted with setting the table, serving and clearing dishes and plates, brushing away the crumbs, checking to see that the glasses were sparkling. He placed and cleared the table linens.

Cook: I regret that I don't remember his name. Brilliant but temperamental, he did not like Missie or Master to interfere with his kitchen except when consultation was necessary. Luckily, he loved Littie Missie and taught me how to make popovers.

Number Two Cook: He did the laborious kitchen work, peeling vegetables, washing raw food in the disinfectant potassium permanganate, sweeping away messes, and generally helping Cook prepare and present tasty dishes.

Tailor: His name too has fled from memory. He dressed us all and the house, too. With his sewing machine chugging away, he created French dresses and coats copied from magazines, summer slip covers, bridge table covers and duvets; with his sensitive touch he hand-sewed the interior seams and hems of clothing so carefully that not one thread could escape. And he made my dolls' dresses.

Fo Sun: (佛孫). The Main Coolie (苦力): He and the Elder Coolie did everything that no one else wanted to do. He also travelled with us to our summer vacations in the north. The coolies laid the fires and cleaned away the ashes; they washed the dogs, cleaned the bathrooms, carried out the trash and garbage and washed and waxed the floors. They took care of summer chores such as spreading books and shoes out in the sun for a full day to prevent mold from forming on them.

Elder Coolie: He instructed Fo Sun in skills required for the different tasks, but he was hunched over with age and no longer strong enough to do much on his own. I believe my parents kept him on as a courtesy, out of respect for his age and past service.

Sew Sew Amah Mary: She came in to do occasional sewing when Tailor was overworked.

Glowing Pearl (光明珠): The daughter of Sew Sew Amah Mary and who helped her occasionally.

Gardener: He tended to the flowerbeds in our garden as well as to fertilizing and keeping the lawn free of weeds. He saw to flower arrangements in the house.

Number Two Gardener: He assisted the Gardener.

Watchman: He planted our vegetables and protected our vegetable garden from intruders.

Mlle. Matrushka: Governess from 1932-1934. I liked her. Brother John adored her.

Frau Neisser: Governess from 1934-1935. We hated her.

Frau Zinner: Governess from 1936-7. We hated her.

Fräulein Erika: Governess from 1938-1940. We loved her.

Contents

I

JAPANESE INVADE SHANGHAI.

SPRING 1932. AGE FIVE

LIFE CAN FLIP *upside down with the tiniest glance. Mine just did.*

I have registered at the Hyatt in Austin to attend the Writers'
League of Texas Conference on Agents. Walking through the lobby
towards the banks of elevators I notice displays of photographs of Hyatt
hotels around the world. I look casually over at them. One shows a
"Grand Hyatt" in a sleek, unusually tall building in a developed area
by a river. I put down my bags and stop to look at it, thinking that it
would be fun to visit one day. What a view from the top of the building!
A closer look: the sign reads, "Grand Hyatt Shanghai (Pudong)."

"Impossible!" I don't believe it. "They must have made a mistake
on the sign." I study the information given about the hotel. Shocked, I
mutter, "It can't be."

Suddenly weak, I back slowly, carefully, onto the edge of a bench
and try to breathe calmly. I peek over at the display again. Could I have
misread the location? The elegant building looks like New York, Dubai,
Tokyo. It cannot be in Shanghai and certainly not in the filthiest part
of the city, Poo Tung.

But still the sign says Pudong and still the hotel soars sparkling
above what is clearly a thriving business district.

I knew Poo Tung, Pudong now I guess, when I was a little girl.

Shadowy memories slowly snake up out of that amorphous area of the soul where the most private joys and the deepest hurts are preserved. Now behind my eyes I see the swamps and tenements and lumberyards, see the warehouses condemned as unfit for coolies of the British American Tobacco Company. That's where the Japanese imprisoned my father in World War II. Unconsciously I wrinkle my nose, sensing in memory the stench of decay. Poo Tung was simply a dreadful place.

Another deep breath. My brain begins to function again. I know that the photograph is real. The hotel is real, in a Pudong that I don't know, and a Shanghai radically different from my home town. What else had happened when I wasn't watching? What is still there of my former world?

I stand up, gather my bags, and go up to my room. My computer plugged in, I search for images of Shanghai while texting my friend Mike Runde, President of the Dulles World Trade Center, and a frequent business visitor to Shanghai.

"Mike," I write, "Is it true that there is a Grand Hyatt in Shanghai?"

"Yes, and it's beautiful," he texts back. He tells me that the whole area is the financial and trade district of Shanghai.

I had avoided thinking about China after my arrival as a 14–year-old refugee in New York in March, 1941. My China life had no relevance to my life in America, and I didn't want to know the later China that I caught from time to time on television. When President Nixon visited in February 1972, the TV showed Chinese sweeping steps near the Forbidden City area like robots in unison. In unison! Where was the creativity and spontaneous fun that I had known? And the Red Ballet – I hated the rigidity and false westernization of the dancers. My China had riotously costumed actors who stamped, raged, cooed, across the stage. I had been taught dance by one of its stars.

The new China seemed foreign and unwelcoming to me. Now, suddenly, that towering Hyatt had pierced through the barriers I had built, and the images of the modern Shanghai dissolved into the

Shanghai that had shaped me. A vivid memory unexpectedly blossomed there in that hotel room, and I was home again, in 1932 a five-year-old American girl.

I couldn't help wriggling around on my chair, impatient for my governess to finish her lunch. The Number Two, Lin Sing, had just served one of my favorite desserts, vanilla ice cream with crackling chocolate sauce, and I had devoured it. Now I was anxious to escape to play with my teddy bears. But Mademoiselle Matrushka was still lingering over her dish, savoring each spoonful. Her long, wavy blonde hair fell almost into the dish as she spooned up the ice cream.

We were having our tiffin, lunch, on the verandah. I especially loved this room for the many glass windows. It was bright even on rainy days; and I could see our garden with its beautiful flowers. A wicker swinging sofa with large chintz pillows was near the wall, and some days, when there was an adult to push it, I could swing on it. My own legs were too short to get it moving.

I was impatient to leave."May I please be excused?"

Before she could answer, my father came in the front door. He never came home at lunch time, and I wondered why he was home so early. After he removed his heavy coat and gloves and put down his papers, he saw me on the verandah. He was wearing an unfamiliar American sort of Boy Scout hat that he took off and placed on a side table.

"Hi. Daddy!" I shouted, getting up and jumping over to him.

"Patty, are you enjoying your tiffin? Yes, I see you are." After wiping some chocolate from the corner of my mouth, he gave me a little kiss. He stood still for a minute, as though he were considering us. I was surprised to see him wearing a strange kind of clothing, like the soldiers I had seen in picture books.

"Daddy, you've changed your clothes!" I said.

3

Father looked scrumptious in a khaki uniform of American cavalry jodhpurs and jacket. He smiled at my open-eyed admiration, then gave me a somewhat bemused hug in acknowledgment of his wearing what he considered to be a fancy dress costume.

I touched the shiny objects nestled in a long band diagonally across his chest."My goodness, what are these things?"

"They're bullets." He looked down at the bandolier that pressed down into the khaki jacket."I've joined a group of businessmen here called the American Shanghai Volunteer Corps. We are sort of soldiers. There's some trouble in the city with the Japs, and our job is to protect you and other Americans from them." I heard people talk about "Japs" for Japanese, the same way that they spoke of "Yanks" for Americans,"Brits" for people from England, and "Frenchies" for people from France.

Lin Sing brought a chair for my father, then some coffee. We sat down, and again he was silent for a moment. Then he turned to Matrushka, who had been listening to this wide-eyed. She had seen the pistol at his belt.

"Mademoiselle," he said,"there has been an invasion of Shanghai by the Japanese Army."

"Oh my God!" she cried."*Bozhe moi!*"

"I don't mean to frighten you, but to inform and prepare you. No one knows what will happen in the next months. I must ask you to be particularly careful in going about the city. While they are north in Chapei (Zhabei) now, we can't be sure they won't come into the International Settlement and French Concession. Try not to go out without a male escort and, for now, stay away from the Chinese parts of the city. You are an attractive young woman and there will be many rough drunken Japanese soldiers in the streets."

"*Da, da, spasibo!* Thank you Mr. Potter! I will be especially careful with Patty, and with my own safety too." Her blue eyes under eyebrows that had been plucked into an exaggerated arched line gave her a constantly surprised look. But now they filled with tears.

I didn't know what an invasion was, but it distressed me that Matrushka was unhappy. I tried to console her the way my parents consoled me. Patting her hand I said, "It'll be all right, don't you fret." She smiled down at me.

Father sipped his coffee "You'll be interested to know that among the Volunteers there's a White Russian Company. Some friends of yours may be among them. There's also a British Company with armored cars and, imagine, kilted Scottish troops with bagpipes! The Volunteers also include French, German, Austro-Hungarian, even Jewish and Filipino Companies."

"What are you Volunteers supposed to do, Daddy?" I asked.

"Our job is to guard the entries to the International Settlement and the French Concession. We are prepared to fight to keep the Japanese out and to keep our homes safe."

Matrushka wiped her eyes with her napkin and grew calmer.

"Spasibo, thank you, Monsieur Potter, for telling me," she said quietly. "It is a shock to think that, once again, we Russian refugees are in danger. We thought we were safe here. Oh my God." Her voice trembled. She reached down to pat my hair. "You may be sure that I will protect Patty with my life." I held her hand tightly, now a bit frightened.

"Thank you. Now I have to make some preparations. It's inconvenient to have our bridge party this afternoon, but I can't cancel it. Lin Sing," he asked the Number Two standing silently by the door, "will you please ask Ah Kung to come in?"

The Number One Boy, as Chinese butlers were called, appeared. He usually wore a long white tunic dressed with a gray silk vest. His soft flat slippers didn't make a sound. Ah

Kung ran the household and managed the service of meals with magisterial, and even inspired, proficiency. He was tall, dignified. I often felt that he somewhat disapproved of me because I was playful and sometimes rebellious. Maybe it was because I was just a useless girl. "Yes Mister Potter?"

"Missie will be back from her tiffin party soon. As you know our bridge guests will arrive at three o'clock and of course you, Lin Sing, and Cook know what to do. Be sure to have the coolies help set up the tables and chairs, and keep the dog away."

"Yes Mister Potter. My can do." He was speaking 'Pidgin English,' the language that grew from several languages initially to enable foreigners and Chinese to trade and negotiate with each other. A mix of Portuguese, Indian, English, and Chinese, Pidgin evolved into the *lingua franca* in communications between Chinese and all foreigners in every area.

"Oh, and please use the new bridge table covers that Tailor made."

"Yes, Mister Potter."

"One more thing, Ah Kung. Please ask the whole staff to come up to my study after our guests leave so that we can discuss what we could do if the Japanese come into the international settlements. I also need to make sure that the families of each one of you are as safe as we can make them. I'm worried about what may lie ahead for us all."

"Thank you, Mister Potter." Ah Kung excused himself.

The three of us left the table and went upstairs to our respective rooms. I raced up to mine on the third floor, hurrying because I had to prepare my teddy bear family for a Japanese invasion.

My teddy bears, my best friends, lived on a shelf in my bedroom. I wasn't interested in dolls, they didn't seem to have much personality. My Shirley Temple doll wasn't as much fun as the girl in the movies, and my Patsy doll bored me too. I refused to answer to the name of Patsy as short for Patricia.

Each of my bears had grand adventures even while living in their shelf world. It was not a perfect home for them, there were no tables or lamps, but I used bits of leftover objects that I found around the house for furniture. The tiniest bear, Edgar, about 1 ½ inches high, was purple; then came Precious, the little white bear; then the yellow Little Oatmeal Boy, followed by other bears of various sizes and colors up to about four inches. I had a problem with their clothing, as I couldn't sew or knit very well yet. Tailor, who worked in the room next to mine, indulged me by making little dresses and jackets for them out of bits of leftover silk and flannel.

I decided that the boy bears had to look more like soldiers, so I tied diagonal ribbons across their chests for bandoliers, and pasted bits of cloth on their heads for hats. I looked around downstairs for burned-out matches in ashtrays to use for guns, but found that our darned coolie Fo Sun had been too quick at cleaning up. No burned matches. Well, I knew I'd find some later if I were quick.

Matrushka came in to tell me it was time for my nap. She laughed on seeing the new bear uniforms, took my hands, and swaying together she led me into singing a French song that she had taught me months earlier:

Malbrough s'en va-t-en guerre
Mironton ton ton mirontaine
Malbrough s'en va-t-en guerre
Ne sait quand reviendra.

(Marlborough goes off to war, Mironton Mironton Mirontaine, no one knows when he'll come back" and mimicking the sound of cannons.)

But now I was getting sleepy, and jumped quickly under my mosquito net, one of my bears with me. I couldn't help looking up at the odious girly pink ruffles around the canopy of my four-poster bed. The matching pink ruffled cover lay over me. The color surrounded my world. The play table and chairs in the room were pink. There was a pink child-size piano in one corner room and a pink desk. Guess what color the walls were.

I hated the color pink. Why couldn't Mother understand that? she had everything in my bedroom painted pink, poo-pooing my objections. She always wanted things her way and paid no attention to what I wanted. Why couldn't she understand that I was not a pink girl! I was an adventurer! But now I was sleepy, stopped pretending that I was yelling at my mother, and drifted to sleep.

I woke when I heard Mother downstairs checking on the preparations for the afternoon. A bridge party was a serious event that took over the entire household.

I sneaked down to look at the rooms. Set up in the living room and verandah were four bridge tables of four players each and additional places for "dummies," observers or spouses. Tailor had made special monogrammed bridge covers for the tables. The presentation included new, initialed playing cards. New pencils and record-keeping pads were precisely set at each place.

They all smoked cigarettes. So at every table was also placed an ashtray made of a silver tael, or "shoe", shaped like high-ranking Mandarin official's shoe, which was a measure of silver. My father would rest his cigarette in the curve of the "shoe", the ash falling into the surrounding silver dish.

Slender porcelain or silver vases of tall flowers and greens were always placed on small tables; larger vases displayed orchids and gingers. Today, our upholstered chairs were placed against the walls to make room for the bridge tables and side chairs. Bright occasional Oriental rugs lay on the parquet floors.

I ran back upstairs as I heard the guests' cars arriving. From my room I could hear their voices greeting my parents. Their tone was somber; they weren't laughing as the guests usually did.

I heard an English woman exclaiming, "Oh Edna Lee, what shall we do! My dear, they are destroying Chapei! You are a journalist, a war correspondent, you must know what's going on better than I do."

Another woman's voice came in, "And how do we know that they will honor our international treaties. It makes me sick to think of Japanese all over our beautiful French Concession. Imagine, Japanese tanks might enter our boulevards."

A man's voice: "Francine, *cherie, calme toi*. We are protected by our French Volunteer Corps. It will go all right."

Father echoed his words when a German couple entered with similar worries.

Matrushka came up to play cards and Concentration with me, and do a little work on my French and German lessons. My brother Johnny was away for the day with some of his friends. He and I weren't allowed anywhere near the bridge players. Sometimes we heard the arguments of couples at the tables when one was complaining about the other's error. I learned the word "trump" when one played a trump card at the wrong time. But this afternoon the group was restrained, carefully polite.

A few hours later, I could tell by the sounds that the party was breaking up. The rattling and tinkling meant that Ah Kung was serving iced tea or cocktails while Number Two was offering platters of *sakuski* and other hors d'oeuvres.

Then Lin Sing walked up to my room to tell me that Missie would like Littie Missie to come down to greet the guests. Lin

9

Sing had numerous household tasks such as spraying the rooms with "Flit" and swatting mosquitoes, in addition to helping Ah Kung at meals and with the dishes. He was sassy and fun-loving. I was always glad to see his square smiling face, his short hair sticking up like porcupine bristles.

Matrushka quickly slipped a fresh dress on me, brushed my hair back into detested floppy curls."Be sure that you walk down the stairs, do not slide," she cautioned."And remember to act like a little lady like your Mama tells you." I wanted to make a face at her but decided that this wasn't a good time to be naughty.

So, dutifully, I walked down the two flights of stairs and into the living room. Mother introduced me to the different guests. The Hungarian architect Laszlo Hudec who had, with my father, designed our house; Count "Cal" Calcina and Auntie Marlys, an Italian-American couple. Charles Ferguson and Isabel; Julius and Florence Reese were Americans. I had been taught to bob into a curtsey and say "Bon jour," to the French guests, "Guten Abend" to the Germans,"Buona sera" to the Italians. That was as many "good evenings" as I could manage.

My father took my arm and walked me over to meet others, saying that these were some of his real estate and banking business associates.

"Patty, may I introduce you to Judge and Mrs. Cornell Franklin, and to Mr. and Mrs. Peter Lin of the Bank of China, he said. Then he introduced me to others, but I didn't learn their names.

My favorite of my mother's friends was Auntie Marlys, the most beautiful woman in the world. When I curtsied to her, this tall, slender lady with glowing dark eyes and hair, thanked me and said, her voice precise, every consonant accented: "You curtsey very nicely, Patty. When you are a few years older I'll teach you how to make a Court Curtsey."

"What is that, Auntie Marlys?"

"That is how you will curtsey to the Queen of England when you are presented to her at the Court of St. James in London. It's a very special curtsey, very hard. You'll find that it makes you feel beautiful — if you don't fall down," she added, laughing.

I was ecstatic at the thought, praying she wouldn't forget me while I was growing up. I managed to pop a couple of the *sakuski* into my mouth. Yummy. They were delicate and flaky and delicious. They reminded me that I had had no tea or dinner.

Mother excused me. I gave a general curtsey to everyone, said "Good night," and headed into the pantry and on into our kitchen where Cook and Learn Pidgin Cook were preparing a simple supper.

It was my dinner time and I was hungry. Lin Sing and Ah Kung were still occupied with food and drinks for the last guests. Cook did not like being disturbed in the kitchen and, on seeing me there, growled:

"Littie Missie, what you do here? You go you Mama." This temperamental man wouldn't let anyone into his kitchen except for my mother when absolutely necessary, and me. Everyone else was scared of him. He would bellow at uninvited intruders like a War Lord, almost shaking the crystal glasses on the shelves in the pantry with his enraged roar. Once I saw him wave his serrated carving knife in the air for emphasis.

But he didn't scare me. I knew I made him laugh. This evening I ventured into the Chinese kitchen adjoining our large one, wrapped my arms as far around his waist as they would go, smiled up at him, and said "Please? Dinner?" He grinned, his smile puffing out his broad face, and filled a plate with *deh tzao veh* (dan chaofan, fried rice with bits of pork and peas and egg), some Chinese greens, and *jiaw dze* (jiaozi, stuffed dumplings), setting it on the little table beside the fat round wood-burning stove in the corner. He pulled out a stool for me.

"*Zhia zhia noong!*" I thanked him. And in the comfort of the tiny warm kitchen I gobbled down the food. Well, I guess I didn't "gobble" as it's hard to gobble down food with chopsticks. I had learned to use chopsticks from the day I could hold them."Just keep the bottom chopstick firmly in the crook of your thumb and ring finger," Mother had taught me."The upper chopstick does the work and is moved up and down by the index, middle fingers and thumb."

That evening I guess I shoveled the food into my mouth, sprinkling the environment with grains of rice that wouldn't stay put. Giggling, I cried out "Oopsy daisy!" The Chinese laughed with me.

I didn't want to leave the Chinese kitchen with its rich fragrances and servants cracking jokes in Chinese; these were my friends. But I finally went upstairs to my room using the servants' back stairs.

Lin Sing had already sprayed the room against mosquitoes and set the *punka* in motion. This was a long thin board hanging from the ceiling, with cords leading to my bed. It swayed back and forth in a slow motion that cooled the air when someone pulled the cords and helped chase away mosquitoes. In the hot humid summer in Shanghai, it helped us get to sleep.

Matrushka had disappeared into her world down on the second floor; now it was our Amah who came in to help me get to bed. Johnny had come home, having sneaked up the back stairs. The door to his room across from mine on the third floor was closed. I knew he was plotting some horror to inflict on me.

Amah brushed my hair, put me in a nightie, tucked me in bed, and, sitting at the end of my bed, began to tell me a story. I loved her stories about the olden days in China, about men who turned into tigers, and fish that multiplied like flowers in the fields.

Father came up just then to kiss me goodnight as usual. Tonight he also unlocked and entered a little room adjacent to my room where a large storeroom held supplies. Amah retreated to her room next door and I crawled carefully from under the mosquito net to join him.

"What are you doing, Daddy? It's nighttime now!"

"Checking to be sure that our shelves of supplies are full. It's the first chance I've had since coming home," he said. He inspected the shelves: bottles of liqueurs and alcohol, cans of New Zealand butter, cans of fruits and vegetables, jugs of water. There were preserves, meat, fish, evaporated milk and cartons of KLIM, a white powder transformed by boiled water into a truly awful liquid. I had learned that milk spelled backward did not create milk.

"Why are these things up here and not in the pantry?"

"This is a sort of secret emergency storage hiding place, Patty. With the war going on around us, we have to be ready for anything." He pointed to a different area of the storeroom.

"Here are flashlights, batteries and light bulbs, oil lamps and oil for them, wooden matches, bandages and medicines, extra "Flit" to control the mosquitoes. Even some New Skin," he remarked, smiling at me. He knew how much I hated that exceedingly painful ointment.

"We need these lamps and flashlights as well as the food, in case the power goes out and we are without electricity. The medicines are also for emergencies."

He completed his inspection, picked me up, and tucked me back in bed. We said goodnight and exchanged hugs. I went to sleep thinking that my father was the world's most wonderful man.

Slowly I return to the present, with a deep sense of peace, of wonder. So

the lady of today, decades later, can still evoke the little girl of long ago.
I can find myself in that little girl. I don't seem to have changed much.
It is a curious feeling to realize that I am still attached to myself.

My computer screen meanwhile has gone to sleep; I wake it and
search for maps. I want to find my home. Irritated and frustrated I find
that all street names are in Chinese. Well, of course, why wouldn't they
be. But they were in English or French when I was there. Now I locate
The Bund by the curve in Whang Poo River (Huangpu River) *and*
from there trace the route down Nanking Road (Nanjing Lu), *then*
on to Great Western Road (Da Xi Lu). *Slowly crossing previously*
unknown over- and under-passes I find my way to the area of what
had been Columbia Circle in the western end of the International
Settlement. My finger briefly caresses the screen.

"There's my home," I whisper.

II

1932. THE MORTAR SHELLING
DISRUPTS THE HOUSEHOLD. AGE FIVE

I DON'T WANT TO leave the screen, so I check out the program for the Conference. No dinner plans, good. I order a sandwich, indifferent to food. My interest, my obsession rather, lives in that computer. I move my finger on the map to northeast Shanghai – to Chapei (Zhabei), enlarge it, and remember the fright that I felt with the repeated rounds of ear-shattering bombing that woke me every morning for several months. Remembering how scared I was, and how bravely I tried to meet the fear.

I woke to an unfamiliar sound: thump-thump-thump, pause, thump-thump, continuing without a break. This didn't sound good. I ran across the hall to Johnny's room, and found him sitting up in his bed with a bewildered look in his eyes.

"Johnny, what's happening?" Two years older, my brother seemed always to know what was going on in our lives.

"It sounds sort-of like I think mortars sound. Maybe the Japs are shelling the Chinese army?" Johnny suggested.

"What's a mortar?"

"It's some kind of very big gun."

Jim, our English setter, had buried his head under Johnny's blankets, and was whining hesitantly.

We went to my room where a large window faced north

toward Chapei, the area under attack. This was an immense part of the city where the handcraft shops and artisans sold their wares. Mother sometimes took me shopping there. Opening the window, the noise became louder. I quickly shut it.

"Oh my goodness!" I whispered."I'm scared. What are we supposed to do? The noise hurts my head!"

"Patty, I don't know. I think we need to see what Daddy says."

Amah had come in from her room that was between ours."Good morning, Littie Master, Littie Missie. My think so Jap man make big noise then soon go way. No fear. Now you dress for school."

I ran over to my Mammy Doll and sank into her soft body for comfort and courage. She was a stuffed cotton doll taller than I, and very dear to me. Near the entrance to my room she sat with her fluffy stuffed legs spread inviting me to sit and cuddle, her arms wide open to pull around myself. In the softness of her lap I felt safety when life was awful. Mammy wore a bright checkered apron and a white cap over her black sprawly curls and there was a great red-lipped smile on her face. Mother told me that my Mammy was like the real life Mammy,"Aunt Mahaley," that she had had as a little girl in America.

I loved the Mammy Doll. She wasn't a real doll to me, she was my comforter."Ohhh," I whimpered, burying my head in her cozy stuffed bosom."I'm scared, Mammy, I don't like the noise!" Slowly my heart began to settle down, and I felt less afraid.

Amah, allowing me no nonsense, pulled me up to my feet, and helped me into the uniform required by the *Kaiser Wilhelm Schule* that I attended: a dark blue plaid skirt and dark blue jacket over long dark blue stockings, and a dark blue hat with white trim. She quickly brushed my curls into those ringlets that I loathed and that always bounced in my face when I ran, and sent me downstairs for breakfast.

Uniting the floors was a beautiful staircase with a smooth banister unbroken by hard angles; it curved in an easy arc between the floors. Just because I was still so upset I jumped up onto the banister knowing that I shouldn't and, whooping "like a banshee" as mother called it, slid down to the second and then to the first floor, landing in a pile on the bottom laughing wildly.

I was met by a scowling Matrushka, who chastised me for my bad behavior.

Everyone was disturbed this morning because of the shelling. The house seemed to vibrate with each round. I now knew that the thumping was the sound of mortars and that they blew up houses and people.

This horrified me. What was happening to the people being bombed? A picture of bits and pieces of people flying around flashed through my mind. Would they be like my doll when my darned brother shot it with his BB gun? The thought made me feel like throwing up."Ooooh, make them stop it!" I yelled."I don't like it!"

But the shelling continued, round after round. After a perfunctory breakfast Johnny went off on his bike; he attended the Shanghai American School, not too far away on Avenue Pétain in the French Concession. Chauffeur Ah Ching escorted Matrushka and me to Father's Studebaker, and we headed off to my school in the midtown International Settlement. Both schools were a good distance away from the area under bombardment.

I always felt safe with Ah Ching. He was a hugely powerful man, with a jolly disposition. He loved us children, sometimes carrying us around on his shoulders, all of us laughing uproariously. His size was so terrifying that one gesture from him would scare away any potential evil-doer.

The thump-thumping had stopped when we got back home to our house in Columbia Circle, an American residential area in the western part of the International Settlement. This and the French Concession were the two areas of Shanghai protected from the Japanese by international treaties.

I was glad to go out to the garden to play. It wasn't too cold outside. Today there wasn't any homework, we had been sent home early as the Germans too needed time to consider what would happen with the Japanese attacks on Shanghai. Matrushka, Johnny and I were served tea in the little summer house by the fish pond.

Our garden of about an acre was surrounded by a ten-foot-high bamboo fence. In the spring and summer, English flowerbeds against the fences held snapdragons. Gardener had taught me how to snap them open; it was fun. I liked to sniff the perfume of the delicate sweet peas, and help by twining them further up their trellises. In hot weather there were chrysanthemums, dahlias and peonies, good luck flowers in China, and beds of smaller flowers.

Willow trees framed the little summer house and the goldfish pond in the center of the garden. This was where I did much of my schoolwork in warm weather. Sometimes I felt sorry for Matrushka, who had to sit there watching the fish swim around while I recited irregular verbs in French or practiced ancient German writing in a lined orange notebook. I liked learning the German writing because it gave me a secret language that my brother couldn't read. Some days Matrushka helped me read *Monsieur et Madame* that taught the genders of French nouns.

Nearby was a grotto built of uneven rocks that I used to walk through but avoided now, because one day a bee had stung me in there and it had really hurt. Beside a rose arbor we had a swing set and a Jungle Jim to swing on and climb. When I practiced turning cartwheels in the garden and jumped shrieking with laughter into piles of newly-mown grass, our Gardener, who had just raked the piles together, wailed *Ai-yah, ai-yah!* Alas!

"Would you like to swing, Patty?" asked Matrushka.

"Oh, yes, only not too high!" I exclaimed."I'm afraid of going around in a circle if I go too high and then I would fall down go boom!"

"Sis, stop talking baby talk." Johnny yelled at me. I made a face at him.

Johnny began tossing a ball to Jim, who loved chasing after it. Once in mid-jump he veered and started chasing Johnny instead, which made us all laugh. Jim had long flowing white hair with black patches. I loved watching him move; he was so graceful that sometimes he seemed to be dancing.

Soon it was time to come in and wash up before dinner. But on my way up, the phone on the second floor landing rang. Lin Sing answered, his raucous voice penetrating every corner of the house.

"*Waah, noong sa ning ah?*" he said."Who you? You wanchee talkee Missie Matrushka? One minute please." He called Matrushka to the phone.

There followed a long frantic conversation in Russian with many exclamations. I was very interested in this, and plopped down on a stair waiting to learn what was going on. Finally the conversation ended. Matrushka walked up to my Father's study on the second floor to speak to my parents. I followed her.

"Mr. Potter, Mrs. Potter," she said,"I am so worried about my friends and family with the Japanese soldiers. They worry about what to do."

"Of course," Mother said.

"They live in bad part of Shanghai, in Hong Kew (Hongkou), where too many Russian refugees live. No protection from Japanese like here in International Settlement. So please, is it possible for me to have a few days to be with my Russian friends and dear ones during difficult time? We need to decide what to do about the Japanese invasion, to think about our future, if we can stay here or if go some other city.

"Of course, Matrushka, of course," Father said."But to reassure you a little, I believe that you are safe. I believe that the Japs will, for now, leave Hong Kew alone and focus on Chapei and their conquests in North China."

Matrushka was still worried."We Russians have had so much pain and hardship escaping from the Russian government after our beloved Tsar and his beautiful children were killed. It is terrible to think of start life again in some other country." Mother had told me that Matrushka had been from an aristocratic family, like the princes and princesses in my picture books, and had to run for their lives on trains and boats and friends' cars to get to safety in Shanghai. Her perfect French and tolerable English, Mother told me, had come from her early education in St. Petersburg.

"You may leave right after dinner, if you wish." My parents agreed to let her move back to her friends' home for a few days without losing her job looking after me. Ah Ching would drive her there after dinner.

Johnny and I usually sat down at the formal dining room table for dinner with Mother and Father. Our parents required us to dress properly: my brother in jacket and tie, and me in a pretty dress with my Shirley Temple curls and ribbon all in place. They tried to teach us table manners: if we wanted to leave the table before they were ready, we had to ask politely in French,"*Puis-je quitter la table?*" and we could not leave until we were excused. Another instruction: "*On ne parle pas avec la bouche pleine.*" We tried not to talk with our mouths full anyway as it looked awful when someone else did

Ah Kung served our dinners, assisted by Lin Sing. This

evening I began fiddling with the delicate filigrée silver and glass coaster under my water glass; a glance from Mother, and I stopped. Candles glowed in slim silver holders, a centerpiece of fresh flowers brightened the table. I loved the way butter was served: sometimes Lin Sing in the kitchen used two rough paddles, like ping pong paddles, to roll pats of butter into balls to be placed on our bread and butter dishes. Tonight he had sliced thin slabs into delicious curls of butter. Slices of bread were served with the crust cut off.

As I munched into a slice of bread, Mother said sharply,"Patty, you know you must break the bread before eating it. Please break your bread. Don't forget that."

She softened."In this way you show respect for the bread broken at the Last Supper. For the same reason we serve fish on Fridays."

I hoped she wasn't going to start telling me again to think about the starving Armenians if I didn't clean my plate. Those were apparently very hungry people who lived far away. But I knew that tonight, because I was worrying about what was happening to people with the bombs and mortars and bandoliers, I wasn't watching my table manners. I picked up some food on my plate with my finger because I couldn't work the fork properly. Mother scolded me again.

"You are eating like an Igorot!" Her most horrible insult. I had heard this enough to find out that the Igorots were a remote Philippine tribe of people with bad table manners.

"Edna Lee," Father said gently,"I believe she is upset about the mortars and the Japanese. And so are you, and Johnny, and I."

She looked surprised."Yes, of course, John, You're right. Patty, I'm sorry I spoke so sharply. We're all on edge. And I want to get out there to cover the story, there's a huge story out there waiting for me to write it, and I can't get there, and that's making me cross."

After that, dinner continued quietly. My father remarked on the Volunteers; Mother reported what she had heard about Chapei.

"Dallas Franklin told me that tens of thousands of Japanese are moving into the bombed areas," she said."Fortunately the parts of the city where the artisans live and work haven't yet been destroyed. It makes me sick to think of what those Japs are doing to the Chinese."

"I heard that the Chinese soldiers are fighting bravely," Father said,"but there's not much they can do against bombs falling from the sky. Large chunks of Chapei are being destroyed."

After dinner Mother talked quietly to Matrushka, then she went up to pack her bag."Please telephone me if you have any problems," Mother said. Matrushka thanked her and said goodbye to all of us. Both Johnny and I hugged her. Johnny, I knew, really liked hugging her and held on as long as he could. I tried to cheer her up, and myself too."It'll be all right, Matrushka. It'll be all right." Then she went out the door, Ah Ching carrying her bags.

We all stood around uneasily."Our gloominess isn't helping the Chinese. How about some music?" Mother said.

Father walked over to the piano in a nook near the stairs."You're right. Come here, Patty, let's have some music." He sat on the piano bench and held me on his lap."Let me hear your exercises," he said.

Oh dear. I hadn't thought about playing my scales because of all the excitement."I'm sorry, Daddy, I forgot." I started crying. I felt awful. Everything I did was wrong today. Music was very important to my father, and I had disappointed him.

"Well, well, now what's this? No need to cry, my little

sweetheart. It won't matter in 100 years, now will it! Let's just see what we can do now with what we've got." He took out his handkerchief and patted my eyes gently. My sobbing and sort-of hiccupping lessened as he placed my fingers on the keys, then tried to help them reach an octave.

"My hands have to grow bigger, Daddy! I can't do it!" I wailed.

"It's all right, Patty, don't fret. Your hands will grow. I remember when my sister Frances was learning the scales; her hands were small, too. But now she plays the organ in the church. Well, we'll see what we can do with little hands."

Dutifully I played the scales with both hands, tucking my thumb under the other fingers on the fourth note going up, and the opposite going the other way.

"That's good," he said. "Each time you play, your fingers learn better to be at ease on the keys."

It was now Johnny's turn. "Johnny, have you also been too busy to practice?"

Johnny got out his bow and two-stringed Chinese *erhu* and began squeaking horribly atonal sounds. He was hilarious playing the five-tone Chinese scale with lots of exaggerated Chinese bowing and facial expressions.

Mother came over. "Johnny, that sounds dreadful!" she laughed. I joined the fun by creating some fearsome "Chinese" opera dances to accompany Johnny's *erhu*, singing women's parts in an artificially high sing-song voice any sequence of Shanghainese sounds that I'd picked up. My voice went from the highest note that I could reach in sing-song down to threatening low grunts for the fierce War Lords. I stamped my feet, waved my arms around, and made hideous faces.

It was time for me to go up to bed. I stopped first in the large cloak room/powder room near the piano. I liked the room; it was pretty, with mirrors against ivory-colored walls decorated with silver flowers. Beside the sink Mother kept a bowl with delicate paper envelopes of French face powder called *papier poudre* scented with the perfume *"Quelques Fleurs,"* and when I opened the door, the fragrance surrounded me.

I wandered on into the pantry beyond that to see if anything was going on and to avoid going up to bed

"What thing, Littie Missie?" Lin Sing greeted me. He was putting away the dinner dishes, helped by Learn Pidgin Cook.

"No thing, just come to see what thing happen this side." I held up one of the dishes to him to put away, but I could tell that he was afraid I would drop it. He said something in Chinese and Chiao Kuei bustled out from the kitchen. She and Cook had been having a loud argument. I could understand the words *"Bu hao"* that she shouted back into the Chinese kitchen."Very bad." Then I heard Cook's voice clearly say *"Hao!"* (Good) in his long angry response.

"Cook makee too muchee walla walla, too muchee talk." she said as she came up to me."Now, Littie Missie, now I take you to upstairs, get ready for go bed." She took my hand and led me gently but firmly out of the pantry.

Amah managed us children with a calm strength. She filled in when the governess was absent, provided nursing when we were sick, scolded us when we didn't behave, taught us proper Chinese behavior, looked after my clothes, and did some maid's work with beds and laundry. It was her calm firmness that enabled the household to function smoothly. Amah was as much a part of my life as my brother and my parents.

We climbed up the stairs to my room. She knew that I was unsettled and upset."Littie Missie, you like my tell you story of old time in China?"

Johnny popped out of his room; he was already in his

pajamas."Please, yes, Chiao Kuei." He too was on edge.

She helped me into my pajamas, then gathered us cozily, one on each side, on her bed in the middle room between Johnny's and mine. She liked to tell us stories at bedtime. There were mystery stories and ghost stories, stories of the Man who became a Fish and of another Man who woke up from a nap to find that he had become a Tiger. Sometimes the stories were about real people of the past.

"Tonight I tell story old old time, talkee one number one big man," she said."Talkee you about Xuan Zang. He number one big man," she told us."Very important."

She settled herself on the pillows against the wall, her arms around us. Now her voice changed into a hypnotic sing-song. 'Venerable Buddhist Monk Xuan Zang wantchee go on horse, on foot, over mountains and deserts to where the sun goes down. Emperor in old imperial city Chang'an say he not go, too muchee danger. But he go, want bring Buddhist stories and good behavior teaching to China. Daytime he hide in farm; nighttime light from moon show him road. He go with horse, carry all he clothes, he papers, on he back. He dress like coolie so Emperor no find he."

"Wow," Johnny said, idly scratching a mosquito bite."He was very brave."

"He go China more far," she said."over very big mountain and big desert where no got water. He very thirsty."

I reached over for a sip of water from a glass by the bed."I'm thirsty too."

"He happy when he come to Jade Gate (Yumen), the door to where the sun goes down. *Ai yah*, bad *joss* come. Bad luck. He guide try to kill he, then go way. Now Venerable Buddhist no got guide, get lost in Taklamakan Desert. He drop water bag and all drinking water fall in sand.

"Oh gosh," Johnny said. "The poor guy."

"He not know what way go, all sand where he look, no sign. He lips get crack and dry. He stop walking. He think what to do, begin Buddhist prayer for make him strong in body and heart. Then he remember one dream where he see holy Mount Sumeru with plenty land he must visit."

Amah stopped for a sip of water too. Johnny curled up at the end of her bed, his blond hair falling over his eyes. We were both growing sleepy. She continued; "By Buddha magic Xuan Zang's horse takee he to the Tianshan (Heavenly Mountains,) where rivers run down to desert, and he refill water bag. Then come to Hami, where plenty fresh water, melons, grapes. He and horse drink, eat, sleep. After rest he fill water bag, and he and horse go more on trip.

"Venerable Xuanzang walk and ride over mountain and river, place name Kyrgizstan, other place. Find India, get too muchee monk, lama, write Buddha teaching in Chinese, then walk and ride back same way, long hard trip. But he save important teachings for Chinese boys and girls, today, tomorrow. All people thank he, say prayer."

Johnny and I were both nodding off. She carried me to my bed, tucked me in under the mosquito net, and turned out the light.

"Now my baby sleep," she said. "No fear, maybe Jap man no come."

I close my eyes, the memory of beloved Chiao Kuei too dear to bear. Tears threaten to fill my eyes. It has grown late; I turn off the computer, set the morning call alert, and slowly fall asleep in the powerful aura of feeling near to my Amah.

III

1932. CHINESE COURTESY IS DRILLED INTO ME. AGE FIVE

I AM SLOWLY LEARNING that today's China is only distantly related to my yesterday's China. I tried to speak Pidgin English at a Chinese restaurant; the waiter replied in perfect English apologizing that he didn't understand me. I'm sorry; while there is no need in today's China for this language, still it was an imaginative and charming way of enabling communication between people of different nationalities. I still, admittedly affectedly, count it as one of my bizarre assembly of languages. I love words, word association, the history of language that I studied at Bryn Mawr. My theme was tracing the origins and evolution of Pidgin English. In this writing, I am happily indulging in that language.

Then there's the interesting difficulty that native-born Chinese have in trying to say the letter "r" and of the Japanese with "l". During World War II Americans, who couldn't tell the Chinese from the Japanese, asked the person to say the word "lalapalooza" — the Japanese would say "raraparooza" while the Chinese spoke it correctly.

My thoughts now wander to the Japanese, and before World War II to May 1932 and the end of the mortar attacks.

Thump-thumping woke me abruptly. Oh—the Japanese again. I rolled out from under the mosquito net, went to the window and opened it. Johnny shuffled in, rubbing his eyes. "Aren't they ever going to stop?" he grumbled. We couldn't see any fighting, but the shelling noises still came from the north. Jim began whining; the noise was hurting his ears. He crawled under my bed.

"Do you think they're going to bomb us too?" I asked."It's louder than yesterday."

"I don't think so."

I shut the window, glad that it was Saturday and no school. It had been a bit scary yesterday, going to school and back, not knowing if Japanese soldiers would pop up at the next corner. I hadn't actually seen one yet.

Johnny went back to his room, whistled for Jim, then shut the door. The noise wasn't so penetrating in his room that faced away from Chapei, and thank goodness Jim stopped whining. His pain was hard to hear. To see if she was up, I wandered into Amah's room, pushing aside some heavy brocade drapes hanging on one of the clothes-lines that crisscrossed the room. I guessed that Tailor was making new curtains.

Already dressed in her black Chinese jacket and trousers, she was sitting in front of the mirror at her spindly-legged narrow dressing table. I sneaked up behind her.

"Good morning, Amah!" I said, covering her eyes with my hands."This is little birdie, tweet tweet!" I paused. The sound of the bombing spoiled everything."My no likee boom boom noise."

"Good morning, Littee Birdie," she replied, pulling me to her side for a hug."Bye and bye boom boom go far away, no fear. Now I finish."

She took a comb and some jars from the dresser drawer, then slathered a clear jelly-like liquid all over her straight, shiny black hair. With a wide, curved, thick-toothed red lacquer comb she pulled it back in tight rows. Finished, she tucked the comb into her hair where it stayed neatly all day. I loved watching her do this.

Her large room held Tailor's sewing machine and ironing board, in addition to her own personal things. Tailor, who slept in the servants' house on the other side of their kitchen, moved in and out of this room as needed. I never heard them quarrelling. He didn't work on the weekends, so I knew that I'd have to wait till Monday for his help with my bears' uniforms and guns.

The thump-thumping continued. I decided I'd forget it by practicing flying for a while, so I went back to my room and shut the door. I'd been trying for some weeks to fly by saying traditional magic words and jumping off the end of my bed. This morning I tried out some different magic words.

"Jumba wamba!" I cried."Vana gumu!" and jumped off, crashing to the floor."Oh pooh."

Up again."Zatahooby! Rebolaving!" Crash. Then again I tried the old words: "Alakazam! Abracadabra!" Crash. Crash.

I gave up, not discouraged."Maybe it'll work next time," I mumbled to myself."I'll make up some new magic words."

Amah came in to help dress me, and I went downstairs for breakfast.

When I went upstairs Mother, dressed in a peach satin robe with long trailing sleeves, greeted me from my parents' bedroom "Good morning precious!" she said, giving me a huge hug."How would you like to dress my hair this morning?"

"OK, Mommy."

This room was all Mother—half professional war correspondent, half society lady/mother. Her unusual ebony desk, with Chinese latticework and a matching rounded stool, were unexpected pieces of furniture. Prominently on the desk stood her Remington typewriter beside a stack of paper, and a black telephone. The six drawers with shiny brass handles were crowded with papers, pencils, erasers; Chinese and English newspapers. Transmitted cables lay cluttered about. Johnny and I loved to climb under that rich, lustrous black desk, pretending we were invisible.

The rest of the room was feminine, with pink and ivory accents on bedspreads, curtains, chaise longue. Glass doors opened to the sunroom overlooking the garden.

Mother's dressing table had three mirrors, like a triptych, and an initialed set of brush, mirror, comb, powder holder, nail set. The scent of her favorite perfume, Chanel Number 5, wafted up into the room from a cut crystal bottle.

As I came in I saw myself in the full-length oval cheval mirror in one corner. I didn't like what I saw; I didn't look like the princesses in the fairy stories in my books. Not even like Nancy Drew or the Bobbsey girls.

"Mummy," I complained,"I don't like the way I look."

"Now don't you worry your pretty little head about that, Patty. You are just beautiful."

I turned this way and that, a chubby little girl with a head full of bouncing curls and a pink ribbon, wearing a Liberty lawn dress smocked across the chest.

Mother sat down on the little stool before her vanity and called me back from my contemplation of myself. I stood behind her, looking at her in the mirror, and we grinned at each other's reflections. Then I began to brush her short wavy blonde hair. She liked it in flat waves because, she told me, this was "the vogue," even if I thought she looked prettier when it was fluffy.

The heavy cruiser U.S.S. *Houston*, Flagship of the American Asiatic Squadron, was in the harbor. That afternoon Father had included Johnny in an invitation by Admiral Harry E. Yarnell, the Admiral of the Squadron of the Asia Fleet, to board his Flagship. Johnny elaborated on the adventure to Mother and me over tea on the verandah that day.

"That was something! Imagine, Sis," he said, striking a pose,"I was on the Number One battleship of the American Asia fleet!"

"Must have been fun!"

"And a Captain—I think his name was Bagley, showed me how the guns worked." He used his arms to mime firing make-believe mighty guns."Rat-a-tat-a-tat. But we couldn't really fire them," he confessed, "because that might start a war. And, Sis, he told me that Admiral Yarnell was based here in Shanghai to protect us Americans."

Father came home; he joined us with a glass of sherry on the verandah while we had tea."It was a lovely expedition," he said."There were not only the *Houston* but also the British frigates *Amethyst* and *Black Swan.*"

"Man, were they beautiful!" Johnny added.

"Are they going to make the Japanese stop bombing us?" I asked.

"I don't think so, Patty. They didn't look as though they were doing anything to help us."

In the following week Mother called us excitedly to her bedroom. She sat at her desk where, with her silver and jade letter opener, she had sliced open an invitation for us children to attend a party given by Sir Victor Sassoon. I whooped with joy.

"What kind of costume are we supposed to wear?"

"Sir Victor wants you to look like a garden," Mother answered."Let's talk to Tailor to see what he thinks he can make for you and Johnny."

Tailor was an essential part of the household. Mother and I walked up the stairs to his work-space in Amah's room on the third floor. He was sitting by the sewing machine studying a French fashion magazine that Mother had marked up.

We discussed our costumes with Tailor."My think so Littie

Missie be one beautiful rose in garden," he said."My can make petals, big skirt like open flower. Glowing Pearl helpee me cut, sew on petals, make little hat of petals." Glowing Pearl was the teen-age daughter of Sew Sew Amah Mary; both helped from time to time.

"What you think for Johnny?"

"My think so Master Johnny be one carrot, green leaf grow out of orange color hat, OK? What Missie think?"

Mother loved the idea, Johnny approved it, and the costumes were underway.

Sir Victor Sassoon loved children so much that he hosted themed parties for some hundred of us of many nationalities every year at his Cathay Hotel. Last year it was a Disney party where Johnny and I were Mickey and Minnie Mouse. Sir Victor gave us wonderful presents, too.

I asked Mother about him while we were trying on our costumes."I'll try to explain," she said."I believe he came here from India with a great deal of money and a brilliant imagination about ten years ago. He rebuilt Shanghai with buildings like the Cathay Hotel and the Grosvenor Mansions. Shanghai soon had the tallest buildings outside the United States. Fortunately he likes to use his money to help people. And to give parties for the children of his friends!"

"Do you suppose he'll have presents for us again?" I asked."Last year Johnny got a really good camera. Maybe I'll get one too?"

Mother just smiled."We shouldn't expect too much more from him." She paused."With this battle between the Japanese and Chinese going on now, I'm surprised that he decided to hold the party. It might be just because so many people are gloomy and need something to laugh about."

So Tailor and Mother bought the pink taffeta, for I was to be a pink rose, not yellow or cream or red. Johnny's costume was of course orange and green. The costumes were ready in time, and, I did indeed receive a camera from Sir Victor.

Johnny and I, when we weren't fighting, loved to play at science fiction, basing our stories on the Flash Gordon comics. We drew fabulous space weapons and flying machines, devising our own versions of Ming the Merciless and Dr. Zarkov. Our designs were carefully detailed. We preserved them in secret scrapbooks, hidden lest they fall into enemy hands.

Johnny had so many advantages. Not only was he older, but as a boy he could bicycle with his friends in nearby parts of the International Settlement and the French Concession, while I had to be driven by Ah Ching with Matrushka or Amah as escort.

Boys were favored simply because they were boys. While I loved and admired my brother, at the same time it was hard to be a little sister, a *Meimei,* in China. I could always feel the favored position of the Little Master, *Gege,* among the servants. No matter how awful he was, he was never at fault.

The favoritism was overt, and I was supposed to go along with it because I was just a girl. Johnny was given the first choicest yummy candy; his were the warmest hugs and the most cooing flattery and the special attentions. Everyone rushed up to him first when we returned from the summer vacations. I knew that our household was as kind to me as their world permitted, that they loved me too, but sometimes I felt inferior and rejected. I dealt with this by learning to entertain myself writing stories and songs. I was too proud to let them see the hurt that I felt.

Sometimes Johnny told me about his adventures. He made friends easily with his wild sense of humor and imagination. He and some friends had created a secret club called the Gunpowder

Gang. They met up in his bedroom opposite mine on the third floor, and there they concocted things that exploded, causing riotous laughter that invaded my world. My own friends and I liked to arrange our teddy bears around my little pink table for pretend tea parties.

He and the Gang had informal patterns of visiting each other, racing around on their bicycles. They learned to swear in Chinese and, while banging tin garbage can lids together, yelled out Chinese oaths at passing Chinese boys. A couple of times they got into fights and ran afoul of the police in our otherwise sedate, safe Columbia Circle neighborhood. I was so jealous of him.

"Johnny," I implored one day, "please teach me some bad Chinese words! I have to know some, too!"

"Don't bother me about that again," he answered testily. "You know that Mom and Dad don't want you to use bad language." He got on his bike and began to cycle away.

"Let me come too!" I called, running after him.

Looking back he yelled, "You're only a girl, you're too little, and you would be in the way. Stop bothering me, Sis."

"I hate you!" I stamped my feet, then jumped up and down in a tantrum. I hated him.

He stopped. I guess he knew that he was being awful to me. "This evening we'll play a game, OK?" and he biked away around the corner.

Johnny also collected cicadas in small bamboo cages, a popular Chinese hobby. It didn't interest me at all; I thought it was cruel to cage the little creatures. The trunks of trees in our garden were dotted with little beige body-like shells that the cicadas had grown out of. In the summer, their rapid clicks filled the air. Then, the boys held competitions on who had the most live cicadas. To acquire them, Johnny applied a sticky wax to the end of a bamboo pole. With this he reached high up into the trees and touched a cicada humming on the trunk. Stuck, the creature was quickly placed in the cage. The cage door slid shut, and presto, one caged cicada.

After school I liked to stand at the pantry door to watch the activity in the kitchen. Because of the prevalence of diseases such as typhus, typhoid fever and cholera, we didn't eat food that was raw if not first washed in a purple disinfectant liquid called "potassium permanganate."

Every day a large sink was filled with boiled water, the purple disinfectant was added, then the raw foods were washed in the purple liquid and rinsed with freshly boiled water. I stood at the sink and stared, fascinated, as the transparent water turned purple, our vegetables vanishing under the color. All of our drinking water was boiled, then cooled and poured into individual sterilized carafes placed in each bathroom and bedroom.

Instead of fresh milk, we were obliged to drink "KLIM." We fought it, unsuccessfully.

"Patty! Johnny!" Mother called every afternoon, a glass of white powdery liquid in each hand, when we'd gotten back from school."Time for your milk!" She forced us to swallow this disgusting drink. Mother always treated it with honey or chocolate to make it palatable but we never became accustomed to it. After that came a tablespoon of Castor Oil that was supposed to make us grow strong. She made us swallow it however much we fought it.

Sometimes she took our minds away from the horrible liquid we were drinking by telling us stories of her adventures as a war correspondent. She had become interested in the newspaper business when she was a college girl in Kansas City,

Missouri."I had twin uncles named Moore, nicknamed Squib and Squib Doodle," she told us. The Moores let her help with their newspaper; then she got summer work at the Los Angeles *Evening Herald* and the *San Francisco Call & Post*.

"I was looking for adventure and serious journalism," she said,"and I found both in Shanghai. I managed to convert the missionary assignment that got me to China in 1918 into full-time work at the *China Press*. I was only 23, and it was thrilling when the International News Service took me on as foreign correspondent." Her byline, Edna Lee Booker, appeared frequently.

She put similar energy and enthusiasm into creating a lovely home for us all. She and Cook spent a lot of time together. Cook went upstairs every morning to stand by her desk to plan the menus.

Chopsticks in hand and apron tied around his roly-poly waist, Cook created Chinese, Indian, French, German, English and American dishes. Mother even got him to learn to make some of the Pennsylvania Dutch dishes that Daddy had grown up with and still loved.

The thump-thumping of the Japanese mortars assaulting the Chinese soldiers defending Shanghai continued for several hours every morning. I began to expect the noise, like the rising of the sun. I went to the window, opened it, looked out, the thump-thumping was louder, Jim whined and hid his ears, I closed the window. The battle continued.

On a Saturday morning, Father asked me to join him in his study on the second floor. The room was also our library, with shelf after glass-covered shelf holding treasured books—a 1911 *Stories from Hans Andersen* with illustrations in color by Edmund Dulac; Edgar Allen Poe's illustrated *The Bells*; the large, heavy, first edition of the *1868 Fables de La Fontaine;* sets of volumes in French and German as well as English; a collection of rare books on Chinese paintings; Father's books of history, science, and thought; Mother's books on Chinese history and porcelains, gardening, current events. Sometimes I was allowed to touch and look at some of the books, they excited me. They were mysterious and inviting, peering out from behind the polished glass. The books were almost like real living friends looking at me through a window.

Father's rocking chair stood beside a standing lamp. Here he liked to read, sometimes pulling me up to his lap to read to me.

His desk and a couple of chairs were in the center of the room. Waiting for him to arrive I walked over to it, touched its blotter top. Father had shown me how to write a letter backward by writing it in ink and then blotting it. I couldn't understand how that worked, but it did. The sides of the desk folded up to reveal intriguing little compartments. I folded one up to explore the contents and found scissors, erasers, a pencil sharpener and pencils, a ledger, and tucked into a cubby hole, some bank notes.

Carefully I closed that side and opened the other. There I saw the pearl-handled pocketknife with which he was often whittling at a dull pencil point, and a pad of scraps of paper. There were guitar picks and safety pins and needles and thread, all in neat sections. I quickly borrowed a pad of paper before Father arrived, knowing I shouldn't but wanting to be naughty anyway, and told myself to remember to return it before he needed it. He scolded me when I forgot to put it back.

I was sitting dutifully beside his desk when Father came in.

"It's time again to give our household helpers their financial compensation, and it's your turn to help me know what has been going on here," he told me. I knew he didn't need my advice, and I knew he knew I knew, and we both knew that Mother kept him informed too, but we loved the game. Johnny and I each had turns with Father at his accounting.

He adjusted his glasses on his nose, asked me to sit unobtrusively a few feet away, and then called in one servant after another. First he consulted the Number One Boy, Ah Kung.

"Ah Kung," he said,"Will you please tell me if any of the staff have been hurt by the Japanese?"

"Mister Potter," he replied,"Jap-man burn too muchee China-man house, take away his pidgin (business) so he no can work. But we family all number one goodee, no hurt family." He stopped."Blong (there is) one new problem for Elder Coolie, Sir. He wife sick, no can get medicine because Jap-man burn medicine shop, she no can work now."

The coolies' jobs, I had noticed, were the lowest of the lowly. I saw them cleaning the toilets, sweeping the floors, carrying out the trash. They washed and fed Jim and tended the fireplaces. We knew Fo Sun, the younger coolie, who came with us on our summer vacations to the beach, better than Elder Coolie, who tended to keep to himself and was old and crotchety.

"Thank you, Ah Kung, for letting me know. Did anyone do extra hard work or was extra helpful?"

"Yes, Mister Potter, Ah Ching muchee help Missie when she wanchee go talk to Jap-man for newspaper story. He tell Missie too much danger, maybe she hurt, more better she no go. She say never mind, she want to talk to Jap-man for write story. Ah Ching say, maybe more better she talk to China-man for newspaper story."

"Thank you, Ah Kung. He did the right thing." Father handed him an envelope with his pay in it. He paused."I know, Ah Kung," he said,"You have more trouble now with worries about Japanese. Missie and I rely on your help. There is a little extra *cumshaw,* (ganxie, "bonus") for you and your family in the envelope."

"Thank you, Sir. Thank you very much." He bowed.

"Now please send Elder Coolie to me."

While Father waited he asked me if I knew of an additional problem any of the staff had had, or who had been especially helpful. He relied on us as well as Mother, because she was often busy with other things, or away.

In addition to Amah, the butlers Ah Kung and Lin Sing, Cook, Learn Pidgin Cook and Tailor, Chauffeur Ah Ching, the coolies Fo Sun and Elder Coolie, our staff included two gardeners. Father wanted to know how each was, really; what was going on with each one's family.

Only Amah lived with us in our house. Adjoining our house through the kitchens was a smaller second house where everyone else but the gardeners lived. I was never allowed to go beyond the Chinese kitchen. We respected their privacy and never entered their quarters.

Several occasional Amahs who helped Mother included Sew Sew Amah Mary and her daughter Glowing Pearl; the Finger Nail and Toe Amah; the Hair Amah; the Massage Amah; these all lived elsewhere.

Elder Coolie shuffled into the room. "Yes, Mister Potter?" He was stooped over with age and arthritis.

"Ah Kung say maybe you wife have got trouble?"

"Yes, Mister. Too muchee trouble get medicine. Must travel other place for medicine. Too far, my no can get, she no can work. *Ai-yah!*"

"Maybe Ah Ching can drive you, you wife, get medicine other place? You think so can do?"

"Yes, Mister Potter. Thank you, thank you, Mister Potter." He bent over in a sort of bow, his hands folded together in front of him, to express his appreciation. Father sent for Ah Ching and so it was arranged for Elder Coolie's wife to get the medicine she needed. Father handed him an envelope with his wages and *cumshaw* before he left the room.

Father asked for Ah Ching.

"Ah Kung tells me that you were very helpful to Missie this week," he said.

"Mister Potter, Missie say she go talk to Jap-man for write story, I say Missie maybe more better talkee to her friends, Jap-man maybe hurt her. My happy she stay home, not go see Jap-man."

Father thanked him, gave him his salary and a special *cumshaw* for his help in restraining Mother's war correspondent instincts, and he left the room.

"Did you hear how Ah Ching got your mother not to talk to the Japanese military leaders?" he asked me. "She wanted an interview to send to her newspaper in the States. He didn't want to go anywhere near the Japanese, and he also feared for her safety but avoided saying 'No.' In China, one must be judicious in the use of negative expressions. One gets around it by saying in Pidgin something like, 'My think so that not so goodee idea,' or, 'My no savvy how fashion do that.' Sometimes it is, 'My think so more better do other fashion.'

He added, "After a while the foreigner learns that the Chinese sense of courtesy makes it extremely hard for them to say "No" and thus finds ways to avoid asking them to do something that they don't want to do.

"Another little lesson for today, Patty," he said, "In China, one does not permit another person to be humiliated in public. Elder Coolie was ashamed that he could not take care of his wife, so I was able to take care of his problem quietly.

"You don't let another person lose face, ever. Not even when he is wrong and you are right. You see, if you correct a person in public, that causes him to lose face. You must put his or her interest ahead of yours, you must make yourself small and unimportant." I guess he kept telling me this to be sure I learned the lesson. I was so small and unimportant and, worse, a girl, that I wanted to make noise so that I could be heard.

"Above all, always, you must protect the dignity of the other person."

One by one all the servants came up to his room. He talked to each one about his situation; had there been drought, famine, illness, hostility, abuse by the Japanese, death; or a wedding, birth, celebration—and adjusted the *cumshaw* accordingly.

I sit back and smile. An AHA! moment. Now I understand why I used to have so much difficulty at Board meetings when I was the CEO, when I found someone emphatically opposing me about something he/ she didn't know enough about. I was simply unable to correct the person directly and publicly, and had to make my way forward circuitously doing verbal lateral arabesques to get my opposing opinion heard, while also protecting the other from being exposed as a jackass. Well of course. In Chinese courtesy, you protect the other person's reputation, you save his or her face. Thinking back to those quiet sessions in my father's study, I realize that I was taught Chinese courtesy from my first words.

Reaching for some nuts to chew on, I wish for a cigarette. Wow. I realize, for the first time, that my values are Chinese. No wonder I find many Americans to be rude and thoughtless.

Maintaining this courtesy is especially hard when you know, as I did, that one of the men on the Board wanted my job. Yet I couldn't expose his inadequacy, I had to save his face.

IV

1932. The Bund; our dog is
kidnapped and comes home. Age Six

THESE DAYS, *I am dipping into English language newspapers published in China. Today the* Shanghai Daily *reports that the First Lady, Peng Liyuan, is listed in* Vanity Fair International *as one of the world's most beautifully-dressed women. Well, well. The story states that her clothes, including her noteworthy handbag, were made in China. Long ago, Mother's friend Soong Mei-ling, Chiang Kai-shek's wife, was also listed as one of the world's best-dressed women. I'm glad that the Chinese feel secure enough once again to parade their elegant leading ladies. Perhaps at last the Mao models have been superseded?*

An article in the China Daily *gets my attention: China has an aircraft carrier, the Liaoning, that conducted takeoffs and landings with domestically-made jets, their J-15s. China hopes to build a carrier-based navy. Modern domestic warships have now sailed far beyond the seas and archipelagos surrounding China, including the Philippines and Japan.*

The last time that a Chinese ship sailed so far was, I believe, when the Admiral of the Western Seas, Zheng He, took a massive armada on expeditions from 1405 to 1433 in the opposite direction, sailing down the China coast and turning left to cross the Indian Ocean, reaching Kenya and Somalia.

I hope that the harbor at The Bund today is full of modern Chinese warships, flags of China flying proudly high. A wave of indignation and anger grabs me when I think of how China's "war junks" were pulverized by an armor-plated British frigate with superior firepower in 1842 at the opening of the Opium Wars. In my childhood, the flags of foreign warships flew proudly in The Bund. But not one with the Chinese flag.

Saturdays were Adventure Days, because there was no school or church to go to. Anything was possible. One Friday I learned that I was to be taken on a visit to The Bund the next day.

I was excited about it, and woke in the early morning; Amah hadn't yet gotten me up for breakfast. Propped on pillows in my four-poster bed, white linen sheets crumpled around me, I opened a precious book, Robert Louis Stevenson's *A Child's Garden of Verses*, to the poem I wanted to read. Whispering the sounds to myself, I touched each word, one by one:

I should like to rise and go
Where the golden apples grow
Where below another sky
Parrot islands anchored lie,

I looked up through the mosquito netting hanging from the ceiling. The thump-thump of mortars had started up again but this no longer bothered me, they thumped on and off as far back as I could remember.

Where the Great Wall round China goes,
And on one side the desert blows. . .

Well, I thought, Johnny and I played on the Great Wall when mother took us once to Peking, so I know what that looks like, that's nothing new. But I do want to see where Parrot Islands

43

anchored lie. Maybe I can climb on a boat in The Bund and just go!

The Bund. I hugged myself in excitement. This harbor area was just about my favorite part of Shanghai—and Mother was taking me on a shopping trip to The Bund this very morning!

Finally Amah came in to help me dress.

"Good morning, Littie Missie," she greeted me."More better you get up now, put on dress to go down town with Missie."

No argument from me! I yawned, stretched, carefully placed my precious book on the bed table, and wiggled out from the mosquito netting."Thank you, good morning to you too!" I said, giving her a hug, my arms trying to reach around her waist."Wonderful! I'm going shopping! Going to The Bund to see the boats!"

She sat me down firmly on a stool in front of my little dressing table to fix my hair, and began to twist strands around a curling brush."Why do I have to have those stupid long curls!" I tried to push her away."They hit my face when I run. Please, Amah."

"Littie Missie, you savvy Missie like you hair like pig ear, tie with pink ribbon."

After sliding into my Liberty lawn dress and sweater, being buttoned up, shoe laces tied, I launched myself, curls flouncing around my face, down the three-story curved banister to land in the first floor hall in a giggling pile on the floor. Amah was calling after me."Littie Missie, you no go down like typhoon! You take step like young lady, like your papa tell you!"

"Papa no home, he go to office, he no see me!"

Lin Sing, the Number Two Boy, in his uniform of white cotton jacket and trousers, was serving breakfast in the dining room. He was a special favorite of mine, younger than most of the staff, He didn't have the dignity of Ah Kung; he was sassier and more spontaneously fun-loving.

"Good morning, Littie Missie," he said."What you likee my bring you?"

"Mmm, one piecee pumelo and one piecee poach eggs on toast, thank you, Lin Sing," I replied. Johnny and I loved pumelo as it was so easy to peel and had no bothersome seeds. Grapefruit was work.

Mother, who had breakfast served to her on a tray in bed every morning, came down and joined me at the table for a second cup of tea."Patty," she said even before she sat down, and I knew from the tone of her voice what was coming: "Patty, the whole neighborhood could hear you shrieking like a banshee as you slid down the banister. Daddy John and I have asked you again and again to go up and down the stairs like a young lady. What am I to do with you."

I mumbled something that sounded like "sorry" but my mouth was full of toast. I wondered again what a banshee was.

"How can I know you'll behave yourself when we're in town! And tiffin at the Chocolate Shop where we might see friends!"

Oh dear, I thought, quickly swallowing the food in my mouth. I'm in trouble."Mummy, I promise I'll behave, I'll do just what you say. I promise I will!"

A few minutes later, Johnny came in."Don't forget that you will be playing with Granny Vincent this afternoon," Mother said.

"I couldn't forget, Mom, thanks. Hey, sis," he said. He ordered bacon and eggs from Lin Sing.

I peeked at Johnny, trying to hide my grin behind my napkin. I knew what he and Granny would be doing with the other members of his Gunpowder Gang. He had told me about these escapades, swearing me to secrecy. One of their more gruesome occupations was to bike over to the battlefields in Chapei after the Japanese stopped bombing. There, where Chinese soldiers lay dead, they collected unfired cartridges from the soldiers' guns. Back at home they would open them up, empty out the gunpowder, and pound it into small metal tubes to simulate tiny cannons.

"We light these little tubes with fuses taken from the red firecrackers," he said. "There are always strings of them around, and then we shoot them at each other from opposite ends of the garden."

"But Johnny, you could be hurt!"

"Yeah we had to stop doing that because an accident nearly blew someone's hand off. So then we fired BB guns at each other instead."

This too had to be halted when a BB hit just below one boy's eye. The Gang then turned to throwing stones at each other, using garbage can lids as shields.

"This got boring," he said, "so we got into stone fights with neighborhood Chinese boys."

When Father heard about this, he spoke very sternly to Johnny. "Don't you realize that you might cause an international incident by real harm on one or the other side? You must stop this, it is dangerous and not funny." So Johnny and the Gang returned to the relatively safer creation of tiny cannons and shooting them now, not at each other, but at targets like garbage cans that made a satisfactory banging crashing sound as they exploded. It sounded like so much fun and here I was stuck with playing games with Matrushka.

This morning, he alerted me to news he had just heard at school.

"On your trip to The Bund, well, I heard that the Japs have brought in around thirty warships and forty airplanes, in addition to about seven thousand troops stationed around the city. I guess you'll see some of the warships."

"Gosh, why do they need all those planes and ships?"

"So they can drop bombs on top of us," Johnny explained with sadistic relish. "You know, like balloons filled with water that we drop from the window. But these bombs kill people." Then apparently he thought better of torturing me. "They probably won't bomb us here in the International Settlement or the French Concession." He added, "I think we're safe. Don't worry."

But now I fretted over the Japanese boats cluttering my Bund. Breakfast over, Ah Ching entered the room wearing his formal driving uniform. "Missie, my takee you shop now?" he asked. "In about ten minutes, thank you, Ah Ching," Mother replied.

We got our things together, which for me was very simple, I didn't have anything to bring. But for mother—well, every time she went anywhere with us, there was great drama. This morning was no different.

"Lin Sing, please talkee Cook four man come for dinner, he must buy muchee coconut for fix with chicken." Yummy, I thought. That meant chicken would be served with a creamy white sauce in coconut shells. "And Amah, would you go up my room, get one piecee pink scarf I forgot on the chair? Let's see. Money, face powder, yes. Patty, go on and get in the car, I'll be right there. There's just one more little thing I have to do." She disappeared into the living room and returned with a swatch of cloth. Ah Ching opened the door of the dark green Studebaker for her when Amah ran out with the pink scarf. Mother thanked her and arranged it around her neck.

"Ah Ching, first we go Bank of China on Bund, then Cathay Hotel, then Chocolate Shop for tiffin, then home."

"Yes, Missie."

We drove along Amherst Avenue (Xinhua Lu, "New China Road"), over to Bubbling Well (Nanjing Road West) with its many shops, and past my school. Then into noisy, bustling

Nanking Road with its great stores and hotels. When we finally turned onto The Bund. I gave a little sigh of joy. I could already see the flags and masts of some of the ships in the harbor. Ah Ching pulled the car to a stop in front of a distinguished building in the center of a block of official-looking buildings.

"Thank you, Ah Ching," Mother said."I go inside bank, Littie Missie may stay water-side to see boats, you look-see she all right. Patty," she turned to me,"I've got to tend to some tiresome business at the bank, and you may cross The Bund with Ah Ching to see the action in the harbor while I am tied up."

I began skipping across the wide boulevard, tugging on Ah Ching's hand as we dodged cars, rickshaws, wheelbarrows laden with goods or precariously perched people. The end of a long bamboo pole slung over a coolie's shoulder, bundles swinging from each end, nearly knocked me over.

"Oopsie daisy!" I laughed.

Ah Ching calmly picked me up and set me down at the edge of the water.

An ocean liner announced its departure with a long, resonant blast.

"Toooooot," I called out in answer."See, Ah Ching, the boat talkee me! He savvy talkee Pidgin!" I could also hear the rhythmic songs of boatmen as they loaded goods onto barges. Deep voices calling out *hai-ah hou-ah* carried across the water.

I looked down on dozens of Chinese sampans. These flat-bottomed wooden boats, about 14 feet long, were crowded in the river beside the dock. They were loosely tied up beside each other, four or five deep, like a floating trailer-park. Some had arched reinforced canopies reaching about three feet across, to accommodate sleeping, cooking, and protection from weather.

"Look, Ah Ching," I said, motioning to one."There's a whole family living on that boat. I guess they have tiffin early because they're cooking on that little outdoor stove." I could see another family washing a baby; others were washing clothes. Everywhere people were chatting and calling across sampans to each other in their rocking, open-air homes. One of the sampans was pulling away, propelled by a man standing at the rear twisting a long oar, the *yuloh (yaolu)*, through the water.

The sounds of the Chinese chatter and of the sampans gently bumping into each other were somehow comforting. In addition to the smells of Chinese food cooking on the sampans, there were the exciting boat and harbor smells of creosote, oil, salt water, fish. I heard the clinking of rigging and the snapping of sails. Words were shouted in strange languages above the sounds of lapping water, the shriek of seagulls, the voices of deck hands and coolies as they loaded boxes and luggage onto wagons.

Further out I could see large junks, with brown or ivory-colored sails, squared, but rounded at the top. The colors and designs on the bow and stern always enchanted me. One- or two-masted, flags flew high above them.

"Littie Missie," said Ah Ching, pointing to one of the junks,"See flag all red? This fashion flag keep dragon quiet. Angry dragon very bad *joss*. Angry dragon makee big wind come, make junk have bad *joss*." Some of the junks were as small as 36 feet; others could reach lengths up to 300 feet and accommodate many passengers on long ocean voyages. Some of them were now moving majestically down the Whang Poo River toward the Yangtze River and the East China Sea.

Across the river in deep water, the graceful ocean liner that had tooted to me was slowly getting under way. Its blue-white-red striped flag showed it to be a French liner. I wondered where it was going.

Some freighters were sitting low in the water."I'll ask Mummy if any of the German boats is carrying teddy-bears," I said to myself."Maybe I could add to my teddy bear family?"

I knew Johnny would like to know what warships were anchored, flying the flags of their nations."Ah Ching, what country boats there today? I see American, British flags." That reminded me that the Japanese mortars were pounding again in the distance.

"Other warship, Littie Missie, fly French, Italian, German flags." Neither he nor I mentioned the many ships flying the Japanese flag. We were both pretending not to see them, nor the very large ship on which Japanese airplanes were landing and talking off.

Mother emerged from the bank and joined us. She took my hand and we quietly looked out over the water. Then she sighed.

"You and I both love The Bund, don't we. It's magical. Can you believe it, not long ago it was just a muddy waterfront. Imagine, Patty, once there were Spanish galleons and China Clippers here on The Bund mixing with the junks! Can you picture it, how extraordinary it would look!" At that moment I forgave my mother for the color pink and the curls and all the rest of our problems; I just loved her.

Still holding my hand, Mother led us back across The Bund to the car. I asked her why there were no Chinese-style buildings facing the water.

"That's because they are Western creations," she replied."The great international banks and the European and American hotels brought their own architects and styles to Shanghai. This made British and American and other international companies feel at home when they were trading world-wide. These buildings offer all the most modern facilities to shipping and trading companies.

"I have to run an errand at the Cathay Hotel," she added."Want to come with me?"

"Yes!" I exclaimed. She knew that the great hotels were

another reason why I loved The Bund.

We walked to the Cathay with its magnificent tower, so tall that I had to stretch my neck up to see the top. As we walked in under the high arched entrance, I became aware of perfume in the air, of elegance, excitement. There was music in the background; a group was playing French songs.

"Mom," I teased, "Do you think they'll play *Parlez-moi d'amour* (Speak to me of love) if I ask them to?" That was my parents' love song. Other times when I'd been at the Cathay there were violins from a gypsy band playing sobbing Hungarian or Russian melodies. Sometimes it was jazz by an Italian or Philippine band. The soft background music added to the adventure.

I looked around the lobby. Immense colorful Chinese vases displaying three-foot-high floral arrangements of greens with peonies, gingers and orchid blossoms, were reflected in long mirrors. Chandeliers sparkled. Tall ferns and palms were placed in ornamental containers on the inlaid marble floors.

"Oh, Mummy, it's just beautiful!" I imagined a time when I could be a real guest there.

Some afternoons at tea-time Mother and I stopped to sit at one of the little round tables. White-robed waiters served us delicate finger sandwiches, garnished with sprigs of baby watercress. We were offered scones with clotted cream, and different kinds of tea with various sugars. Lemon slices were de-seeded and pierced with one clove each.

But today Mother just sat me down in one of the chairs by a table, and went to take care of her business. I didn't mind being alone; I liked to listen to accents and languages from all over the world. The different kinds of national dress didn't surprise me for I was accustomed to them, but I still found them exciting. Punjabi turbans and Farsi scarves were worn by some women. Japanese ladies with shimmering obis swayed as they walked in *geta* raised sandals.

Mother joined me at the little table.

Some men in long white gowns passed."Mom, why are those African men wearing dresses?"

"Those men come from Somalia, a country in Africa where they wear gowns I guess to protect themselves from desert sand storms," she said. Some of the Somalis were draped with brilliant generous scarves.

"Look at those Chinese ladies in their bright silk *cheongsam* dresses. Isn't that silk beeeaautiful! That's something else we both love, silk." The dresses had high Mandarin collars and side slits that sometimes showed the ladies' knees.

Elegant Philippine ladies walked by."Those ladies are wearing dresses made of *piña* cloth," Mother told me."That's an unusual fabric made from the fiber of pineapple leaves. And those Philippine men escorting them are wearing embroidered *piña* shirts."

Now a group of American and European women came in, casually displaying silks and furs. One, I saw with surprise, was wearing a coat made of leopard skins. Oooh, I wanted one of those! Then I asked Mother about what looked like a little fox that another was wearing over her shoulder. Its head and paws with fingernails were hanging around her neck."How can she wear that poor little fox? Look, Mummy, I can even see its eyes looking at me! That's just awful!"

"It's supposed to be very elegant," she answered."I don't like it either. I won't wear one."

She looked around wistfully, it seemed to me, and sighed."Let's walk over to one of the shops in the arcade. I have to find a lamp to match the swatch of cloth I brought."

In a shop exhibiting fine porcelains, she stopped by a lamp with a fat belly. Painted on it was a lady in a huge skirt; the color matching her swatch of cloth."Perfect," she said to herself.

I asked her about the dress."Why is she dressed like that? I've never seen anyone with that funny-looking kind of dress."

"Well, Patty," she replied,"The picture shows a lady in France hundreds of years ago when they wore dresses like that with very full skirts. The lamp came from France.

"I really want to buy that lamp," she said, somewhat petulantly.

"Why don't you, Mommy? It's so pretty."

"Oh, your father doesn't want me to spend money we don't need to now, when things are so uncertain with the Japanese."

"I'm sorry, Mommy, I wish those mean old Japs would go away."

We walked back through the lobby and out to the car.

"Ah Ching," she said,"Please drive to Madame Garnett's salon. Patty, I forgot, I just have to pick up a jacket, it won't take long."

I didn't mind. Not at all. Mother looked so pretty in Garnett dresses; my favorite was a light blue suede dress with matching jacket, the color of her eyes. The skirt swirled around her legs when she moved. And she had suede shoes to match. I liked accompanying my Mother to her salon simply because the dresses were so beautiful.

We walked out with a package. Ah Ching was parked in front, talking to an emaciated rickshaw coolie who was apparently begging from our wealthier Chinese chauffeur."Oh Patty," she said under her breath, "Just think of the contrast. Luxurious living is not expensive here in Shanghai." She seemed to be talking to herself."Life is cheap in every sense of the word."

She asked Ah Ching to give him a few coppers. Then we got in the car again."There's just time for a light tiffin before we go home," Mother said. Ah Ching helped us into the car. The

Chocolate Shop was nearby on Nanking Road, near my father's office."Why doesn't Daddy come with us?" I asked

"He's very tied up in business just now," Mother answered."Something to do with the Japanese."

The Chocolate Shop was sunny and informal, with little round tables for four, and ironwork side chairs. It looked like one of the restaurants we went to in California when we visited my grandparents. Here the menu offered delicious ice creams, pastries, sandwiches and salads. Mother ordered chicken sandwiches for us, with tea for her and root beer for me. We both ate our tiffin quietly, deep in our own thoughts, then Ah Ching drove us home.

Our road took us along my second favorite street: Nanking Road, that ran from The Bund through the center of the International Settlement.

This, I believed, must be the busiest, most glamorous road in Shanghai with its splashes of red, gold, green. People from all parts of the world—Chinese, Indian, African, European, Russian strolled along its sidewalks. Many rickshaws crowded the street, the coolies pushing, squirming, and swearing past cars while Chinese chauffeurs in trim uniforms, like our Ah Ching, honked at them.

When we got home I thanked Mother for taking me on a wonderful expedition, and went up to my room. I spent most of the afternoon playing with Jim in the garden.

I was called in for tea around 4:30. As we children wouldn't be dining with our parents and their guests this evening, Lin Sing served us "high tea"pudding and fruit as well as tea and scones with jam. Johnny, his hair wet and his hands suspiciously clean, joined Matrushka, Mother and me on the verandah. I knew that he had again been digging for unspent bullets in the Chapei battlefield, but I didn't give him away. Mother took jasmine tea with tiny jasmine blossoms floating in the cup. I had tried this, but found that it tasted bitter. She liked tea scalding hot — too hot for me to sip. Johnny and I had tea with milk and sugar, which she called "cambric tea".

Amah came in. It was time for us to go upstairs, she said, so that the room could be cleared for the dinner guests. Matrushka and Mother went to their rooms on the second floor, and Amah, Johnny and I continued on up to ours.

"Amah," I asked as sweetly as could be, "I was very good today, and Johnny good boy too. When the coconut chicken is ready, can you bring two piecee upstairs for Johnny and me? Please?"

"My think so can do, Littie Missie."

Johnny rewarded me for my thoughtfulness by inviting me into his room, where he showed me a few of the bullets that he and the Gunpowder Gang had collected.

I tried to pretend that all was well even though I knew it wasn't normal to wake up every morning to the sound of war or to have Japanese soldiers lurking a few miles away. But one day I couldn't pretend any longer: our dog Jim disappeared.

One day he just wasn't there. Johnny and I and the whole household called for him and searched throughout the neighborhood, but no happy bark came in response. No laughing dog bounded up to us. I was broken-hearted.

A few weeks later when my parents were having a dinner party, Ah Kung silently and unexpectedly bent down to my father and spoke to him in an aside. Father excused himself, got up and went out to the kitchen. Mother told me later that all the guests were worried about what could have gone wrong, but no one said a word about Father's leaving the table.

He followed Ah Kung to the kitchen, and as he opened the

door a large wet dog bounded up to him. It was Jim, soaking wet and starving, with his tail wagging like a windshield wiper, his body wriggling with joy, his tongue hanging out and with a big smile at finding his way home again. Father immediately asked Lin Sing to bring us down to the kitchen.

"Littie Master, Littie Missie, good news!" he said happily."Dog Jim come back home, he in kitchen now." I was half-asleep, but the news woke me instantly.

"What? Jim's home? Really truly?" I cried."Gee whiz," Johnny yelled,"That's great!" and we ran down the servants' stairway to greet him ourselves.

Jim was beyond himself with joy, running from Johnny to me, licking us and pawing us; little yips of joy slipping out of him.

"Oh Jim, you look so thin!" I said, patting his chest. Johnny said he looked as though he hadn't eaten since his disappearance. Tears began to pour down my cheeks and I felt as though I were shaking inside. I sat down suddenly on the kitchen floor, still hugging Jim.

Father patted my shoulder."It's such a relief to have him back, isn't it. But now he needs a bath and some hot food." Reluctantly I let go of him.

Father asked Cook to prepare a meal for him. He summoned Fo Sun, putting him in charge of giving Jim a good bath and wrapping him in a warm blanket. Then he returned to host the dinner party.

We were allowed to stay up until Jim was warm, dry, and fed, then waved goodnight to Father in the dining room. He joined us briefly."We and our guests have been speculating on what caused Jim to disappear. The consensus is that he was kidnapped by the Japanese, and escaped. Quality dogs are being stolen for use by the Japanese army in fighting the Chinese."

Jim, Johnny and I went up the stairs. Jim ran right to his usual bed, his tail still thumping almost as loudly as the mortars in the mornings.

We decided that Father was right, that Jim had escaped his Japanese captors, swum across the river, and with his sense of smell and natural intelligence, found his way back home.

One morning there was no thumping of the mortars, my daily wake-up call. I opened my window; there were just the non-threatening street sounds of horns honking, rickshaw coolies muttering in Shanghainese, children playing. No exploding mortars.

"Johnny!" I called."Johnny, come here! It's quiet outside!"

He came in rubbing his eyes."Come to the window!" I said."Do you hear the mortars?"

He listened carefully. Slowly a look of joy came over his face."I guess they've gone! That's great!"

I learned more at the dinner table that evening. A ceasefire had been arranged between the Japanese and the Chinese. Johnny and I were glad that Chapei was no longer being burned and bombed, but learned from our parents' conversations that the terms of the treaty harmed the Chinese.

"I don't know how long this so-called peace will last," Father said.

"How can it be that Japan is allowed to garrison several Japanese units north of the main parts of Shanghai, above Chapei? leaving China with only a small police force, and allowed none of her own troops?" Mother exclaimed."It's terrible! It's a terrible treaty!"

"It was arranged by the League of Nations who know nothing about China," Father told her."They naively believe the Japanese guarantees of peace." But he put away his Volunteer Soldiers uniform, hoping for the best.

Now the Japanese mortars shelled the city apparently only whenever they wanted to create an incident, or practice firing mortars and cannons. The occasional thump-thumping became unpredictable, but always occurred in the morning, with week- or even month-long interruptions. Our lives began to return to their pre-February 1932 patterns.

The terms of the Shanghai Ceasefire Agreement that the League of Nations forced on China are appalling. How did the League ever come into the picture? What right had they to decide China's future? Why was China so punished for defending her greatest port? This decision helped the Japanese take over Shanghai five years later. Their troops were already in the city.

V

1932-33. THE GERMAN SCHOOL AND A LONG WALK HOME. AGE SIX

SANDY, MY YOUNGER SON who is an expert on military history, is visiting; we're watching a World War II movie on the TV. The Nazis start singing the "Horst Wessel Lied," and I join right in:

"Die Fahne hoch,
die Reihen fest geschlossen,
S.A. marschiert,
mit ruhig festem Schritt..."

(The flag high,
The rows tight,
The S. A. marches
With quiet firm steps.)

Sandy starts to laugh in a sort of amazement. "Where did you learn that? The German school you went to?"

I liked the German school. The Kaiser Wilhelm Schule, with twelve grades, was in a sturdy stone building beside a nice playground in midtown Shanghai. At One Great Western Road it intersected with Bubbling Well Road. During my early years there, before Hitler and the Nazis spoiled it, the atmosphere was quiet, focused on learning, and lent a sweetness and innocence to my life. Neither Johnny nor I asked or knew why we were sent to different schools. Maybe we fought too much when we were together. Maybe they wanted one of us to know German and the other, Chinese.

The German flag flew above the school; opposite it was the Lutheran Church, and a business area called the Deutsche Eck (German Corner) was at the intersection.

The school didn't believe in coddling children. At age five, in Kindergarten, I was being taught geography. We learned not only about Germany and Europe but also about China and the location of the many provinces. It was fun drawing neat blue lines for ocean and brown and green lines for land and forest. Another subject, arithmetic, was more difficult, since I had to do the numbers in German: *Fünfzehn geteilt durch drei ist fünf --* Fifteen divided by three is five. Arithmetic was hard enough for me in English.

But the writing lessons in the ancient German script gave me a secret language. No one outside of school could read it; it pleased me to have this arcane skill.

We girls had lessons in embroidery, and in this class I had a head start through Tailor's instruction. In music we sang German folk songs and the German national anthem, *Deutschland Über Alles*. We gave recitals and concerts, for the German and for the international community on special occasions.

Sometimes I played with my teddy bears. My best friends, Renata Rall and Nina Wilhelm, also brought teddy bears to school. We built little homes for them between the roots of trees, making furniture out of bits of bark, leaves, and acorns. Some days Renata or Nina or both came to my home with their little bears to play with mine. I was proud that my boy bears were wearing army uniforms with bandoliers and matchstick guns with which to protect the others against the Japanese.

At Christmas we decorated the live, fragrant school Christmas tree with ornaments that we made of *papier maché*, red and green paper chains, and lacy cut-outs of golden and silver paper, singing *O Tannenbaum* as we arranged them. Every now and then my mischievous self sneaked out and I bellowed the song in English: *"Oh Christmas Tree, Oh Christmas Tree,"* disrupting the people around me and earning furious looks from the music instructor.

The teachers carefully attached real candles to the tips of the branches where they wouldn't set fire to the tree. As the teacher lit each little white candle with a long taper the hushed, familiar, inspiring tones of *Stille Nacht, Heilige Nacht* rose and echoed in the auditorium. I learned to sing the second soprano harmonies and enjoyed the sounds of the chords as well as the sense of wonder that embraced us.

Every year there were Christmas pageants in the auditorium. At one, I was dressed as a snowflake. Tailor, helped by Sew Sew Amah Mary and with Glowing Pearl beside him cutting out and hemming many little snowflakes, made a pretty dress of overlapping white flakes, and a cap with fluttering bits of flakes. I proudly wore these in the pageant. Other snowflake girls and I performed a little dance.

I learned about Father Nicholas and about putting sticks and stones into the Christmas stocking of children who had been naughty. All children, good and naughty, had stockings with Christmas pastries like Stollen, fruit and sugar candies, *Pfefferknüsse*, chocolates, and figures made of marzipan.

The Kaiser Wilhelm Schule took part in a children's program with the Shanghai Municipal Orchestra held at the Lyceum. Children from six or seven schools took part in singing Christmas carols in their respective languages—French, German, Russian, Italian, English. I liked hearing the different kinds of songs celebrating Christmas.

I had a real adventure that spring. One day Ah Ching, despite his almost infallible reliability, forgot to pick me up from school and somehow Matrushka, Amah, and Mother all had other things to do. After the bell rang announcing the end of the school day, I sat on the front steps for a long time waiting to be picked up. All the other students were picked up, all the adults left, but no one noticed me. I finally decided that my family had forgotten about me, but that I could find my way home and that I'd just have to walk there by myself. I picked up my school bag, resolutely placed the strap over one shoulder, and set off on the five-mile walk home.

It was a hot day. I headed confidently down Bubbling Well Road, staying on the sidewalk as much as possible. Sweaty gaunt rickshaw coolies came panting alongside me as they pulled their passengers. Cars jammed the street. People stared at me with curiosity, but no one spoke to me. Little as I was, I didn't look up at the tall office buildings and elegant shops high above me as I passed by, and ignored the action on the street; I just focused on the road ahead and on what was underfoot as I trudged along.

At intersections I carefully moved across the streets with a crowd of people for safety. Near the Race Course I noticed elderly gentlemen in long robes who had brought their favorite birds in cages for a stroll. Amah had told me, when we saw them on our drives, that the birds kept the old men company. Sometimes, she said, the men had competitions about their birds: which one had the best song, the best color, the friendliest disposition.

Finally I reached Great Western Road. Passing a vendor of fragrant hot noodles and dumplings I stopped, sniffing the air longingly. But I hadn't a penny on me with which to buy some.

"Littie Missy wantchee one piecee dumpling?" the vendor suddenly asked as I gazed at the trays of steaming food at my eye level. His smile was sweet.

I wasn't wary of a strange man's offering; no one had ever hurt me, nor did this kind man. I held up my empty hands, fingers spread open."My no got cash, my no can have."

The vendor picked up his chopsticks. My eyes opened very wide as I watched him. He selected a dumpling filled with goodies, placed it on a torn square of old Chinese newspaper, and handed it to me."My think so littie Missie hungry," he said."You likee?"

"Oh, yes! *Zhia zhia noong!* Thank you!" I said, gratefully stuffing the treat into my mouth. It was delicious."Ummm, too muchee goodee," I mumbled, smiling broadly, my mouth full. After I'd swallowed every crumb I thanked him again."You blong (are) one piecee so nicee man. *Zhia zhia.* My go home now."

The vendor grinned at me, several teeth missing in his gnarled old face. I saw that one of his eyes was pale white. How could that be! I wondered.

Continuing on my journey, I began to notice that the gray road underfoot was filthy and unpleasant. There were droppings from water buffalo and camels mixed with chewing gum wrappers, leaves, mud, spit, motor oil, food, newspapers. Smells of burned peanut oil, incense, sweat, opium, tobacco arose together or separately, were wafted over to me by occasional breezes as I walked the long blocks. I had to duck sometimes to avoid the wet slimy spittle that the rickshaw coolies hawked up as they trotted past me. Each one left a wave of unwashed body odor as he grunted along.

I was getting tired, cross, and beginning to limp. Now there were fewer office buildings and more residential areas. My long walk was almost over.

When I finally crossed over the little creek at the entrance to Columbia Circle, I sighed with relief. Shifting my school bag again from one shoulder to the other I limped a few more blocks, then, finally, saw Amherst Avenue and found my home.

There was satisfying hysteria after I knocked on our front door and stumbled in, dropped my school bag, and plopped in a chair. The household had realized that I was nowhere in sight. Amah told me that Ah Ching was frantically driving Mother along the back roads looking for a lost little girl. My father was on the phone with the police and trying to rouse someone at the German school. The school should not have left me alone on the front steps, I heard him shout. When he saw me as I came in he dropped the phone and gave me an immense hug, tears in his eyes."We were so afraid that maybe we'd lost you," he said, kissing my cheek."Let me look at my little sweetheart!"

Soon Mother and Ah Ching returned. They were stunned to see me safe in Father's arms. Mother rushed up to me and hugged me."Oh my precious, I was so scared!" She started to cry, holding me tight. Ah Ching was mortified that he had not picked me up at school.

"*Ai yah! Ai yah!*" he moaned. Poor Ah Ching, I thought. He is so ashamed. So I went up to him, patted his arm."It's OK, Ah Ching," I said,"I had fun walking home." I was trying to do what I had learned from Father: I was trying to save his dignity.

My long walk home had brought me for the first time into close contact with the emaciated rickshaw coolies. Before my expedition, I had not thought about their lives. I had now become aware of their panting and wheezing as they pulled their passengers.

I asked Father about this."Daddy, I think it's bad that the

rickshaw coolies have such an awful job. They have to run along pulling fat people when they are sick and coughing and should be home in bed with tea and medicine, like we are when we are sick. I don't like it."

"It is a complicated situation, Patty. I agree with you that it's an awful life for them. But they have no other way of earning a living. Without their work as rickshaw coolies they might just starve to death." He started to turn to his evening newspaper, then added: "Many of the coolies are addicted to a drug called opium and are so thin because they buy the drug with the money they earn, not the food their bodies need. There is nothing I can do to change their circumstances; the only thing we can do is to give them extra large *cumshaws* when we take them. I know it's not enough. I am truly sorry."

"It makes me angry, Daddy."

"You are right to be angry. I'm proud of you, daughter, for caring about other people the way you do." He paused, thinking, then set aside his newspaper."Why don't you and I cheer ourselves up by reading a story book together?"

One day at school that spring of 1933 the Headmaster called a special meeting of the entire student body and faculty. We all looked at each other questioningly, not daring to talk as we entered the auditorium.

There were huge unfamiliar banners on the walls. I couldn't help whispering to friends as we pointed up to them. Chairs scraped the floors, clothing rustled, people coughed. I became so nervous that I surreptitiously took the forbidden chewing gum my mouth and stuck it under the seat of my chair.

The Headmaster rose to the podium. He looked at us all for a moment, quietly, as though memorizing our faces. With evident sorrow and a gravelly edge of discouragement in his voice, he stated: "Good morning," in German. (Everything was conducted in German.) He paused, cleared his throat. "I am instructed by the new government in Germany to tell you that the régime of Fűhrer Adolph Hitler has replaced many of your present teachers with new young teachers who better represent the goals and ideals of the Fűhrer and the National Socialist, called Nazi, Germany."

He pointed to the huge red and white banners with heavy black swastikas that had appeared overnight on the walls. These swastikas, he explained, were the symbol of the new Germany. In Germany, he said, there were now Nazi rallies, parades, marches and meetings.

"From now on," he announced, "your formal greeting will change from 'Good morning,' 'Good afternoon,' or 'Good evening.' Now you are to say *Heil Hitler* at all occasions with your arm extended upward. Like this." He raised his arm to point up at an angle. "This is in acknowledgment of the greatness of our new leader."

Then he turned to the stranger with a harsh, angular face standing beside him. "May I introduce you to your new Headmaster. He has replaced me. We wish him well in his new position."

There were gasps around the room. I didn't know what to think; the idea of such a change in the school put me on edge.

Our well-liked Headmaster continued his remarks. He spoke about the fine quality and excellence of the students who were now under the new Headmaster's care, said that he and his family would be returning to Germany.

He raised his arm slightly and quietly said *"Heil Hitler."* I could tell that he was uncomfortable saying it. He paused. His eyes moved from student to student across the rows tenderly, affectionately, sometimes half-smiling. Then after a small bow, he left the room.

"Heil Hitler," the new principal shouted, arm raised high. He spoke about the *Führer's* glory; we should feel awe; we should always glorify him in our behavior and our language; how lucky we were to attend a true German school even in China. He closed with a snap of his heels and his arm shot up and his *"Heil Hitler"* rang out. I returned his *heil* with an uncertain, nervous wave, and returned to our classroom. I didn't know how I should act but decided to follow the lead of my friends.

On going outside that afternoon, we saw that a new German flag with a huge swastika was flying over the school.

At dinner I told my parents about the change at the school.

"Daddy, Mummy," I stuttered, my nerves unsteady,"I don't know what to do, the new headmaster and this Heil Hitler stuff scares me." I hesitated."I don't like holding up my arm and yelling Heil Hitler."

"Maybe it is like our elections at home," Father said, slowly considering this news,"when we change from one president to another. Let's wait and see what happens. Why don't you go along with it unless it gets too unpleasant for you?"

That seemed like the wise thing to do."I guess I can handle a weak Heil Hitler."

"For a while anyway, and see what happens in the future."

I remember that walk; how I had to avoid the constant spitting of the rickshaw coolies; their skeletal bodies with bones almost poking through their skin, the sound of their labored grunts as they ran, their feet slapping the filthy cement. Their running shoes? Straw sandals. Even in the winter, in the snow, the rickshaw coolies ran in straw sandals pulling their fares like oxen for a few pennies. An ache pushes up from within me and I have to get up and walk it off. I was angry then and I am angry now at the indignity to humans, the pain. Thank God for the invention of the pedicab.

VI

1933. I REMEMBER EACH ONE OF YOU.
AGE SIX

I STRUGGLE TO haul the trash down the stairs and out to the sidewalk. It's been raining; I step carefully, hoping I won't slip and fall on the wet driveway ramp. It really hurt, the last time. Back in my house, I stretch my back and rotate my head gently.

Well, I chastise myself, I don't want servants underfoot. I think briefly about my childhood. People say that I was so privileged to have had a childhood with live-in servants doing all the work. And so I was, although I didn't know it. More and more however I love, need, the quiet to think and feel and listen, to release the creativity so long restrained and postponed by duties. It's my turn, now. So I outsource or ignore what I can't, or don't want, to do. And in the quiet, the people of my long-ago come close, closer, and nudge at me."Remember," they whisper."Remember us."

All of the people who kept us going had the lively Chinese sense of fun, and they loved Mother, who liked to spoof people. One day in late March she and Cook were planning an April Fool's Day party for us and some of our friends."Cook," she said,"What you think, slice some soap very thin, make some holes to look like Swiss cheese, for sandwiches?"

"*Hao, ding hao,*" Cook said, laughing."Very very good idea. Maybe for dessert my makee cotton ball cream puff for profiteroles? Pour real chocolate sauce over?"

"Wonderful, Cook, that's a wonderful idea! Patty, what do you think?"

"I think that's just awful. That's an awful party. Mother, you can't do that!"

"Well, maybe we'll surprise you a bit. Don't you worry your pretty little head about it, darling." She and Cook made some other plans, then she asked him to send up Ah Kung.

As the Number One, Ah Kung ran the household under Mother's instruction and I noticed that sometimes he ran Mother too. She almost always took his advice.

"We are going to have some children over on April One, April Fool's Day," she said."Will you please arrange for the dining room table to be removed, replaced by the Japanese sukiyaki table? The little children can sit on the floor like the Japanese do."

"Very good, Missie. You think put cushion for children to sit?"

"Absolutely. There will be—let's see—ten children in all to sit around the sukiyaki table."

"Serve Amah, governess, on verandah? What thing serve, Missie?"

"All same as for the children. Patty, would you leave the room for a minute? Ah Kung and I have to have a private conversation." I guessed that they would "secretly" plan some real food for us, so I gladly left.

On April Fool's Day we children all sat on the floor around the low sukiyaki table. Sure enough, we were served soap sandwiches and cotton cream puffs smothered in chocolate sauce. Everyone groaned and complained until Mother appeared with Ah Kung carrying trays of real sandwiches and cream puffs.

"April Fool!" she cried, laughing, and we all began to laugh.

"The soap sandwiches were delicious!" one guest said."And the cotton balls yummy!"

I don't know how we would have managed without our butler, Ah Kung. One evening, when there were guests to dinner, Ah Kung presented the platter of roast duck to be carved by my father. Amah told me the story as relayed to her by Lin Sing.

As my father began to carve, the duck slid off the platter onto the floor.

"Please bring another duck," he said calmly to Ah Kung.

The duck mess on the floor was collected and returned to the kitchen by Lin Sing. In several minutes, another duck complete with orange decorations was presented to my father. He began to carve it. It too slid off the platter onto the floor.

"Please bring another duck," my father, still calm, asked Ah Kung, as Lin Sing cleaned up the new mess on the floor.

Another perfectly presented duck appeared. This time, he managed to keep it on the platter. Amah told me later that the same duck had reappeared those two additional times, perfectly and invisibly reconstructed and decorated by Ah Kung and Cook.

I heard from Lin Sing about another time when Ah Kung had saved the day for my parents. That morning they were at the Races. Father expansively invited ten friends to join them for lunch at home. Mother frantically phoned Ah Kung to alert him to the potential disaster—no guests had been anticipated, nothing was prepared.

"No problem, Missie. My can do," he replied.

When everyone arrived at our house an hour later, an elegant sit-down luncheon for twelve was ready. Lin Sing told me that Ah Kung, who knew which friends of my parents were going to the Races and would probably be guests afterwards at our house, had phoned each of their Number Ones. Explaining the situation, he got Ah Ching to drive to the respective homes to collect the meals that would have been served there, and he and

Cook rebuilt them.

I loved the enormous kitchen and Cook spoiled me even though I was a girl. A bread oven had been built into one wall. Here, Cook baked several loaves at a time, their fragrance inviting little fingers to poke into them. And sometimes when I thought he wasn't looking, I did reach up, open the latch, and poke my fingers into the warm center of a loaf to pull out a yummy bite.

One day Cook invited me into his kitchen.

"Littie Missie, my have got one number one goodee present for you." He reached into the bread oven and with a broad smile wrinkling his chubby cheeks, brought out a wee little loaf, about six inches long, carefully handing it to me."My bake for Littie Missie. Now no more take Missie, Master bread." His eyes twinkled. So he knew my secret! I held the little warm loaf in my hands, turned it over, then reached into its heart and pulled out the warm squishy bread.

"Oh thank you, thank you," I mumbled, smiling up at him, my mouth full of delicious newly baked bread.

Another time, Cook decided that it was time to teach me how to make popovers, one of my favorite dishes. I kept swiping them from his kitchen.

"My think so Littie Missie big now, can do make popover all same Cook," he said, smiling broadly, the wide spaces between his teeth like dark pickets among the white teeth."Number one, put apron so dress not dirty." He wrapped a white cloth around me, then walked me through every step in preparation of popovers until we poured the mixture into hissing hot tins, then gently shutting them in the oven."Now we wait. Littie Missie go play, my watch popover."

Chauffeur Ah Ching was also a problem-solver. One of his accomplishments when he saved Mother's face became a family story. He had been teaching her to drive. One day, with him beside her in the car, she drove successfully to a tiffin party. She sighed with relief, then, instead of braking, she stepped on the gas pedal. The car crashed into a cement post that held up the gate and fence around the host's garden.

After a moment of shocked silence Ah Ching calmly said: "Never mind, Missie. You no talkee this Missie. You and Missie chow, my fix. No man savvy, Missie. Missie no lose face, my no lose face."

Mother straightened her clothes, put on a carefree smile, and, pretending confidence, went in to the party. The group of ladies had tiffin, then a bridge game, tea, and then, oh dear, a walk in the garden to see the roses. She began to think of ways to explain the wrecked gateway. But to her surprise, the cement post was erect, as was the rose-covered bamboo fence. What kind of miracle was this?

She learned that Ah Ching had quickly brought in friends of his—a mason, a carpenter, and a gardener to repair the damage. He had saved her face and thereby his own.

During this period of relative peace, it was safe for me to go on expeditions around the city in areas that were free of Japanese soldiers, in addition to the safe international treaty areas.

Near our house was a dusty parade route where we occasionally watched Chinese mourners shuffle along to the temple or cemetery. One day when Amah and I were out walking we came upon a noisy funeral procession.

"Littie Missie," she said,"This blong one number one big man, have much wife." So we stopped, and from the side of the road, we watched the parade of mourners.

Musicians were banging on large brass gongs and crashing cymbals to announce the funeral procession. After them came a motorized hearse hung with elaborate embroideries, the eldest son and family following on foot in order of status in the family. A narrow length of white cloth linked the hearse to the family. More white cloth was pasted to windshields.

"What for white cloth, Chiao Kuei?"

"White cloth mean all person very sorry that man die. For China-man, white color mean sad, man die or other bad thing happen." Most of the mourners were dressed in long white robes with white caps.

A special long joss stick had been lit and was carried throughout the procession; it represented the soul of the deceased.

Next we saw representations of the deceased's favorite objects made of tissue paper stretched across bamboo frames — his Mandarin throne chair, his house, his car marching along the dusty road.

"Look, Amah, at his beautiful house! And there's his boat!"

I was fascinated by the palanquins decorated with red lacquer and golden dragons, borne by coolies with bamboo carrying poles on their shoulders. Amah told me that they hid his favorite women behind veils. Reaching high above the heads of the procession were portraits of the departed, decorated with good luck sayings in gold letters.

"*Ai yah*," Amah muttered from time to time as we waited on the sidewalk for the procession to pass."My think so this man have got too muchee goodee joss. He have got plenty *dong dee* (Shanghai slang for "money"). She told me a wild story about how the man got so much money by blackmailing families into giving him their money.

"Look see, Littie Missie!" She exclaimed as she pointed out an especially elaborate palanquin."My think so he have got too muchee wife, too."

Then came the professional money marchers. Truly horrible to me, these were people hired to show the riches of the deceased.

Heavy chains of actual coins swung from long oblong holes that had been cut into the skin every few inches along the underside of their arms. They walked slowly, their arms outstretched, swaying slightly with every step under the weight of their burden. There were grotesque elongated holes in their ear lobes, swinging chains of coins hanging from them. Some of the coins were "coppers," flat round coins of relatively little value made of copper, with square holes in their centers. More expensive, heavier coins were solid silver "Mex."

After watching these money marchers, for a long time I couldn't look at the ears of mother's friends who wore earrings hanging from holes in their lobes.

School was over; it was summertime in Shanghai. The mugginess and humidity turned every activity into an effort. Hair drooped and sometimes dripped. Prickly heat irritated the skin. Mold luxuriated on leathers, linens, under wallpaper in older homes, on any enclosed damp surface. Bureau drawers expanded and stuck. The pages of books warped.

When I looked out of my window one morning I saw that our garden was filled with rows of boards on sawhorses that the gardeners had set up. Fo Sun and Elder Coolie were making trip after trip from the house to the garden, carrying leather books, shoes, Mother's purses. These were aired and dried in the sun all day to prevent mold from forming on them. The coolies spread the books opened wide to expose them to sunlight.

Then Lin Sing, Tailor and Amah, helped by Mother, gathered all of our winter clothing to be hung out, brushed and aired. In the late afternoon, it would be stored in the camphor wood closet on the second floor. They brought down all our wool blankets, giving them a good shake and beating them with a long-handled, fan-like, flat whisk. That done, they tramped back upstairs to pack the blankets into cedar chests.

When I asked her why all this was going on, Mother explained that it was to protect our winter things from mold and moths.

Inside our house, bamboo floor mats woven in curving designs replaced our thick oriental rugs; those were also taken outdoors, brushed and beaten, and then rolled up with camphor balls to preserve them until fall. Thin flexible woven bamboo mats were placed under our sheets to help keep our bodies cool. This year, I saw Tailor making gray linen slipcovers with yellow piping to protect the fabric of the upholstered chairs and sofa in the living room.

The businessmen like Father packed away their dark suits and vests and brought out white Bermuda shorts with short-sleeved shirts and light summer jackets, often seersucker that wouldn't wrinkle. I was so proud of Father when he wore his white shorts and knee-length white socks; he had elegant legs.

Some days we went for sports and fun to the nearby American club."Daddy John and I are going to the Columbia Country Club for a luncheon," Mother said one day."Maybe you and Johnny would like to go there too to play with some of your friends? At least there'll be no danger from the Japanese soldiers there." Mother liked us to call my father "Daddy John;" I think it was an attempt to maintain us even in China as a traditional Southern family. We preferred to call him simply Dad or Daddy.

The Club was in a real sense the cornerstone of our Columbia Circle community. Most of our neighbors came over to my parents' parties, or bridge and poker games, and my parents to theirs. When I went to play at other children's homes in the Columbia Circle area, I saw that they were much like ours. The servants and the governesses and Amahs all knew each other.

We loved the sports and the parties in the Columbia Country

Club. Tennis courts, a swimming pool and a squash court were there for us, and a large bowling alley. Under the Spanish-Mexican style arcade was a long verandah for dining and dancing. Mother once showed me a photograph of some grown-ups at a costume party; I saw Father with a woman I didn't know, and Mother with a man I didn't know.

"Why aren't you and Daddy together?" I asked.

She giggled. "That photograph was taken at a 'Red Dog' party at the Club where we were all dressed as Civil War couples," she told me. "That's when Daddy John and I met and fell in love. He called on me the next day with flowers, cream-colored roses, you know, like the ones he gives me every year on our anniversary."

I had fun at the Club and so did my parents, who knew we were safely watched over by an assortment of nannies, Amahs and governesses of different nationalities. Mother and Father joined other couples enjoying their whiskey sours and gin fizzes on the verandah on the other side of the building.

After lunch—I usually had American-style hamburgers smothered in catsup—and ice cream, our parents collected us, found Ah Ching, and we drove the few blocks home.

One day when we arrived I was surprised and pleased to see that Matrushka had returned. She and her friends had decided that the International and French parts of the city were now safe, and were going to stay. Many of the Russian refugees in the Hong Kew part of the city, however, could not find rooms in the international areas to rent at prices that they could afford, and were trapped with the Chinese peasants in poverty.

We went occasionally to an area about a half-hour drive west in the outskirts of Shanghai, where we had a vegetable farm. A stretch of the road leading to the farm was lined with Chinese peddlers selling domed birdcages made of fine bamboo sticks, with a little gate that slid up and down. Each cage held one bird.

"What are those men doing with the birds?" I asked Amah, who had accompanied us this time.

"One bird in cage want to fly away; man who buy bird open cage, let fly away, all same let spirit free," she said."All same what Buddha say." I tried to understand this idea, but could only feel sorrow for the poor bird that had to sing in its little cage until set free.

On our plot we grew our own vegetables to be assured of their cleanliness; but even so, the tomatoes, lettuce, string beans, potatoes and other vegetables, when brought home, were washed in boiled water and that purple potassium permanganate. The land was protected by an iron fence and a gate with a lock, and guarded by a gardener/watchman who looked after our vegetables.

In the middle was a small Chinese tomb made of gray stones, about two feet high and three feet long, with a curved tile roof. We never learned who or what was in the tomb; we didn't dared ask.

A stream about five feet wide traversed the land. Two white stone slabs, each about a foot wide, bridged it. A four-inch space separated the slabs. And under them, I could see and smell the stream pungent with rotting stuff and covered with green slime. I was terrified of falling in. My brother went cavorting across the slabs while I had to get down and, panicked, crawl across, no matter how often I tried to walk across. Every time we went to the farm I tried to walk across the bridge; every time, paralyzed by fear, I had to crawl.

The smells of mothballs, camphor and cedar all evoke Shanghai. With a whiff of those round camphor pellets I am again in the attic in China with trunks of winter blankets, sweaters, Harris tween jackets, camel's hair overcoats, woolen socks. We still have a few precious pieces of

77

clothing from that time—my father's camel's hair bathrobe made by Tailor, which Lila now wears when she is cold. Two of his hand-hemmed handkerchiefs are treasured in my jewelry box. And when life is just too hard to bear, I find solace in pressing his handkerchiefs against my cheeks, just as I did when I was a scared little girl. My heart has never grown up.

VII

1934-35. I am taught Chinese and Western culture.
Age Six-Seven

It is one of the minor curses of my life that, while I can extend my arms into lovely arches, my legs are trapped by unyielding hamstrings, and I can't kick high enough to do a split. But I love, love, ballet. The impossible grace, the seeming long minutes balanced in mid-air during a leap, the rhythms and lines of bodies in a pas de deux. My daughter-in-law has sent me the link to David Hallburge's and Natalia Osipova's Giselle. So beautiful that it is hard to breathe while watching the performance — it is literally breath-taking.

The Chinese half of me equally loves the dramatically different Chinese dance. We've seen examples in Crouching Tiger Hidden Dragon *directed by the magnificent Ang Lee. One of the remarkable people in my life was the leading dancer/singer in Chinese theatre who taught me, just a little girl, many aspects of Chinese dance. Traditional performance dance always takes me to Shanghai.*

My parents did everything they could to make sure that Johnny and I acquired some degree of Western culture while also absorbing the Chinese culture that surrounded us. They took advantage of everything that was offered. We were enrolled in a Saturday morning music program hosted by the Shanghai

Municipal Orchestra, where, in the concert hall, we were introduced to Western music and to the strings, woodwinds, brass, and percussion instruments in addition to the piano, guitar and violin in our home.

I especially liked the French horn for its physical beauty — the shining brass tubes, wide or narrow, circular or crossing gracefully over the circles — as well as for its sound that always made me sit up straighter and my eyes open wider.

Artists on international tours sought out performances in Shanghai. I was thrilled one afternoon when Mother took me with her to see a world-famous Russian ballet company on tour in Asia.

"The lead artist dances like the great Nijinski," she said excitedly as we settled in our seats and began reading the program. "He must be a beautiful dancer."

The opening music enthralled me. I was holding my breath for the curtain to rise. Then it slowly revealed the stage. The lead male dancer, dressed with leaves woven into his hair and costume, entered with a great leap through a window. He flew, really flew, staying up in the air an unbelievable amount of time.

"Mom," I whispered, "that's impossible, what he's doing! Oh, it's beautiful!"

As the program went on he sometimes seemed to be doing a split in mid-air, his legs reaching almost horizontally to the right and left. In one part of the ballet he leapt straight up and twittered his feet across each other rapidly before coming back down, and then flew straight up again to repeat the motion.

"He's doing an *entre-chat*," Mother said, astonished. "My goodness, he must be doing a good eight twitters with every upward leap! I am sure that its not an *entre-chat dix*, as only Nijinski himself could ever accomplish that. Patty, that is an extremely difficult dance step, where the feet cross quickly back and forth many times before coming to ground again."

"Mummy, just look at him! He can't be doing those things he's doing! He's really flying! Oh, he is beautiful!"

I couldn't focus on anyone else on stage, just this one magnetic person. Later at home I tried to do an *entre-chat* and managed one before my legs got tangled and I fell down.

Chinese artists and actor/dancers were among my parents' close friends. They took Johnny and me to the Chinese opera from time to time. I loved the garish, clashing colors of reds and yellows and ochers and the equally garish, clashing sounds of drums, gongs, and theatrical sing-song voices. Mother whispered to us what was going on in the wildly dramatized legends. Warriors in vivid costumes wore hideous masks, with hair twisted and glued into top-knots; long swords poked through to protrude on both sides. Special Mandarin shoes with three-inch soles raised them above normal height.

The great Chinese male opera/dance star, Mei Lanfang, who played the leading female roles, was especially kind to me.

"His name means 'plum aromatic orchid' in Chinese," Mother told me,"very appropriate for a female part, don't you think?" Mei Lanfang was a man with slight body, expressive eyes and long flexible hands. His voice had a wide range that accommodated the high soprano theatrical sing-song.

A friendship grew between us when he called on my parents. He was charming as he taught me some of the craft of the Chinese dance.

"You use every part of your body, Miss Patty," he said, taking my hands in his and moving them around."Sometimes you lift one finger to show strength, like this." He extended one arm, almost uncurling it from his body, the fingers curled under the horizontal palm, and then slowly raised the pointer finger up, holding the pose while uttering horrible sounds in Chinese."Or sometimes you stamp you feet to show angry," he said."Beauty of harmony or ugliness of anger can be created by gestures." He showed me how to curve and bend my hands expressively and how to hold my fan and use my eyes."You play with you fan covering half you face and make eyes friendly, that means you want the man to like you."

Once he clothed me in a dancer's dress with two very long — at least three feet — gauzy silk scarves that were extensions of the sleeves. Because I was small, they had to be pinned back about two feet. Then he rotated my wrists, using their momentum to throw the filmy sleeve-scarves forcefully upward so that they soared far above me and then fell in slow shimmering waves."So beautiful!" he said."This movement means trouble for other person."

He asked me to shake the long sleeves wildly, creating nervous eddies of the silky gauze, to indicate trembling with fear."Throw the sleeves out, and wave your arms around gracefully," he said."That will make lovely circles; this means anger. And waving the sleeves around you body, like embrace, says that you happy to see important older man."

I tried over and over in our living room to make magical leaps like the ballet dancers, but landed on the floor in a heavy clump. Warlord-style stamping and waving fans and scarves around fared no better. Finally my parents decided that I should have dancing lessons that were neither Chinese nor ballet. So I learned how to waltz and foxtrot with other Western boys and girls at a class in town.

A succession of interesting people came to visit. Various Amahs who helped to keep Mother looking pretty and healthy came to the house regularly. I liked watching them and hearing them.

Nail Amah applied the pale pink polish that Mother preferred on her fingers and toes. I tried a bit of polish on the nail of my pinkie but Mother made me wipe it off immediately. I was too young, she said.

Massage Amah came every week. One day I asked Mother what she did."It isn't just that the massage helps me relax, but also, Patty, I learn so much about everyone else!" she confided."This same Amah goes to the homes of many of my friends." Indeed, as I went past the closed door to her bedroom I could hear Massage Amah chatting about parties being given, families that were quarreling, new people arriving or old residents leaving, what the Japanese or the Communists were up to. I smiled on hearing Mother's voice murmuring encouragement from time to time. Mother was an ace journalist and she got her stories in some amazing ways

Hair Amah came as often as Mother needed. While she let me arrange her hair from time to time, she needed another level of expertise for parties.

She was visited also by women who were her friends. Especially fascinating to me were very old Chinese ladies with bound feet. I knew about the "golden lotus" feet that truly well-born ladies had to endure and had watched some of the elegant women with bound feet making their way slowly and carefully across the lobby of the Cathay Hotel. Some of Mother's Chinese lady friends walked with very tiny steps, swaying slightly and moving slowly on feet about three inches long. I thought that their beautifully embroidered silk shoes would fit one of my dolls.

After one had left I asked Mother why the Chinese peasant women didn't have to suffer the bound feet, but the elegant women did. It pained me to see dignified bejeweled Chinese ladies shuffle along so slowly, while some other women could walk normally. It made no sense.

"The custom began about a thousand years ago," she told me,"when an Empress was born with club feet, little deformed feet. It was decreed that all ladies should have tiny feet. As time passed, no high-class gentleman would marry a woman with big feet. The girls' feet were bound when they were about four years old."

"Oh my goodness, I wouldn't have let them do that to me! It must hurt something awful!"

"Nobody's allowed to bind feet any longer," Mother said."Thank goodness."

My new pink and white bathing suit, created by Tailor to fit my almost seven-year-old body, never got to jump into the happy blue Wei Hai Wei ocean with me.

"Why can't we go to the beach?' I complained."Why not!"

Mother tried to quiet me down."The situation with Japan is just too risky in North China now," she said."The Japs are fighting the Chinese army in Mongolia, just north of Shanhaiguan, the easternmost Chinese fortress. Everyone is very jittery about what is happening up there."

There had been intermittent skirmishes and battles north of Shanghai among Japanese, Koreans, Russians, and Communists ever since I could remember, but those hadn't directly affected my life.

"This year we'll stay home." Father then sweetened the prospect of a bleak hot summer in Shanghai: "How about swimming lessons for you at the Country Club?"

"OK, that would be nice," I said, somewhat mollified.

"We have to remember that here in Shanghai we are protected from the Japanese by the treaties that establish our safe homes in the International Concession. Outside of Shanghai, except in a few other Treaty cities, we have no such protection."

"Don't they have the Royal British Navy up in Wei Hai Wei?" Johnny asked."Isn't that where the British warships are based when they're not in Hong Kong?"

"Yes, Johnny, you're right. But we can't be sure we would be protected if the Japanese made trouble. I am not willing to bet my family's safety on the possibility."

So we found interesting things to do in the summer months. Most of the time Johnny and I played at the Country Club. I had basic swimming lessons while Johnny learned to do swan dives and jack knives. He made spectacular belly flops, too, and depth bombs that splashed everyone near the pool. I paddled around, crawling really, in the shallow section. My swimming teacher didn't have much luck with me. I was scared of letting go of his hand and started yelling when he left me to float on my own.

Mother also took advantage of the summer months to give us riding lessons. I learned to ride at the Ascot Riding School in the French Concession with a former Russian Cossack officer, Mr. Belorukov, as the riding master. The head of the school, he loved teaching me to canter.

"*Da, da*, Mademoiselle," he called out. Then in heavily accented imperfect French he encouraged me to let the horse dance on the air: "*Maintenant donnez-lui d'encouragement, laissez-lui danser sur l'air.*"

Johnny and I liked to play scary games about the war and Chinese warlords. I was a year older now and allowed to bicycle around the neighborhood with Johnny. We tried to frighten people, gathering our courage and defiantly yelling the names of warlords:

"Wu Peifu!"

"Chang Tso-lin!"

We were too scared of the Communists to shout out the name

of Mao Zedong, who was alive and active, unlike the deceased war lords, and we didn't want to say the names of the Japanese generals.

"Bang bang bang!" we shouted. I waved a toy gun around. Johnny aimed with his real BB gun.

We also scared everyone and ourselves by setting off long strings of firecrackers, the two-inch red firecrackers which were sold everywhere and which gave off an exciting gunpowder smell and wonderful little pop-pop-popping blasts. I loved the smell of the gunpowder.

My parents sent me on Sundays to the modern new Christian Science Church. Here I learned about Mary Baker Eddy, and also learned another of life's truths: despite what Mrs. Eddy said, pain, real or imaginary, hurt. But I also learned about Luke and Leviticus, Isaiah and Jesus. I could recite the Ten Commandments and the Beatitudes, and knelt by my bed every night to say *"The Lord's Prayer"* as well as *"Now I lay me down to sleep,"* to thank God for my blessings, and to bless different family members, friends, and animals.

Mother told me that she had been a Methodist like her mother, and had studied at Scarritt College in Kansas City, Missouri, to become a social worker and missionary at the McTyeire School in Shanghai, run by the U.S Southern Methodist Mission in China. She had converted that into a career as a war correspondent.

Once Father showed me a clipping by the editor of the *China Weekly Review*, J. B. Powell, about Mother. He wrote that *"Miss Booker has the distinction of having gained the first interview ever granted to a foreign woman correspondent by either Chang Tsolin, Mukden's war lord, or Wu Peifu, China's national hero."*

On a long afternoon on a boat deck she told us how this happened. She had befriended Madame Wu Peifu, wife of the fearsome warlord, and was invited as a guest for several days into their home.

"I spent hours in the women's quarters waiting for something to happen," she told us."When news did break, I heard it as soon as my hostess did, and could act on it before any other reporter. Madame Wu sent me off to war with a picnic basket, imagine!" she laughed.

Madame Wu enjoyed her personality — Mother's quick sense of humor and genuine interest and courtesy always made friends for her among the Chinese and wanted to help the woman journalist get the rare interview with the Marshall.

It was Marshall Chang Tso-lin's son, the young General Chang Hsuehliang, who arranged for her to meet that warlord and his family.

Mother's drive as a journalist was hard for us to live with. Her almost ruthless determination ruled the family. Everything was on a deadline and had to be done *chop chop*. Immediately. No excuses, no *maskee* or "never mind." She wouldn't quit whatever it was that interested her until it was done to her satisfaction. Her newspaper stories always met the deadline. But nothing else ever did without high drama.

She was cuddly and cute, playful with a dimpled smile and blonde hair. Her legendary energy and determination were balanced by her sense of humor and her total loyalty to those she loved. The Chinese, from highest rank to peasant, all adored her.

Some days we were taken by our parents and Matrushka to the parts of Shanghai dominated by the Russian refugees. Early one evening we went to the Russian Tea Room in the French Concession. Matrushka began singing softly to the Russian songs performed by the orchestra with balalaikas, teaching me some of the words of *Ochi Chornya, Vera, Vera,* and *Sierze* as she sang. She told me that this Tea Room, a favorite of all Shanghai's Russians, reminded her of her former homeland. It was too expensive for most of the refugees, however.

Father had had some good luck that he wanted to celebrate with us."Well, isn't this a nice party," he said, very pleased."This afternoon we're going to have a Russian specialty, *blinis*."

"Oh, Mr. Potter, how wonderful!" Matrushka cried."Real *blinis!* I haven't had any for so long."

He signaled to a waiter wearing a white blouse with a dramatic sash tied around his waist over loose trousers. Well-shined cavalry boots completed his costume.

"We would like *blinis* all around, yes?" he looked around our table of five people."Yes indeed, darling!" Mother replied. Her eyes were shining and her trademark dimples appeared on both cheeks as she smiled."With Beluga caviar please!" Father also ordered lemon grass vodka, with ginger ale for Johnny and me.

During all this I was fascinated by the waiter's large twitching moustache. He saw me observing it and gave it an extra twitch. I giggled."*La petite demoiselle*, she like my moustache?" I giggled again and hid my face with a napkin. He left to give the order, then returned with the drinks, the *blinis,* the Beluga caviar and the sour cream and chives for the *blinis*."Oh, these are like little *crèpes*."

Then the waiter taught me the words *da* and *nyet* while preparing my blini. "Some caviar? *Da?*" he said."*Da*," I replied, grinning."Some rocks and dirt?" "*Nyet nyet!*" I laughed. From then on I played with the words, laughing at the drumming sounds and rhymes that I could make with da da, ddda ddda and no no nyet no nyet yet.

After a while I looked around the room. At other tables there were men accompanied by beautiful Russian "vamps" with high cheekbones, gaudy jewelry and furs, and with what I guessed was lots of "oomph."

Matrushka knew some of them. After she had her share of the delicate buckwheat *blinis*, she asked to be excused to speak to one of the women.

"Mrs. Potter," she said, "May I join my friend Olga for a few minutes? She escaped on the train with me from the murderers in Russia. There are so many of us here now, they say around 20,000. Imagine! And I am so thank you and Mr. Potter for giving me a home and nice work with Patty. So many friends are starving or working as guards or as waiters, like our waiter Dimitri, who was a businessman in St. Petersburg."

She rose, then paused, smiling shyly. "I am grateful to live in a nice house, and not like so many other Russians who have to live so close to Japanese in that terrible Hong Kew. And I don't have to be charming to men, like the young women we see here, like my friend Olga, in order to eat. Thank you."

She left to join her friend, returning soon, and we left to go home. The music stayed in my head and I annoyed everyone by singing *Ochi chornya* and *Sierze* in endless repetitions. I was also thinking about what she had said. I guessed that many people, not just the rickshaw coolies, had hard lives. When later I told my friends about the adventure, one told me that some of the Russian men refugees couldn't find any work because they couldn't speak English, French or Chinese, and were forced to pull rickshaws like the coolies.

As we drove home through the French Concession, I noticed bright signs in Russian next to those in French. Many Russian businesses had found homes on the tree-lined boulevards.

"Oh, Mr. and Mrs. Potter," Matrushka suddenly exclaimed, "You might be interested — look, over there to the right — that is the new Saint Nicholas' Church, it has just been built!" Ah Ching slowly pulled to a halt in front of an unusual building with onion-shaped domes reaching high, and an elaborate entrance."It was built by the efforts of us White Russians in Shanghai."

"It is beautiful," Mother said."One day we'll take time to visit it."

A busload of Japanese men stopped in front of the church. They climbed out of the bus and posed for a photograph, the church their backdrop. The photographer had a large black camera box with an accordion-like extension, just like Mother's. The air became filled with noisy Japanese exclamations.

"Probably a lot of spies among them," Father muttered. I cringed and hid my head in my mother's shoulder.

"Darn them," Johnny said angrily."Why don't they take pictures of what their bombs have done to Chapei instead."

"The blankety-blanks!" I yelled. I knew that meant something bad.

"Let's drive on," Mother said, patting Johnny's head."I can't stand seeing them either. Patty, watch your language."

Surprising, the bits of life one remembers, specks of memories clinging here and there to the fragile web of a life. Recalling Matrushka's return evokes memories of a world rich in drama, in sorrow, in elegance and in penury; and the film that my daughter Lila has brought brings that world vividly to the forefront of my mind.

"I brought a great movie for us to watch!" she announces as she comes in the door.

"What is it?" I'm looking forward to seeing it. Lila picks great movies.

"It's called 'The White Countess' and is about your period in Shanghai." Lila knows that I am writing a book on growing up there. The movie is about a White Russian émigré family that escaped to Shanghai from the Communist purges, and what happens to them and to the patron of the Countess when the Japanese invade the city.

"But she didn't say the famous line everyone knew – 'No got Mama, no got Papa, no got Whiskey Soda,'" I note.

Also featured in the movie is a struggling Jewish refugee family that is crowded into a little house now shared with the Russians. The family of Jews, too, had fled to safety in Shanghai, far from the Nazi purges in Europe.

"Is this familiar to you?" asks Lila.

I nod. "Oh yes," I breathe. "So familiar that it hurts."

Scenes in the movie of almost forgotten moments of my early life surprise and shock me.

VIII

1934. CHRISTMAS; MOTHER HEADS
NORTH TO COVER THE WAR.
AGE SIX-SEVEN

I HAVE ARRANGED *green boughs over the mantle; I have balanced on the top rung of the step-ladder to hang the mistletoe with satin red ribbons on the entrance hall light (touching the ribbon with pleasure, recognizing that my love for satin, real satin — soft, pliable, sensuous, arises from my childhood); I have put in supplies of food in preparation for Christmas dinner. All the children and grandchildren will be present.*

Now I forage in the attic for the boxes of special Christmas tree ornaments that I have made from designs by my children and grandchildren. I unwrap my older daughter Lila's, the planet Saturn in a night sky; younger daughter Tina's heart with everyone's initials on it. Will's dragon, Henry's Greenie, Thomas' rainbow. Kit's and Sandy's. Remind myself to get Glenis to draw one for me to make. Humming, I bring them out, and they speak to me.

I turn now to the woven rattan trunk with its scraps of labels from long-ago voyages still stuck to the top; it creaks as I pull it towards me.

"Hello, old friend," I murmur, patting the trunk, smiling. There is a trace of my mother's initials, "ELP," in heavy black ink.

I unfasten the sturdy woven clasps and raise the lid, reaching in for other boxes of ornaments. Nestled under them, tucked in a corner, is a

toy wardrobe trunk with a child's hand-written label in uneven block
letters:

ROTARY DOLL HOSPITAL FOR REFUGEE CHILD.
CONTAINS: DOLL, CLOTH, DRESSES FOR DOLL.

As I touch it, a sharp memory of Japanese soldiers with open
bayonets gleaming stabs at me. Their somewhat nauseating odor. I
shake my head to clear it away. I won't let them in.

Now the scent of sandalwood surrounds me; in the big trunk there is
a collection of delicate, almost filigree, hand fans carved of sandalwood.
I breathe deeply, give a little involuntary shiver of joy, and smile."It
smells like home."

In December, everything in the house changed to prepare for
Christmas.

I loved our home at Christmas. My parents decorated every
room on all three floors. The banister from the third floor to the
first was wrapped with fragrant pine garlands and red satin
ribbons. An aroma of sandalwood always permeated the house
because the intricately carved sandalwood cabinets and other
sandalwood objects throughout the house perfumed the air. The
sandalwood blended with the scent of the pines to imbue the
entire house with wondrous magic.

During the season my parents entertained frequently. The
family specialties were Father's flaming plum pudding dessert
and Mother's eggnog from an old Virginia recipe. Father's skills
at carving roasts and game were matched by Mother's elegant
table settings.

My father brought out his centerpiece for the dining room
table: a Christmas landscape he had built before I was born. This
was a country winter scene on an oval board about two feet long

and one and a half feet wide. When I stood up on a chair I could see it all. There was a path through a field that led to a house about six inches high. This year Father had to repair the picket fence made of matchsticks that surrounded that house, and he let me hand him each little picket to glue in place. Real lights shone inside, and smoke, created by a piece of incense, rose from the chimney. It pleased me to see that on the grounds were a pond with a boy and girl skating on the mirror "ice," and a little horse and buggy.

I wanted to touch them and play with them, but made myself sit on my hands because I feared I would break one of the objects that Father had worked so hard to create. Especially the little buggy. Ooooh, I wanted to play with it! The fields showed stubble in rows, with a scarecrow in the middle like the Scarecrow in the Wizard of Oz book in my room. Haystacks were tied up in little triangles, and a couple of crows perched in the fields. A tiny Santa with packages sat on the roof. Over all was a dusting of "snow".

When the scene was almost ready, Father in his tweed trousers and rolled-up shirt sleeves crawled under the table, soldering iron in hand, doing something with a string of lead, and this brought electricity to the scene. And when the light came on in the little house—what a celebration!

This Christmas was a bit strange. I was not allowed to go into Father's study. I became very cross about it.

"Why can Johnny go in the study, but I can't?" I complained."It's so unfair!"

"Hush, Patty, be a good egg and stop whining," Mother said."I promise that you'll be happy about it later. Just not yet."

"But why, Mommy? Am I being punished for something?"

"Oh, no, darling, not at all. You'll see."

On Christmas morning my parents called me into the study. With a flourish, my father whipped the covering off of a large object on the floor. And there stood a three-story doll-house, Santa on the roof standing near the chimney, with smoke from incense wisping out of it, like in the tiny house in Father's centerpiece. There were real glass panes in the windows, electric lights with little flashlight bulbs blazing, even a tiny live goldfish darting around in a real fish pond in its real garden.

I couldn't believe what I was seeing.

"We all kept it a secret, Sis!" Johnny exclaimed, jumping around with excitement."Mom and Dad designed the house," he said, and Father told me that Zung Kee—an accomplished carpenter in Poo Tung—had constructed it. The gardener had put in the plants and the goldfish; Tailor had made the curtains and had laid the rugs running up the stairs. It was left to me to shop for the furniture for the house.

When I'd recovered from my amazement, we carried the house to the third floor into my bedroom."Please put it over in that corner," I asked, quickly moving a child's chair and table out of the way. The next business day Matrushka and I, driven by Ah Ching, went shopping for dollhouse furniture at Wing On department store on Nanking Road. An elegant salesman in a long gray gown, cuffs on his sleeves immaculate, helped me. I selected tiny chairs and mirrors and beds; bathroom pieces; dining room finery including candelabra; rugs and garden furniture.

As soon as we got home I began placing the pieces carefully, each in an appropriate spot, into the rooms of what was now called Teddy Bear House. Little by little I gave the bears new wardrobes to live up to their elegant new quarters; after all, moving from their plain bookshelf to this mansion required new clothes. The bears were so pleased with their new quarters. I crocheted and knitted tiny hats and scarves and sweaters for them. Tailor gave my bear soldiers proper uniforms with matchstick guns.

One day there was a visit that was not joyful. Good Chinese friends, with an ancestral home in the far north near the Great Wall, who currently lived in Shanghai, came for tea and scones. They brought their children, so Johnny and I were included in the party. During the conversation we learned that the Japanese had destroyed much of their ancestral village. They didn't know the fate of their grandparents.

"Edna Lee," the wife, Alice, said,"It is so hard to understand. We are at risk in our own homes. But the Chinese government doesn't seem to be strong enough to drive out the Japanese. The national Chinese army seems to be fighting somewhere else, while the Russian and Chinese Communists are fighting the Japanese near Shanhaiguan. It is hard to sort out what is happening."

"It is going to be a hard Christmas for many people. How may we help you?" Father asked.

"We must go up north to see what is left of our home and family," the husband, David, answered."It is a dangerous trip to take, but we feel that we must see to their wellbeing. However, we can't risk taking the children with us. We have to keep them safe. I have arranged for them to stay in Shanghai with cousins, and they will be able to continue with their schooling, but we would be so grateful if you would phone our cousins from time to time until we get back, and help with any emergency that might arise."

"Of course, gladly!"

The conversation made me think about our own lives, about how safe we were in our part of Shanghai, and how dangerous it was for others. Just as I had contrasted my life with those of the rickshaw coolies on that long walk home, once again I felt lucky to live in a safe area.

We also had visits from Chinese businessmen bringing presents to my parents.

"Good morning, Mr. Ho," I said to one portly Chinese gentleman elegantly dressed in a formal Chinese silk costume following ancient customs, who arrived one Saturday morning when I was on the verandah. I knew him from last year's Christmas visit. He was carrying a long bundle under his arm."Please sit down, I'll get my parents."

Father and Mother greeted him, offered him tea that he politely declined, while presenting the long package."A little remembrance for you for Christmas," he said."My company so much thank you for friendly business." Mother unwrapped the package and revealed a bolt of bright red silk."This is so beautiful, Mr. Ho," Mother thanked him."The silk is very fine and the color magnificent."

"It is small thing," he replied. Father spoke up then, saying that it was a most welcome, most generous gift.

After he had left I asked,"Why do Mr. Ho and the men like him bring us these presents?"

"Mr. Ho is what is called a *comprador*, that is a Portuguese word meaning a man who buys and sells. In China, it refers to a man who helps with communications and actions between the foreign and the Chinese business communities," Father said."At Christmas, it is customary for the Chinese businessmen to make gifts to the foreign businessmen and their families to promote good business relationships. The custom began with the first traders, who were Portuguese down in Macao near Canton."

One evening a month or so after the New Year we had a small dinner party with Mr. Peter Lin, an investment officer with the

Bank of China, and Mrs. Lin. The other guests were Christopher Chancellor and his wife, and their son Johnny. My brother and I were included because Johnny Chancellor was a friend of ours. I'll never forget him because he once picked up the little pink desk in my room and accidentally dropped it on my toes.

The conversation was about the war. Mr. Chancellor questioned Mr. Lin about the current situation with the Japanese; there was fighting going on in north China above and below the Great Wall, near the historic fortress town Shanhaiguan. My father had explained quietly to Johnny and me before dinner that Mr. Chancellor had taken over the British news agency Reuters in China. The evening was an opportunity for him to obtain accurate background information from a knowledgeable, trusted Chinese businessman.

"The situation is even more complicated than it appears," Mr. Lin said."Many foreigners are not aware of the problem created by the presence of Communists, both Russian and Chinese, who sometimes fight the Japanese, but sometimes attack the national Chinese government army, and sometimes both. Additionally there remain elements of the Boxers with their deep hatred of foreigners to contend with."

Mother made a reference to the efforts of the national government to unify China; that it was imperative for all Chinese to stand together against the Japanese who were encroaching more and more on Chinese land.

"Did you know, Mr. Chancellor, that Mrs. Potter was an ace war correspondent before becoming a mother?" Mr. Lin asked.

"Really? Where was this?"

Mr. Lin referred the question to Father."I don't know where to begin. Shanghai; the Tokyo earthquake. Well, perhaps her most memorable writing came from North China. Edna Lee is noted as the first woman journalist to interview both Marshalls

Wu PeiFu and Chang Tso-Lin."

"I say, that's very interesting! When was this?" Chancellor asked."We are certainly thinking about that area these days."

"In 1922, when Edna Lee was invited by Madame Wu to stay with her pending a great battle between the two war lords. She met separately with Marshall Chang, I believe up in Mukden, in what was then Manchuria."

"Hush, John, let's not talk about me when we have Reuters at the table! Mr. Chancellor, I'll never forget the Reuter's Pacific Service dispatch on the death of Dr. Sun Yat-sen in 1925."

"Another time perhaps we can elaborate on Mrs. Potter's extraordinary reporting on Dr. Sun when she was smuggled onto his warship in the Canton harbor," Mr. Lin suggested."When was that, Edna Lee?"

"Oh goodness, Peter, I can't remember." I knew she was embarrassed to talk about herself.

The discussion continued until dessert, when Father presented his Cherries Jubilee.

Champagne was poured and Father toasted the guests and the New Year. The two Johnnies and I were excused to play upstairs. I could hear Mother's voice, knowing that later her typewriter would be clacking with a background piece for the International News Service on the British, Chinese, Japanese, and Russian Communists warring back and forth over the Great Wall. I was proud of having a mother who was one of the first women war correspondents in China.

"Mr. Chancellor," I heard her ask, "Do you believe that the British interests at Wei Hai Wei are more imperiled by the Japanese advance beyond the Great Wall into China proper, or by the Russian and Chinese Communists?"

It didn't surprise any of us that Mother headed north with her typewriter and camera a few days later.

Mother was a newspaper reporter until the day she died. Her softness turned to steel when she was after something. Nothing, no one, could interrupt or temper her determination. She conquered obstacles by tenacity, feminine wiles, canniness, intuition and imagination. She was kind, adorable, ruthless, and one of the great war correspondents of the 1920's and 1930's.

IX
1934. Summer in a British Treaty Port, Wei Hai Wei. Age Seven

I am standing on a long fishing pier that reaches well out from the dock, early for the meeting of the Rockport Writers Group. As I wait for the others to arrive, I enjoy the loneliness of the pier and the reach and retreat, the constancy and inconstancy, of the waves beneath and around me. I try to see below the surface, but it is opaque; I can't see anything but the blurred, quivering reflection of my face framed by the moving clouds above me.

I peer more closely, take off my sunglasses, determined to see what is below; there are interesting things down there. Maybe some relics from the Karankawa Indians; or from the World War II shipbuilding works. But the ocean is hiding its secrets. Slowly I begin to sense what was below the surface of another ocean, at the other end of the world. There, I realize as I stare into the ocean of my past, is where my deepest contentment was nurtured. Seeing, now, myself as a child in Wei Hai Wei.

I reached down over the edge of the sampan into the clear cool water, splashing it lightly as the clumsy boat swayed forward, carrying Johnny and me toward a favorite fishing spot. The visibility was good--twenty, thirty feet down to the beige sand below. A school of brilliant purple fish swooped by; little objects in the sand might be rocks or shells. Scooting along the bottom was a starfish.

Our boatman, Lao Lu, was grunting *yu loh, yu loh* steadily and rhythmically with each pull on the one long oar. He stood at the end of the sampan, his wiry body weaving back and forth like a Venetian gondolier. One of his sons came with us to help with the fish that we hoped to catch.

"Look at all the jellyfish," Johnny said."Wow. That one must be two feet across! like a large round pillow."

Jellyfish of all sizes floated around us. The clarity of the water made them even more iridescent, their bodies like pulsing bubbles with long tentacles swaying under them.

"Why don't you go swimming now, Johnny?" I asked, teasing."You can jump right over the edge. Lots of friends in the water."

"Great. After you, Sis."

I reached over, splashed the water again lightly, then scooped up a handful, tossing it into the air.

"Whee! Look, Johnny!" I cried as a quick shower of drops catching light from the sun flew from my hand."I made a rainbow!"

Wei Hai Wei had been our beach home from the beginning of my memories.

Every summer we escaped the smothering heat and humidity of Shanghai to sail north in a comfortable coastal tramp steamer. Most of our friends left every summer for cool seashores, scattering to Treaty Ports such as our Wei Hai Wei, Pei Ta Ho (Beidahe), Tsingtao (Qingdao) or Chingwangtao (Qinhuangdao). Others went inland to Kuling (Guling), a resort high up on Lushan, a mountain area cooled by breezes.

Mother had found on her expedition north that the fighting was well above Wei Hai Wei. The Japanese were focused on establishing their positions in towns around the Great Wall. So we felt safe in returning to our favorite summer retreat.

But before we could sail up the coast in the steamer, I had to get on it. This was an immense challenge for me, because I had to climb up a wobbly ladder made of slick wet wood slats and held together by knotted wet ropes. A Jacob's Ladder, I heard it called. Holding with all my might onto the ropes on either side of the swaying ladder, the ocean rolling below me, slat by slat I finally reached the deck.

The boat itself was a pleasure. Nothing to do but lounge on an extended deck chair and watch the clouds and the flying fish. Every day at eleven the ship's officer played a little xylophone melody to announce that the mid-morning bouillon was ready. So I sipped the bouillon, ate the toast that accompanied it, and went back to doing nothing at all.

Our servants too were able to enjoy the trip, because we needed no help from them. Amah, Cook, and the younger coolie, Fo Sun, came with us for the summer. My father, who had to work in Shanghai and could join us for only a few weeks, was left with Ah Kung and Lin Sing, Chauffeur Ah Ching, Elder Coolie and the gardeners, to keep the house running comfortably for him. Matrushka didn't come with us; with a reduced work-load, Amah could take care of Mother's, Johnny's and my needs.

Our boat steamed up the China coast and the Shantung (Shandong) Peninsula to reach the harbor of Wei Hai Wei at the end of the peninsula. I learned that its name, *Wei Hai,* meant,"Mighty Ocean."

"What a beautiful place this is," Mother murmured half to herself as we stood by the rail, the ship slowly entering the harbor. Liu Gong Island protecting the harbor, lay at our right, the town on the left. I saw powder sand beaches and a stand of pine trees on low cliffs that I knew were covered with blue bells.

An officer said that, centuries ago, Wei Hai Wei had been a simple fishing village, but raids by Japanese and Korean pirates caused the Chinese to build walls to protect the town. The 14ᵗʰ century city walls were almost two miles in circumference, the man said. Johnny got into a lively conversation with him about the pirates.

Finally we anchored. Lao Lu and his son met the boat in their sampan; suitcases were placed onto the little boat, and he *yuloed* us to the dock. We passed quickly through customs, and were on our way. Our servants followed us in another sampan with our heavy luggage.

The dock was noisy and full of laughter. Crowds of children in bright cotton shorts crowded around us.

"Melican! Melican!" they cried, pointing to us."*Ni hao*? (How are you? in Mandarin).

"*Hao, ding hao,*" I shouted back happily."Very good."

One pointed to his brown eyes, then to my blue ones, and laughed. A number of people who looked like traders, and others looking for work, wandered around. One carried our luggage to a cart to follow our carriage.

Father had arranged for a horse-drawn *gharry* (a sort-of carriage) and a *mafu*, or driver, for the summer. The driver led us carefully through Wei Hai Wei with its ancient high gray walls. Narrow streets were crowded with bicyclists, mutts, and oxen pulling wheelbarrows loaded with people and produce.

The road toward the beach was sweetly familiar when our horse clippety-clopped away from town. Driving along the shore I at last smelled the ocean again, the salt air teasing my hair. Long silvery fish were spread out to dry on rough nets over flat angled rocks on my left, the distinctive smell not unpleasant to me but, rather, welcoming. Farmers were threshing wheat, rhythmically flailing it on large rounded earthen surfaces.

Other farmers hoeing sweet potato patches called out greetings and waved. There were farmers working on tightly planted terraces climbing up the hills. Children in brightly colored shirts, and pants split for convenience, shouted to us as they helped with the work. We passed pine forests and climbed up over cliffs — and then we could see the ocean.

The beautiful Wei Hai Wei beach lay before us.

Our agent had engaged an experienced local houseman to serve as the Number One Boy.

I jumped out of the carriage and raced up to the cottage that we rented every summer on Half Moon Bay, on a low cliff overlooking the bay. From the terrace I saw Liu Gong Island a little distance out from us, in water of such pure blue that it seemed to be an extension of the sky, with white caps bouncing in a staccato dance. Several British warships were anchored offshore, their flags bright. Near them, a large spirited tri-sail junk and small junks bobbed at anchor.

Then I remembered the only problem with this lovely place: there were no toilets; there was no sewer system. We had to use an outhouse a few feet from our home. The first summer that I remember, when I was around four, I was afraid I would fall into the dark smelly hole when I needed to use the toilet. I knew I was little and could easily slip in. Sometimes I had nightmares about sliding down into it and woke up screaming. Mother or Amah had to help me until I was confident that I wouldn't fall in.

Otherwise, it was perfect. Mornings we ran across the cliff and down to the beach before Mother got there. Some times I turned to watch her, big roomy purse in hand and white sailor hat on her head, as she walked jauntily on the path through the pines and blue bells across the cliff and down to the beach.

We decorated sand fortresses with dribbled wet sand and

created aquariums. After the grown-ups arrived John and I were allowed to paddle in the shallows where the surf eddied around small dunes.

Our red and white beach cabaña was lined up with those of Mother's friends at the base of the cliff. She joined Italian and British friends stretched out in long beach chairs to chat, sipping Lime Rickeys or iced tea presented with intricately designed iced-tea spoons.

From their beach chairs Mother and the other ladies with children planned parties; the best was a scavenger hunt. We children, dressed as pirates, sailed off in a junk to a secret beach looking for treasures and found "pieces of eight" make-believe coins.

Lao Lu decided to teach me how to fish.

"Missie Patty, now you catch you dinner," he said."Maybe littie girl catch big fish! More better big fish not catch littie girl." We both laughed. He found a short lightweight bamboo pole for me, tied a string and a bobbin to it, and added a hook with a worm desperately wiggling around on it.

"Johnny, me, catch plenty worm in early morning. Best time catch worm." I could see that we had a good supply of slimy wiggly icky ones that I wouldn't touch, in an old tin.

"Where is Master Johnnie?" I asked.

"He fish on river, my take you better fishing place. I teach you."

We headed out in the sampan on the happy blue ocean, he *yulohing* us to where he could see there were fish. He then helped my arms to throw the line over the side while holding on to the pole. It was harder to do this than it looked when others did it. But once the pole was safely over the side I loved to watch my bobbin and the hook. In an ocean as clear and clean as a glass of blue-tinted drinking water I could see what was coming along to nudge at my worm. And I caught and pulled in several of the fish.

On the beach one day I ran into a British girl whom I knew in Shanghai, Bronwen Hughes, who was here with her mother and brothers. We saw much of them as the weeks passed. We all had little boats called "punts." Wearing my life-jacket and in my punt that we named the *JITTERBUG* I had the freedom that I didn't have in the city to go exploring. The punt was a little flat-bottomed and square-nosed rowboat with a paddle, perfect for shallow water and boating from beach to beach.

One day Bronwen and I punted down to the beach at the foot of the East Cliffe Hotel, the choice hotel for summer visitors. She and I recognized languages and accents from Italian, Scandinavian, French, and of course British and American visitors. No German."The Germans go to Tsingtao for the summer," Bronwen explained.

We loved watching the different kinds of people in the afternoons having tea or cocktails on the broad verandah of the hotel. Elegant women in floating silk chiffon dresses mingled with men in Royal Navy uniforms or in light summer suits. Mother had told me about "Sin-sin Jelly Belly," the Number One tailor, who had made many of the men's suits. I laughed whenever I thought about the silly name.

Bingo games were held on some evenings. The Bingo Master called out numbers by nicknames in a penetrating, high-pitched British accent. It was "man alive, number 5," "time for fun 1," or "flea, number 3," "two little fleas, 33" and "a flea in heaven is 37." The number 80 was "eight and blank". The nickname "trombones" was for the number 76 and "66 clickety-click" for 66. Of course Mother won, she always won, and collected the prize, a glass bowl.

Johnny wasn't interested in the summer fashions at the East

Cliffe or the bingo games; he was involved in playing war with Bronwen's brothers and other boys. But some days we rode our mules together, after we put on our hard white *topee* hats as protection against sunstroke. We raced up and down the beach laughing noisily as we encouraged our steeds to greater speed. Soon some of the other summer visitors politely asked us to ride more quietly; we were creating havoc where they had hoped to bask serenely on the beach.

The summer came to a close; it was time to pack up and return to Shanghai and to school. We loaded one sampan with our luggage and gear. Reluctantly we climbed into Lao Lu's sampan and were *yuloh*'ed back to the harbor. I kept looking back at the beach; it slowly disappeared as we neared the steamer anchored offshore. Lao Lu and I hugged each other before I climbed out. A few more minutes, precious minutes; then we headed back to Shanghai.

I sit back in my chair, unconsciously rotating my wrists, my mind far in the past. How rare, how beautiful, how far away, how forever gone are the summers at peace by the seaside in China. I visualize them as paintings by Degas or Renoir. Ladies like my mother in old-fashioned white dresses or loose slacks, wearing large hats. In the scenes there are bright flowers — bluebells — among the pine trees on the hillside behind the ladies; and sampans, junks and sailboats bob on happy blue water.

In my memory, the local citizens — the Chinese working for us or serving us in stores in town, and even the Chinese officials — all have kindness in their eyes and courtesy in their manner. I have never again known such consideration, especially to a little girl.

But now I stop to wonder about their lives. What happened to them after the two summer months of service to us foreigners? Did they have to earn enough during those sixty days to keep them and their families comfortable in the cold northern winter? The harder, more experienced part of me suggests that some of that kindness and courtesy was a façade presented to earn more dollars when the rich foreigners were around. Well, if they did, I don't begrudge them for it. I would have done the same. I believe, however, that their kindness was genuine, and so also was their need.

Now the romantic side of me checks out Wei Hai on the computer. I move the map around, enlarge it into a blur and shrink it into a tiny square, but I can't find Half Moon Bay. I do find monstrous monuments on heavy terraces, I find lots of construction and factories. I want to cry.

X

1934–5. Life in Shanghai.
Age Eight

Father's scrapbooks are *a family legend. He made one for Johnny,
one for me, one for the whole family that we call the Big Book. In it
are photographs from the time of my father's youth, when he created
a camera in an old watchcase and took pictures with it. Some of these,
about as big as a thumb nail and in a blue color, are on two pages of the
Big Book. Photographs of his sisters and his mother and the old Stauffer
Homestead in Pennsylvania are included. There follow photographs of
his progression from the Philippines to Shanghai and the Anderson-
Meyer Company, then the China Realty Company, and finally the
Bank of China. There are delightfully old-fashioned photographs of him
wooing young ladies in the Philippines and then Shanghai — then only
photographs of my mother, young, and the two of them page by page
growing older as they voyaged life together. The Big Book follows us all
through our adventures until Father was too old to keep the pictures
current; and no one has replaced him. The heavy old books are here with
me now; and when my children and grand-children are visiting, we like
to turn the fragile pages ever so carefully to peek into those long-ago
adventures that still live in photographs, letters and cards.*

Almost every summer my father, as with most of our friends'
fathers, wasn't able to take a vacation. This year he had had to

stay in Shanghai to deal with circumstances caused by the short Japanese invasion. He, Ah Ching, and Fo Sun met our boat when we returned from Wei Hai Wei.

"How you've grown, Patty!" he said, hugging me. "Let's see, you must be almost nine years old now! And Johnny, look at you, as brown as a bear." He hugged him, then kissed Mother. "I'm so glad you're back, Edna Lee."

"You must have been awful lonesome, Daddy," I said. "I really missed you. I wish your darned old business hadn't kept you away from us."

"Yes, I admit, I was lonesome. But when we get home I'll show you what I've been doing to keep busy."

The next day, after we'd unpacked, played with the dog and settled in again, Father invited us into his study. He reached over to a shelf and pulled out a thick heavy black scrapbook. "I've made a special scrapbook just for you," he said. "See where I've carved your name?"

On the center of the cover large white letters spelled out: PATTY LEE POTTER.

He opened it up. There I saw, pasted in one by one, the poems and drawings that I had sent him from Wei Hai Wei. In the next pages there were some of my old workbooks from the German school, and French dictation that Matrushka had given me to do, that he had saved. Some of the pages featured photographs of me playing on the beach, and some newspaper clippings mentioning me were there too. "Daddy," I said, wonderingly, "Daddy, you did all this while I was away? You did all his for me?"

"Well, I missed my little sweetheart."

"Oh, thank you, Daddy!" I hugged him. I was shy to tell him that it made me feel that he really loved me.

He had made a similar scrapbook for Johnny.

Matrushka had left Shanghai while we were away for the summer. She and some friends had moved to a city in the southern part of China where there were neither Japanese soldiers nor Russian Communist organizers.

My new governess, a German lady named Frau Zeller, arrived soon after we returned.

"Frau Zeller is the widow of a fine German businessman who unfortunately died bankrupt," Father said, telling us about her before she arrived."She will be able to give you good care as well as help with your education. I expect you to be polite and cooperative."

Johnny and I hated her. She was always displeased, and expressed her boredom with having to deal with me. There was a perpetual frown on her face; her thin lips curved downward into an upside-down smile. She was thrilled to find that I went to the German school. The only thing she liked to do was to accompany me in the car with Ah Ching. A few weeks later Father called me into his study.

"I understand that you are rude to Frau Zeller and don't obey her," he said."What is this all about?"

"Daddy," I complained,"I don't like her. She doesn't like me."

"Have you considered that if she doesn't like you it may be because she doesn't like your rudeness to her?" He paused."Well, I realize that she's not young and pretty and fun like Matrushka, but she was one of a kind, we were lucky. Please try to get along with Frau Zeller. Your mother and I need her help."

I tried to adjust to our fearsome governess, but I was never good enough for her.

"How are you and the Frau getting on?" Johnny asked one day.

"Terribly. She's awful strict with me, more than Daddy even."

"Do you think it's us or that's how she always was?"

"I think she always was awful. She probably drove her husband to death after spending all his money."

But I knew that it was true that Johnny and I didn't behave like proper German boys and girls.

Frau Zeller dutifully escorted me to school and back; to piano lessons with Madame Paci and to horseback riding lessons with Monsieur Belorukov. She helped me with my homework and taught me songs to recite in French for my parents' guests. They said they loved it when I sang, for instance, "*Sur le Pont d'Avignon, l'on y danse, l'on y danse*" and acted out the lively dance.

One day Father, knowing that I would be downtown with the governess to do some shopping, invited me up to his office. Ah Ching drove us to a modern building on Nanking Road. There I climbed up a high flight of wide white marble stairs that turned to the right half way up, and found myself on the second floor where a tall dark-eyed and dark-haired lady waited for me. She was middle-aged, nicely dressed.

"Good morning, Patty," she said. "I am your father's secretary, Mrs. Petigura." She led me back to my father's office.

Father rose from behind a large desk to greet us, showing the governess the view over The Bund, then we all sat down. Soon a Chinese office boy in a long white robe brought pots of tea, almond cookies, and steaming jasmine-scented hand towels.

While she was out of the room I asked Father about the strange long scarf his secretary was wearing

"Miss Petigura is of Parsi birth," he replied. "The Parsi religion requires women to cover their shoulders with the scarf."

"Even in China?"

"Parsis went to India hundreds of years ago from Persia, now Iran," he explained. "They fled because people of their religion,

Zoroastrianism, were being persecuted by the Muslims." He told me about a leader named Zarathustra who had established this religion."They believe that there is continuous war between the forces of good and the forces of evil, and that the good forces will win if people do good deeds and have good thoughts."

"Why did she come here from India? What kind of name is Petigura?"

"It's a Portuguese name. She fell in love with a Portuguese merchant who went to India for business, and then was sent to Shanghai with more than he had expected—a bride. But regrettably he died of typhoid fever, and she has to work now to support herself and their children. I am very lucky to have her help," he added.

Frau Zeller, Father and I left after tea. I found going down the stairs frightening, as there was no banister for me to hold to. Father took my hand and helped me down, step by step; we continued on to walk into the street and around the corner to the Chocolate Shop, where we had ice cream sundaes.

Another special trip downtown was with Mother, who was able to include me as a guest at the wedding of Chinese friends. This was held in an elegant building in the French Concession.

Mother and I walked down a short flight of stairs into a modern chrome and glass reception area.

Gigantic bouquets of peonies, ginger and chrysanthemum were arranged in large porcelain vases on brightly decorated tables. The scent of incense burning on joss sticks vied with that of the flowers. Miss Petigura had told me that the word *joss* was a distortion of the Portuguese word for "God," or, *Deus*. People would burn joss sticks when worshipping their god.

Red silk banners with gold characters decorated the walls.

"Look, Patty," Mother said, pointing to a pair of gold

characters on red silk framed in dark wood. "The pair is the Chinese saying for "'Double Happiness.'"

喜喜

"They look like the ones you have in our living room!" I exclaimed.

"Yes, those were given to us by Chinese friends when Father and I were married. When we go home I'll show you where our names are."

Then she giggled. "See those characters up there on the left?" She pointed to a different group of characters. "One is the character for 'good luck,' and it is matched with the same character upside down, to joke that it would definitely arrive."

Strings of small red paper lanterns hung from the ceiling.

"Why is everything red?" I asked.

"Red is the color of joy in China."

Guests were sitting at round tables, each with plates of finger foods and candied fruit. They were decorated with small red rice paper parasols as favors for the guests. Carafes of wine and glasses gleamed. Mother picked up one of the red paper napkins at our table to show me the bridal couple's initials imprinted in gold. Other Chinese characters, also in gold, I recognized as the Double Happiness characters.

The ceremony was both Chinese and Western in mood and style. The young bridal couple entered the room quietly. Their red silk and satin clothing shimmered as they moved. An ornate headdress balanced on the bride's hair, which was combed and plastered with gel into a bun. A curtain of beads covered her face until at some moment, mysterious to me, it was lifted by the groom and he could see her face.

The couple knelt to pray at an altar; the service was led by a

Protestant minister. At the end of the service they walked to a specially arranged low altar. They knelt in front of it, facing the guests. A group of people was seated separately from the other guests on chairs facing this altar.

"What's going on?" I asked my mother.

"This is the tea ceremony at which the ancestors are honored," she whispered. "The photographs on the altar are of the ancestors, and their living parents and family are on those separate chairs."

The bride poured tea from a delicate Rose Medallion service like ours at home, carrying a cup to each family member. Mother explained that it was the custom for the bride first to serve the groom, his parents and grandparents and all of his uncles, aunts, brothers, cousins, sisters, before she served her own family.

I didn't think that, when I married, I would serve my husband's family before my own. It also struck me that they were putting her to work even before she finished getting married.

As the families sipped the tea, each member in turn put a fat red envelope on the tea tray. Mother explained that the envelopes were stuffed with gifts of money or jewelry.

The tea pouring ceremony complete, the bride and groom together lit an ornately carved wedding candle that displayed the phoenix and dragon symbols. This symbolic joining of the two families was followed by the signing of the Chinese wedding contract and the end of the rituals.

The guests, who had been quiet through the formal service, now began calling out congratulatory phrases and toasts.

"*Gong xi fa cai!*" — may you make a fortune!

"*Ganbei*" — bottoms up!

Mother took my arm and we slipped out quietly as the party became rowdier. When we got home she showed me the pair of wedding inscriptions that had been given to her and Father when they married. I was proud that they were up there on our living room wall.

I went on upstairs to my room after thanking Mother for taking me with her to the wedding.

There was much for me to think about. I began spending more time by myself, especially in the summerhouse in the garden where no one bothered me except for schoolwork with the governess. I wanted to write down some of the ideas and songs and poems that were in my head. This was not as easy as I'd thought it would be. Mother and Father wrote all the time, Johnny too. But my English got all mixed up with German and French spelling.

Father corrected a letter I wrote to my grandmother in which he turned my *bleu* into "blue," my *haus* into "house," and my *braun* into "brown." I struggled with spellings that made no sense to me: the word "said" for instance. How was that spelled? Sed, or sayd, or zed? Then, the word "was." I knew that "wuz" wasn't right, so I devised my own spelling, a sort of an "a" with a squiggle on it, attached to a "z". Those, too, got corrected.

My first story was "The Little Robin and dwerfs".

This was followed by "King Loyold of the Seas", illustrated.

My handwriting was too slow for me; soon I began to pick out a few words on Mother's typewriter. It felt very daring to hit the letters, creating one word after another, making up the spelling if I didn't know it as I went along. I'd already found out that Father often corrected the spelling in Mother's writing. That made me feel better about all my mistakes.

"The Misteries of smart Little Sophia", a 13-page typed story of three chapters was written in the summer, 1934, in Wei Hai Wei. My best poem so far began:

"Agnes Agnes quickly come

"Into the Land of Memory"

I didn't know any Agnes; I just liked the sound of the word in the *Agnus Dei* that I'd heard in church. I loved writing music, too, and enjoyed entering the notes onto the staff sheets, later playing them.

Except when friends came to play, my bedroom was my own world in which my teddy bears and I had many adventures, where I could experiment with flying, and where I was free of people telling me how I was doing everything wrong and to behave like a little lady.

I practiced magic words in different orders when I was trying to achieve the facial beauty that I wanted. One of the Oz books had a princess with a closet full of heads. She could unscrew the head she had on when she was tired of it, and screw on another; she could be blonde with green eyes or black haired with purple eyes, round-faced or oval. This ability, I really really wanted; my own face was always the same and I yearned for changes. I checked out my closet but there were no shelves appropriately placed for a collection of heads.

I was awakened one night around two a.m. by a crashing noise in my bedroom. Then a curious sound:

"Ribit, ribit, ribit!"

Frog talk? in my bedroom?

Impossible. I sat up to be sure that I wasn't dreaming.

"Ribit, ribit." There it was again. Now there were some croaks and more crashing of furniture--from my dollhouse.

I turned on the table light by my bed, climbed out from under the mosquito netting, crept over to the house and switched on its lights.

A frog with huge protruding eyes stared at me through a window. I jumped and screamed.

Frogs were hopping up and down the stairs, trampolining on and off the beds, croaking frantically as they tried to escape

In came brother Johnny and his friend Granny Vincent, both laughing wildly. My bratty brother and his Gunpowder Gang had caught a dozen or so large frogs that evening. His friend had stayed overnight, and the boys let them loose in the dollhouse while I was asleep.

Amah came shuffling out in a wrapper and flat black cloth slippers.

"*Ai yah, ai yah!* What thing!" she cried as she came in. She took in the frog situation and gasped."Littie Master, how fashion you scare Littie Missie! You number one cheeky boy!"

More of the household arrived. Frau Zeller, with her perpetual scowl, smelling unwashed, came stomping up from her second floor room. Her orange hair was set in green curlers."*Ach, wass für ein schrecklicher Bube!*" she hissed."*Hier kann Man gar nicht schlafen!*"

My parents arrived and sent for Fo Sun to catch and dispose of the frogs. Frau Zeller clumped back to her quarters, still muttering in German about how bad Johnny and our whole household were, and we all returned to the quiet of what was left of the night. Johnny was suitably punished the next day. I had to hide my giggles and act injured over the episode, but in truth I admired his brilliance.

Little by little, month by month, the atmosphere at the German school changed, reflecting the major events in Germany.

Nazi policies began to affect Shanghai A selection of children now took part in a group called the *Hitler Jugend* (Youth). During recess, those boys and girls were drilled, marching around with their legs sticking straight out.

"Renata, why are they sticking out their feet like that?" I

asked."It's the new way to march," she replied."It's called 'goose step.'"

They goose-stepped with their right arms held high, shouting "*Heil Hitler.*" The boys' new uniforms were khaki shorts and shirts with red, black and white armbands, a "swastika" in the center. The *Hitler Jugend* often sang songs glorifying Germany and the Nazis. My friend Wilhelm (not his real name), a handsome blond blue-eyed muscular model for the German ideal, was the group's leader. I thought they were like the Girl and Boy Scouts, just boys and a few girls marching around having fun in their little costumes, and, anyway, I wasn't included since I wasn't German. But they made me uncomfortable.

Our Nazi musical repertoire was enhanced by the Nazi anthem, the *Horst Wessel Lied.*

Another day we learned to sing *Die Wacht Am Rhein,* a military patriotic song about protecting the Rhine River from invaders:

Lieb' Vaterland, magst ruhig sein,
Lieb' Vaterland, magst ruhig sein,
Fest steht und treu die Wacht, die Wacht am Rhein!
Fest steht und treu die Wacht, die Wacht am Rhein!

(Dear Fatherland, no fear be thine
Dear Fatherland, no fear be thine,
Firm and True stands the Watch, the Watch at the Rhine!
Firm and True stands the Watch, the Watch at the Rhine!)

I asked Father if he knew the song, but he didn't, so I taught it to him. I also told him about the *Hitler Jugend.* He seemed surprised.

It seems to me that one of my parents should have become interested in what was going on at the German school. I assume that my father was preoccupied with trying to make a living in very uncertain circumstances, and my mother was charging off after a news story when she wasn't being a hostess and going to parties, or improving things around our house. My brother thinks it may have been because Father was passionate about languages, having mastered seven himself, and coming from a German-speaking Swiss background. They may have thought that I was exaggerating the situation and creating a drama to draw attention to myself.

And after all, how long did it take for most people to recognize the Evil of the Hitler regime?

XI

1935. ADVENTURES ON A TRIP TO AMERICA. AGE EIGHT

ALL THESE YEARS *later, I still break up laughing, remembering our unexpected trip from China to America in an old German freighter. Some days when I phoned Johnny in Martha's Vineyard where he lived, we convulsed with laughter when he mentioned Mother's bit with the tarantula in the jungle in Vietnam and my sighting of the odious German officer flying overboard. We laughed again over the antics of the monkeys in Vietnam and Cambodia and Singapore.*

But then I stop laughing, thinking about the Vietnam War and the suffering of so many people. Here on the Texas Gulf Coast, many of the shrimpers are descendants of the Boat People who fled their country in terror when the Americans left. Some local Vietnamese, Thais and Cambodians have become athletes, shopkeepers and restauranteurs, testimony to their brains and spirit; a friend is a banker, another a landlord. The fine architect who drew the plans for remodeling my home is Smith Nguyen, a second generation Vietnamese.

There was great friction initially between existing shrimpers who did not want to work day and night, and the newcomer Vietnamese who, homeless, were desperate to earn money and would work all night as well as all day. Of course they brought in more shrimp than the native shrimpers. I'm told about a movie, ALAMO BAY, *filmed in nearby Fulton in 1985 and directed by Louis Malle, that accurately presents the early problems between shrimpers.*

A Thai friend tells me about one of the descendants – Dat Nguyen, the famous football player. His parents fled to Rockport after the war. Many years later they were able to found "Hu Dat," a popular restaurant featuring Chinese and Vietnamese food. Another success story: Ang "Joseph" Cao (LA, R) from nearby Louisiana was the first Vietnamese American to serve in US Congress. I'm glad that some good has come after so much sorrow.

It wasn't the Japanese or the Germans who forced us to make an unplanned, rushed trip to America. I learned about it one night in the spring of 1935 I was restless and couldn't get to sleep. Finally deciding that I needed something to nibble on. I crawled out from under the mosquito net, put on my slippers and crept down the stairs. As I passed Father's study I was surprised to hear the voices of my mother and father. Why were they were up so late? I stopped to listen.

Their voices were clear."Yes, John, I did cancel the plans for our tea dance. It's hard to believe that this is happening!"

"I completely trusted that crook Frank Raven," Father said."Well, so did everyone else. Thousands of us have been bankrupted. With his virtuous air and his polite missionary wife, we thought he was an upright banker. But he was a damn embezzler! You'll see, he'll go to a federal prison for years for this!"

There were a few moments of silence. Then, Mother:

"Do we have anything left?"

"Just enough to keep our home going and to look after our household servants; we don't want them to suffer. We closed down Raven's American Oriental Banking Corporation today. Can you believe it, he absconded with all of everyone's money, bankrupting many thousands of us who had entrusted our money to his bank."

"John, there's no way you could have known. He was so charming. No one would have dreamt that he was a crook on a massive scale." She paused."I guess everyone knows."

"Yes, Edna Lee, everyone knows. Did you hear that our neighbor B killed himself last night?"

Overhearing this, I was so shocked that I could hardly breathe. What if it had been my own father?

"Oh how dreadful. Those poor souls. I must go to see his wife tomorrow. Oh, John, what shall we do?"

I could hear father shuffling through some papers."My sweetheart, I'm afraid there's nothing for it but for you and the children to go to back to your mother in California until I can rebuild our accounts. And it won't be first class on a great liner, sorry. This afternoon I located a freighter leaving for Hamburg in a week. It carries only twelve passengers, and I have put the three of you on it. That's the best I can do. Oh sweetheart," he paused,"I'm so sorry about all this."

"I've just time to at least wire home a story about this disaster," Mother said.

"You have to focus on leaving as few pending expenses as you can. Close up your credit accounts."

"Oh Lord."

"At least it will be an interesting trip, although with few comforts. You'll be boarding the Norddeutscher Lloyd's *Mosel* in Hong Kong in a couple of days, and then you'll be off on a new adventure through the Straits of Malacca, stopping at Saigon for a week before continuing across the Indian Ocean and through the Red Sea. New adventures for you!"

I could tell that he was trying to be cheerful, but it sounded like crying. Poor Daddy, poor Mummy, I thought.

Then,"How awful all this is! It seems like a bad dream."

Now I could hear Mother crying. I knew he was holding her, wiping away her tears. I crept quietly up the stairs and back into my bed, tring to understand what was happening to us and to me.

All I knew about money was that it was in people's purses or pockets, and brought things I wanted. I didn't have any at all, so not having any was hard for me to understand. I was so upset by trying to figure this out that I couldn't sleep, and finally went to Johnny's room and woke him, telling him what I'd overheard. He was shocked, especially on hearing about the neighbor who killed himself; his son Billy was one of Johnny's Gunpowder Gang. We talked for a long time, then Johnny said:

"There's nothing we can do now. Let's try to sleep. In the morning I have to see Billy."

" Ok. Night."

The next days were frantic as we packed up what was essential for the long trip. It was especially hard as no one knew when we could return. I took a couple of my bears with me for comfort, and some colored pencils and coloring books; Johnny brought a journal in which he was going to write a book about the trip. He carried Mother's typewriter downstairs, she couldn't live without it; and I helped pack her camera and hats and shoes. I said goodbye to Frau Zeller, glad that I wouldn't see her again. But I was in tears at leaving Amah and the others of the household.

Ah Ching drove Father and us to The Bund.

We pulled up in front of a long building, Butterfield & Swire. Crowds of sweaty dockhands were shouting and shoving each other; passengers with tickets and passports in their hands wandered around looking confused. Some coolies carried trunks held by straps over their shoulders and across their foreheads as they hustled down the pier and over onto the tender. We didn't have a lot of luggage for this hurried trip. I glumly watched Johnny's and my steamer trunks, along with Mother's big wardrobe trunk, being loaded onto the tender.

Father handed to Mother the "medicine bag" that he had created for our trips. This was a black leather suitcase that opened up in the middle, with trays of essentials on each side and bulky bottles in the center. He had woven a handle of thick twine, attaching it in the center so that the suitcase stood upright. His supplies included small vials of brandy for stomach-ache, sweet oil for toothache, aspirin for everything. There were various ointments, adhesive tape in different widths, castor oil, vitamins, witch hazel, alcohol. There was vinegar to clear the sinuses, and scissors and knives of different sizes. Iodine and New Skin and an anti-insect bite ointment were also tucked away.

"I hope you won't need any of this and that you and the children will be well and safe until you come back to me," Father said. Mother thanked him. Then they held onto each other for a long goodbye.

It was my turn now for a goodbye kiss. "You know I'll write you, Daddy," I said, hugging him. "And I'll write poems for you, too."

"I hope so, my little sweetheart. I will miss you very very much." He paused. He had worried, tired lines around his eyes. "Try to be thoughtful of your mother. She is very unhappy." I nodded. "We're all very unhappy."

But Johnny was impatient to start on the journey. "Come on, let's get on the tender, or we'll miss the boat!"

The three of us climbed onto the tender, found seats, and turned to wave back at our father and Ah Ching.

We chugged across to the B & S ship waiting in the deep water. Now we had to walk on a rickety gangplank up from the bouncing tender across the water into the ship. I was terrified of falling into the ocean and hung on tightly to the flimsy handrails, grateful that it wasn't another Jacob's Ladder. Once on board I found my way to the railing on the deck where I could see the action. It was exciting to watch the ship's preparations for departure: the last tender bringing passengers, luggage, and freight; the creaking sounds as the anchor was raised; the bumptious uniformed officers pushing little eight-year-old girls out of the way; looking over at the other passengers lining the rail with me.

The ship moved by inches, then by feet. I hurried to the stern to watch the curls of the wake as the ship turned to follow the curving Whang Poo River through Shanghai into the mighty Yangtze River and then southeast toward the South China Sea, destination Hong Kong.

Mother, Johnny and I crowded into one cabin for the two-night trip to Hong Kong. Everyone was tired. I just wanted to look at the ocean all day. But finally the mountains in Hong Kong rose up over the horizon. As we neared, I made out buildings high up the Peak.

"There's hilly billy Hong Kong!" I shouted to Johnny.

"It's beautiful," he said with awe. "I'd like to live here one day."

Our ship maneuvered slowly to our mooring through the magnificent Hong Kong harbor crowded with liners, warships, junks, ferries and sailboats. Disembarking onto a tender that brought us to the B & S pier, our luggage was transferred with us to the Norddeutscher Lloyd pier. There we boarded another tender that took us and our luggage to our freighter, the SS *Mosel*, moored in another part of the harbor. I was appalled when I saw the gloomy, ungainly little ship. I couldn't believe that we were going to travel on her. The SS *Mosel* was an ugly duckling among the sleek liners in the harbor.

Disembarking from the large liner had been easy; but boarding the freighter from the tender was hard for me. I clutched the handrails as I slipped and slid up the wet sharply angled gangway. The seamen cheered when I finally reached the deck. With a huge smile of relief, and shaking my curls that were wet and sticky from salt spray, I thanked the men, easing into their German.

"*Vielen Dank.*"

"*Bitte schön, Liebchen,*" they answered, delighted to find that I spoke German."You are welcome, little girl!"

The boat got underway quickly and headed south to circle down to Cochin-chine (Vietnam). It didn't take long for us to get to know the ship. There was a group of cabins and public rooms in the stern, a high bridge over the dining area and kitchen, and a large flat area for freight at the front of the ship. All the passenger facilities were as small as feasible to permit more room for freight.

We met the other passengers that evening at a small reception: a pair of Americans in addition to the three of us, four Germans, three Italians. Then we moved to the dining room for dinner, where we were served on large round tables with white tablecloths. I watched the horizon move gently up and down through the round portholes encircled with shiny metal studs as the ship reacted to the motion of the waves.

Johnny and I were the only children. We had our own cabins, but no private bathrooms. The use of the available facilities by the twelve of us passengers took some planning and agility. I had to walk down the long narrow hall to use the toilet; the floor in the hall was made of some metallic element that rattled and clanked as I went. Reddish-orange rust lay in cracks where the floor and the wall were joined.

One room off a hallway held the bathtub. To take a bath, I

had to put on my blue and white cotton kimono (a Japanese name for the wide-sleeved cotton robe worn by all foreigners in Shanghai) and head down the hall at the allotted time, carrying all my equipment. When I found that the bath water was piped in from the ocean, gritty with salt, I found less need for tub baths.

"Johnny, the bath water is full of salt!" I complained.

"I know. Just pretend you're swimming in the ocean."

Every day I was up early on the deck of our ship, excitedly squinting in the morning sun at the horizon for signs of our first stop, Saigon (Ho Chi Minh City) in Cochin-Chine. There was an inviting smell of creosote in the air. To me, that meant, adventure. The railing on our freighter was already warm as I leaned over it. I had never been south of China and was almost vibrating with excitement. Soon Johnny joined me at the rail.

"Look over there," I said, pointing. "That's land, not clouds!" Finally, land!

Soon I saw blurred white specks of low-lying buildings. When we docked, seagulls with demanding shrieks shot down to the boat looking for scraps of food.

We watched from an upper deck, fascinated, as the covering over the great hold was pulled back to reveal the ship's cargo. Our crew got into action with cranes and winches and suddenly we saw that they were hoisting cars, and crates, and—animals?

"I don't believe it," Johnny said, laughing. "They're transporting water buffalo in those hemp slings! I hope the hemp is strong enough! And look at the miserable horses struggling to get free."

The cargo was maneuvered over the pier, then lowered slowly onto the dock to a cacophony of shouting voices. Sweating bodies caught each bundle or animal, pulled it safely onto the dock and freed it from its sling. Crates were piled on top of each other under a corrugated tin roof. The angry buffalo and horses protested with a mix of neighs and snorts and brays at being dragged to a corner of the area to waiting trucks. Clanging anchors, chains, and horns added to the confusion of sounds.

We had arrived at the first stage of our long voyage to America. Mother, Johnny and I joined the other passengers in disembarking onto the humid dock.

"We'll be here for a few days taking on a cargo of bags of rice, the Captain has told me," Mother informed us."Do you want to sit on the boat in the heat, or would you rather have a jungle adventure?"

"What do you think we think!" Johnny said, sassy."Gee whiz, yes! Patty too!" I nodded."Golly yes!"

The passengers organized a caravan of three cars to take us all on the long trip from Saigon deep into the Cambodian jungle.

"I show you the mysterious, majestic Angkor Wat and Angkor Thom," our guide told us in French when he met us early in the morning."Angkor was the capitol city of the Khmer Empire a thousand years ago."

Humidity hung heavily in the air around us as we drove along. Opening the windows was pointless since there was no breeze to cool us off. We passengers were soon sweating heavily."Perspiring," Mother said, because "ladies don't sweat."

The jungle road was shaded by tall trees with thick foliage. I became aware of the gibbering of monkeys high up in the branches; they seemed to be laughing down at us. We stopped and got out to watch them.

"I believe they are called long-tailed macaques," Mother said.

Suddenly everyone began screaming. A half dozen of the monkeys, their long tails swaying high above them, had scampered down apparently to look us over. They bared sharp little teeth in their narrow grinning faces, tails waving around. We rushed back to get in the cars while yelling at the monkeys to leave us alone.

"I'll bet they bite really hard!" Johnny exclaimed."Let's not try them out," a passenger replied.

After trying to get in the cars' doors and windows that we had quickly closed, the monkeys climbed up onto the hoods and roofs where they jumped up and down. Our drivers began to drive away slowly. Finally the monkeys leapt down and formed chattering groups on the ground, staring at us. But we were free of them.

Later we made another rest stop. The damp heat fogged up our sunglasses immediately. My hair hung in wet ringlets. We were nowhere, on a bumpy one-lane road surrounded by strange gigantic trees, more monkeys watching us from the branches.

"You see those trees?" our guide said."They are called *banyan* trees. The trees have regular roots, but some of their branches grow down to the ground. There, they root and new growth rises to widen the tree, and the process repeats itself over hundreds of years." He pointed to a huge banyan that looked like an ancient ogre who let his gray hair grow out. Mother wanted to take a photograph of it, and put her hand against a tree trunk for balance. Suddenly she screamed.

"There's a giant spider here!" Her hand was an inch away from a huge ugly hairy black spider. She was scared to move. The passengers gathered around her, looking nervously at the monster spider. I grabbed Mother's hand and pulled her away.

"A tarantula," a man said. On hearing this, Mother nearly fainted. Johnny propped her up.

As there were no bathroom facilities around, we all had to go behind the trees and shrubs. After Mother's adventure, the three of us never went off alone.

The drive went on and on through the jungle. The only sounds were the high-pitched chatter of the macaques and the calls of birds as they flew from one tree perch to another. Then I saw a clearing where an enormous gray structure with unfamiliar architecture towered over the trees.

"Is that it, Mom? Is that Angkor Wat or whatever it's called?"

"Yes, Patty, that is what we came to see. The lost city of Angkor, the lost Khmer civilization. Oh my. Will you look at that."

The cars all stopped, and we got out to see the beautiful, mysterious, structure.

It was late, so it was decided to spend the night at the little French hotel called the Siem Reap, and tour in the morning. It was fun to have French food after the German food on the *Mosel*, and to practice our French. After dinner we were ushered to a spacious bedroom with large ceiling fans, one bare light bulb with a long string cord in the center of the ceiling, louvered windows, and heavy white mosquito nets over the beds.

In the morning Johnny cautioned me. "Remember, don't drink any water unless it is bottled, like at home, and don't forget to shake out your shoes like Daddy taught us. This place is tropical, like the Philippine island where he was nearly bitten by a scorpion, and the ones here would also like to crawl into our cozy shoes."

After breakfast we drove back to the area with the strange buildings, then walked across a wide moat leading to the temples. Marking the way were stone guardian lions. Before us we saw a fantasy—tier upon tier of gray sandstone statues of Buddha, or gods, or goddesses, rising up in a beautifully proportioned central structure, higher than anything we had ever seen. The central temple, the guide told us, was designed to represent Mount Meru, home of the *devas*, or spirits, in Hindu mythology.

It was flanked by two smaller buildings.

"The Khmer Empire, whose people inhabited Cambodia for centuries, had a religion called Hindu," the guide told us,"and their greatest temple was Angkor. This is Angkor Wat, the largest Hindu temple in the world and also the world's largest religious monument."

Johnny asked about the statues with four faces, and the one with many arms reaching in different directions."That one with eight arms," he pointed," is the great god Vishnu, to whom Angkor Wat is dedicated. Some of the important Buddha have four faces. There are carvings and deep *bas-reliefs* covering the walls, telling the tales of a thousand years ago."

Trees had taken root in many of the courtyards of buildings, and some had overtaken the buildings, the roots crawling all over them. I asked our guide about this.

"The little temple covered by roots? The silk-cotton tree. Others similarly covered in roots have been overtaken by the strangler fig, or, *ficus strangularis.*"

Suddenly Johnny yelled "Ouch!" and began jumping.

"*Oh mon Dieu*, he's been bitten by fire ants," the guard said, reaching into his knapsack."They are everywhere here, like the monkeys. I always carry ointment that will help." Mother applied the ointment to Johnny's legs, and from then on we all avoided standing in spots that we thought might harbor the ants. We walked around Angkor Wat and then the larger ancient Khmer capitol, Angkor Thom, nearby. I became tired in the heat.

"Mummy, can we leave soon? I hope?" Johnny had fire ants, but I had prickly heat.

"Say MAY, not CAN. Of course you can, and in this case, you may, because I'm ready to leave too." We returned to our hotel, exhausted.

In the morning our caravan retraced our drive south, turning to follow the Mekong River that led us to the capital, Phnom Penh.

"What an enchanting place," Mother exclaimed, as we drove toward the shimmering spires of the Royal Palace."The villas and avenues have a French elegance.

After lunch we watched a performance of Khmer classical dance. Young women, beautiful in gleaming gold-colored silk dresses, were arranged in ascending rows on the marble stairs of the Royal Palace. They wore headdresses of golden spires that, I thought, matched the spires on the Palace. Sparkling jewels decorated their dresses and their bodies.

"Look, Mummy," I whispered to her,"their hands curve back just the way that the Chinese women dancers do."

,I had never heard music like theirs before, neither the lively rhythm nor the sounds. The music programs that we had attended in Shanghai had taught me about the sounds of instruments; I didn't know this one. The primary instrument sounded like a xylophone, but with deeper ringing, harder, tones. After the program I asked the guide."It is called a *roneat*," he said.

I loved the program, but was ready to go back to the boat.

At Singapore, our next stop, we were not allowed to disembark. Throughout the day I was out on the deck to see the action. Here the loading and unloading didn't interest me so much as a family of long-tailed macaques hanging in the trees and sitting on a retaining wall facing our ship.

"Hello, you monkeys!" I called to them, comfortable because I knew they couldn't jump across the dock and the water to get to me with their sharp teeth. They chattered back to me. I began making faces at them, waving my arms around. This caused them to wave their arms wildly. When I jumped up and down they jumped. I began laughing at their antics. They were definitely sassing me back. Soon some of the passengers, who had been passing nearby on the deck, joined me at the railing waving their arms and making faces. The macaques copied them. When I stuck out my tongue, they copied me. They even mimicked my hysterical laughter. This entertainment ended only when a ship's officer came by announcing afternoon tea. I thought later that the only difference between us and the macaques was that we didn't have tails.

That evening we were underway again. We steamed along through the Strait of Malacca, past Penang, then northwest into the Indian Ocean, just as the Admiral of the Western Seas, Zheng He, did, in an armada of giant junks in the 1400's that I'd heard about at school. I was thinking about what an amazing sight that would have been when a sudden lurch of the ship caused me to grab my chair.

A monsoon had caught us in that huge ocean and for ten days in intense heat it threw us around. The horizon appeared and rapidly disappeared when I looked out of a porthole. Heavy rain and ocean swells rocked the boat. I bounced from side to side when I walked down the corridors. I asked a ship's officer if we were in danger of capsizing.

"Oh, no, *Liebchen*," he reassured me."The *Mosel* has an excellent stabilizer that will keep us safe." I didn't know what a stabilizer was but it sounded helpful. I wondered whether the ancient traders too had been caught in a monsoon, and became quite sympathetic to them, because they probably didn't have stabilizers.

The large round dining room tables had one-inch protective sides, called "heavy weather strips," that had been raised to catch dishes before they could crash to the floor with each roll. The dishes slid back and forth as we clung to our chairs. I learned how to time putting my fork in my mouth and not in my eye between rolls of the ship. And I always drank my soup quickly because I didn't want to lose it in my lap. The cook, Ajib, made marvelous creamy cold cherry soups with large pearls of tapioca floating in them.

The ship finally escaped from the monsoon. Johnny and I began looking for things to do during the long hot days. We were allowed to visit the Bridge and also the Engine Room, which I loved. It excited me to see the gleaming tubes and to hear the churning of the engines as they turned over. A huge compass in the Bridge fascinated me. Once, the officer on duty picked me up in his arms and let me turn the wheel so that I could see the needles point our change of direction.

The sailors had slung a canvas swimming pool over the hold, tying it to cleats by lines through fat round holes. The simplicity of the construction and the pumped-in ocean water made me feel almost as though I were bouncing around in the ocean itself.

We were all growing bad-tempered in the tropical heat that continued day after day without a break. One day there was a fracas on board. A passenger told us about it later. A third-rate German officer said something offensive to the cook, who did not take well to it. In the sweaty close quarters of the little freighter, the insult was heightened by the irritant of the noisy pumping of the engines and the constant rocking of the boat. The cook's temper flared. Furious, he went after the officer with the long, wavy *kris* that he also used as a cleaver in the kitchen. Swinging his muscled arm, he managed to kill him. Everyone was silent, especially after the officer's body went flying overboard. No one had liked him; he was a prototype Nazi.

We entered the Gulf of Aden. The *Mosel* slowed down as we passed an Italian troop ship carrying Italian soldiers. The ships were close enough for passengers to wave at each other. Johnny horrified me by letting loose one of his piercing Tarzan yells; the Italians laughed and yelled something back to him. I joined in with the little Italian I remembered, from the opera *Madame Butterfly*:

"*Un bel di vedremo*" (one beautiful day we will see ...) I shouted across the ocean to them, waving happily.

The soldiers called back something in Italian that I assumed to mean something like "I hope so." They were handsome young men, with broad smiles.

Mother's antennae began twitching when she saw the Italian troop ship. I could see that her war correspondent instinct sensed a story. At the entrance to the Red Sea was a major port, Djibouti, then part of French Somaliland (Republic of Djibouti). The ship stopped to unload cargo at this busy port at the edge of Ethiopia.

We were stunned at breakfast the next morning. "Children," Mother said, "I have an appointment to interview Ethiopia's Emperor Haile Selassie in his capital, Addis Ababa, later today, and will be back tomorrow. I've been able to get a ticket there and back on the train. I can just get in for an interview with him and catch the train back before the ship leaves." She added, looking us over before leaving: "Johnny dear, you'll look after your sister, won't you, while I'm gone? I'm sure you'll be all right? I really need to get this story." My brother was all of ten years old, and I, eight. She was counting on our fellow passengers to keep an eye on us.

My brother and I hung over the railings all day after she had gone. I was fascinated by the ebony-skinned laborers steering slings of cargo into the hold. I had never seen people who looked like them. The men were gaunt and tall, wearing nothing but a sort of diaper, their long, skeletal mahogany-colored legs stretching down to feet bare but for straw sandals.

We studied the unfamiliar terrain visible beyond the dock.

There were palm trees unlike any I had ever seen. The melodic sounds of the Amharic language were also beyond my experience. I began imitating the sounds until the looks on people's faces made me feel that I'd said something inappropriate.

Mother returned the next day, kissed us hastily, and immediately disappeared into the cabin to get at her typewriter. She wrote and cabled several stories on Italy's plans for Ethiopia, and Ethiopia's aversion to those plans. Over dinner, she told us about her adventure to Addis Ababa and her rare meeting with the Lion of Judah, Emperor Haile Selassie. He was, she said, the 225th successor to his legendary ancestors, King Solomon and the Queen of Sheba. Well, I thought, that's hard to beat.

"When I arrived," she said, "the Ethiopian chieftains were in a formal assemblage dressed in their sumptuous war garments; they had come to confer on the situation regarding Italy. I learned that, indeed, the Italian army was on its way to reclaim its former ownership of the country. The Ethiopians were determined to resist the invasion."

She caught her breath; she had been talking at the speed of her typewriter keys, her words running over each other. "Haile Selassie is trying to modernize his nation, but is finding that resources and time must be diverted to meet the threat from Italy. Those young Italian soldiers are destined for war," she said. Her stories became by-line front-page features in the U.S. newspapers and she was pleased to earn a little money for us on the trip.

Two days later we entered the Red Sea and moved slowly north through the Suez Canal. A capricious tidal flow between the waters of the Red Sea and the Mediterranean Ocean caused our ship to wait until the depth of the canal had adjusted to permit transit.

We stopped at Port Said at the Mediterranean end. Once again I hung over the rail to watch the activity in the hold and on the dock. I couldn't see what the cargo crates contained, just noticing the thick coils of rope, gleaming wet, on the deck. Johnny and I wrote secret messages in code to each other, also throwing some overboard for a passing wave to capture and carry into the unknown. He controlled his Tarzan yell here, as we were too close to the workers for it to be anything but unpleasant, or even frightening if they didn't know about Tarzan.

At sea again we wove our way through the Mediterranean, past Greek islands, Malta, and Sardinia, and then turned north into Marseilles in France.

Here another unloading and loading of goods was accomplished, then we steamed off again. I was on a deck chair reading when Johnny yelled out:

"Patty! Come here! Look at the Rock!

"What rock," I muttered, deeply in my book.

"It's the Rock of Gibraltar where we'll see some Barbary Monkeys!"

I got up and ambled over to the bow of the ship to join Johnny. "Wow. That's really an impressive rock!" But the monkeys must have been taking a rest, there were none in sight.

Off again, around Spain and France, and we docked at Amsterdam in Holland. Here Mother got a cable from Father.

After she had read it, she gathered us to her side. "Children," she said, "I've a cable from Daddy John. Things aren't going so well in Shanghai, he says, and he can't send us any money just yet. Somehow we have to cut our expenses so that we can get to California. It's going to be hard on us until we get to Grandma's." During the next day Mother was sending wires to London and New York to change our plans.

We were suddenly boarding a coastal steamer across the

English Channel to London. This was a very unpleasant short trip: high seas splashed salt water over the decks and onto our luggage in the hold. Some of our bags and our clothes turned bright green. We couldn't stay in London, as we'd all hoped, but immediately boarded the next ship to America, the Norddeutscher Lloyd *Bremen*. In our fancy clothes hand-made by Tailor we traveled across the Atlantic in Steerage, the lowest cheapest level of the ship.

Neither Johnny nor I felt any need to complain. Finding out how to manage without money was part of the whole adventure. Going from ten live-in servants to traveling in Steerage meant an adjustment in priorities, but we found just as much to exclaim about.

In New York Mother arranged for friends to put us all up for a few weeks while she worked with her publisher and got a badly needed advance on a future book. Unfortunately it wasn't nearly enough to restore our fortunes. One afternoon the three of us stood in front of the F.A.O. Schwartz toy store on Fifth Avenue.

"I want the toy red airplane in the window," Johnny cried."Please, Mummy. Please!"

"And I want the teddy bear!' I stretched my arms out toward it.

"No," Mother said."I'm sorry. No."

I knew we were making Mother feel guilty just for the sake of it.

We boarded a comfortable Greyhound Bus bound for California. The trip across America, seeing these parts of America, was fascinating. We drove for days past fields of wheat and corn. When we finally reached the Painted Desert and Petrified Forest everyone got out to look at the sights. Then we crossed the Mojave Desert and Death Valley, climbed up and over the

Rockies, and finally we reached the comfort of our grandparents' home in Rialto, California.

Johnny and I loved visiting our grandparents. The Bookers lived in a comfortable house with a garden and a large shaded porch in front, a garden with a storehouse in back, and a storm shelter/storeroom under the house.

Every now and then we had a little earthquake when the dishes standing up in the dining room breakfront rattled and I heard the quiet clanking of my great-grandmother Mary Katherine Moore Livingston's quarter-silver samovar.

"Aren't you a bit scared when the house shakes like this, Grandma?" It was kind of exciting.

"Pshaw, child, I'm so used to it that I hardly feel it."

Some afternoons when we all relaxed on the front porch, Grandmother told us stories. She was writing a mystery story series starring a girl detective. She wrote, longhand, chapter after chapter on pads of lined yellow paper, keeping the pages in the bottom drawer of the pine chest in her bedroom. Every few weeks she brought out the new stories to read to us. At other times Mother's sister Auntie Lou and Roland Craig and their sons, our cousins Donald and Richard Craig, drove up from their home in Long Beach. Richard was a little younger than I was, and we liked to roughhouse together on the floor until Mother stopped us. "Patty, remember that you are a little lady!" she said. "Act like one!"

It was a time when many Americans were unable to get work, a period called the Great Depression. Many people here were still in trouble. One day when I walked to the Post Office I saw a man in a dark suit faint right at the door, a letter in his hand. I was certain that he had received bad news. Other people came up to help him and he was driven away.

My grandparents seemed to be doing all right despite the

Depression. At least they had shelter and food. They grew a small crop of vegetables in the back yard, and they had a chicken coop. The iceman came weekly in an open truck pulled by an ugly old workhorse, blocks of ice protected by straw in the flat back of the truck. With giant tongs he carried a block to the back door of our screened back porch, where the icebox stood with its bottom door open for the block to be inserted. He also brought milk that was put on the upper part of the icebox beside the eggs from our chickens. Sometimes I helped grandmother churn butter from the cream of the cool milk, but my arms grew tired from the repetitive motion.

Every now and then Grandfather killed a chicken in the back. The first time I saw this, the squawking bird was placed on a stump where he held it in place with one hand while he hit the neck with an axe held by the other arm. The headless bird then jumped down, wings flapping.

"Grandpa, the chicken is still alive!" I screamed, when the chicken for our dinner was running around the yard, blood streaming from its neck. The head lay by the stump. "It's just awful, Grandpa!" I cried. "Now don't you fret, Patty," said Grandma. "It's really dead, this is just a nervous reaction."

"Do you want dinner?" Grandpa asked gruffly. "If you do, someone has to kill the chicken. Would you like to? It's no fun for me." Grandpa was strict with me, and no fun at all.

I loved my grandmother, but missed my life in China. It wasn't just that, here, I was expected to share in the housework. That was normal, and I did the best I could with a broom and dustpan, and wringing out the wet laundry. Johnny was vigorous with the vacuum cleaner. But some American ways were foreign, or even offensive, to me. Without realizing it, like a human blotter I had absorbed Chinese behavior and thinking. Internally, a good part of me was Chinese. I slowly came to realize that I was split, not just between two continents, but also between two cultures. Some days I felt that I was like a jigsaw puzzle with many pieces lost. I missed so much, even the little geckos that ran up our walls at home.

I wasn't happy at my new school. My spelling tests were covered with red corrections. But when I looked at the words, I found that I had spelled them correctly: *colour*, not color, *traveller* rather than traveler. It was irritating to get bad marks on my spelling when I had spelled the way I had learned in China, and had spelled correctly. Apparently I was more British than American in my schooling. The teacher told me that I had to learn the American, not British, spelling, and kept the low grade to force me to learn the "right" way.

Then some girls began to correct my pronunciation. Velda Fouts and Patty Connor and I had formed a secret club that met hidden in a field with high reeds. I knew that they were friends and meant well. But even they corrected me.

"Why do you talk with an English accent?" they asked me."I don't," I muttered back, somewhat testily."I speak the way we speak where I live."

"Well, you shouldn't say "tomahto' but 'tomayto', like we do," one said."And here we say 'eether,' not 'aither'." I decided that I wasn't going to stay in Rialto long enough to bother to change my spelling and pronunciation, and told them so. I was surprised that the people cared about my accent, whatever it was. In my world there were many ways of pronouncing words in English, all of them right. Why should the Rialto accent be the only right way to speak?

There were other children who did exactly what I had been taught not to do. They were pushy. They contradicted other people in public, whether they were wrong or right. They put themselves first instead of last. No one had taught them about making the other person important. They did not know about the importance of "saving face" of the other person even if he was your enemy.

I saw this especially one day soon after I arrived. Someone shoved me aside to get in front of me in line. I didn't want to be in a wrestling match, especially because, being smaller, I knew I would lose, so the big bully took my place ahead of me. I didn't like that. The same bully once told his parents to "shut up" which really shocked me. Yet he was permitted to get away with it.

It wasn't so with my friends, who had kindness and respect for others bred in their bones.

Another problem: I was blind to people's features. Asian and Mexican children attended the school along with the white children, and the white children generally didn't mix with them. I couldn't relate to this, and befriended them no more or less than I did the non-Asian, non-Mexican children. I didn't notice shapes of eyes or colors of skins, not because I was nicer than anyone else or making some statement, but simply because I just didn't see the differences. It was like being color-blind. One day when I had innocently mixed the groups, I got into trouble with my regular friends. Apparently in our multinational environment in Shanghai I had become accustomed to people of all colors and faces. I did see stupid or bright, mean or kind, beautiful or ugly. Malformed people repulsed me; seeing them threw me mentally back to the dreadful poverty, open wounds, and unrepaired bodies of the beggars in Poo Tung and the Old City.

I was Chinese in my thinking, but I was also American. If someone hit me, I hit back. Once my brother threw me into the rose bushes in front of Grandmother's house. A thorn scratched the side of my face from the temple to the jaw. Blood running down my cheek, I looked around for revenge and found a board in the garage. Hiding it behind me I crept up to him, whacked his hand with it, and broke his thumb. I felt a glow of triumph.

"You've broken my thumb!" Johnny yelled.

"You've torn up my face!" I yelled back.

An adult arrived, we both got treated. A gentle healing cream was applied to the side of my face and Johnny's thumb was wrapped in a splint.

The most difficult time for me when my darling grandmother arranged a surprise for us: dinner at the Chinese restaurant in a nearby town."You must be missing your Chinese food," my grandmother said."Here you can have some real Chop Suey."

"Goody! Yummy!" I said. But: *Chop Suey*? What is that, I asked Mother quietly on the side."The name means bits of pieces of vegetables and meat thrown together, often over rice," she said."It's a sort of Americanized version of no Chinese dish I ever had in China," she replied."Just do the best you can. They are trying to do something nice for us."

So we drove to the restaurant. The table was set with regular knives and forks. I asked for chopsticks, but they didn't have any. We picked up our forks. I was afraid that I was going to start giggling and didn't dare look at Johnny. I pushed the grayish slimy food and the squashy rice around on the plate, drenched it all with soy sauce, and managed to work my way through half of it.

I became more and more homesick. I wanted my bedroom and my Amah and my regular friends and food. I wanted my world where people were polite to each other and protected each other's dignity. And something else I missed: the smells of China. The sandalwood, the incense, the gunpowder from little firecrackers, the ginger. I even missed the smells I didn't like— burning peanut oil, stagnant canals. Here in Rialto there were smells, but they were puffing out of cars and busses. Well, to be truly honest, I loved the California fragrance of orange blossoms and eucalyptus trees.

But I wanted to go home…

I wanted to go home where I belonged.

A cable finally arrived from Father saying that things were better financially now; we should come home; the children needed to get back in time for the start of their new year at school. Mother was radiantly happy and made reservations for us to sail from Los Angeles to Shanghai on the next ship.

Even today, after decades of living in an American environment, I still feel sometimes like a jigsaw puzzle with key pieces missing — perhaps the edges that hold the entire design together. I know I belong here, I know that I have dear and thoughtful friends and a good life, but, still, I often feel incomplete.

XII

1936-7. A GRUESOME GOVERNESS; TRIPS
AROUND THE CITY.
AGE NINE

SITTING AT MY DESK, *now considering the Shanghai that I had experienced, it is my pre-1937 time there that gives me joy. I had buried my memories of my Shanghai life. It had become a place that frightened me, where Japanese cruelty increased from month to month, and when nice German friends turned into Nazi monsters. My feelings, my fright, had been too deep to dare exposure; I was like a sea anemone that shudders and curls into itself when touched.*

Now at last I can look back into my Shanghai, especially the time before the Japanese destroyed my life – thinking of the significance of the chrysanthemum blossom contrasted with the garish stamping angry-faced opera dancers and the raucous laughter of Chinese men telling jokes. The refined chilled almond soup balanced by crude contented belching after a good meal and the messy grains of rice scattered around each place at the table. The canniness about money and the inability to be overtly rude even to an enemy in public. The individual character of each distinct part of Shanghai and yet the cohesiveness of Shanghai as a whole city.

And I can at last revisit those last months of peace before the Japanese invasion.

We returned to a Shanghai that had not changed much, nor had our lives. My father had managed to hold the household together during the difficult months, and it was a joy to be greeted by the dear faces of our staff. The awful governess Frau Zeller was not among them, and that brightened our lives too.

The absence of a governess for me, however, made life more difficult for my parents. I was nine going on ten, and needed an escort if I went out of the house, even to walk in the neighborhood. It was different for my brother. He was twelve now, and in addition he was a boy. I was jealous of the freedom he was allowed. In addition, I was deeply lonely. Mother was away a lot with her writing or preoccupied with the Shanghai international social life. Father was downtown on business, Johnny had his Gunpowder Gang, and all I had was school and occasional visits with my German girlfriends.

One day when I felt especially forlorn and Mother was away I decided to have a birthday party, even if it wasn't my birthday. I really really wanted a party. Since Father was never involved, so far as I knew, with planning parties, I didn't mention it to him. I hand-printed and sent invitations to a "birthday party", and our chauffeur drove me to town to buy party favors and decorations.

"Ah Kung," I asked the butler one day, "my have one birthday party two week time. Please you helpee me have party cake, ice cream, party sandwiches?"

"Missie savvy you have party?"

"No, she not care, she like party. Never mind Missie."

But Ah Kung was way ahead of me. He didn't want to get into trouble with my mother, and knew that this little girl had no business hosting a birthday party for herself, especially on a day not her birthday. He mentioned it to my father, who in turn contacted Mother. Learning about my initiative, she rushed back to Shanghai and cancelled my party to prevent what looked to all the grownups like a disaster in the making.

I was sent to my room to be punished. I didn't want them to hear me cry, I was too proud, so I hid my head under the pillow on my bed and sobbed out my loneliness and the humiliation imposed on me into the darkness under the pillow. I don't think she ever knew how unhappy I was or how deeply she had hurt me. She and I never mentioned this fiasco.

It was now clear that we needed another governess to keep me company and to take me around the city.

I was thrilled when my father told me that I was to have a new governess. Maybe she would be like Matrushka who had always been clean and fresh, and had never scolded me like awful Frau Zeller.

"Don't expect too much, Patty." Father warned me."Frau Neisser may not be so sweet as Matrushka, but let's hope she'll be better than Frau Zeller."

A few days later the phone rang. It was answered by Lin Sing. *"Waah, noong sa ning ah?"*

"Iss Herr Potter da? I vish to speak mit Herr Potter. Qvick, I am sehr hurry!" a cracked voice demanded.

This turned out to be Frau Neisser. She wanted the car to bring her to our home. I blamed her piercing harsh voice on the telephone and waited eagerly.

When at last she arrived Mother had returned, and told me to stay in my room. But if I couldn't see Frau Neisser, I certainly heard her. The grating voice reached me upstairs and I winced as she spoke. After a few minutes mother called me.

Mother's bedroom door was slightly open, and I could see a part of Frau Neisser's 1915-style dress. That wasn't very encouraging. Then, as she moved, I saw her hair—bobbed brilliant red hair with an inch of white at the roots. It was only after I went in that I knew the worst. She had a bumpy pointy nose, scarlet lipstick smeared over withered lips. She looked like the old hags in Hans Christian Anderson fairy tales.

She settled into the bedroom on the second floor like a gloomy cloud over us all. My brother and I hated her more every day. Mother, who pitied her greatly, didn't have the courage to fire her because she wept miserably whenever anyone mentioned her leaving, and besides, I needed a governess. She did speak excellent French and German with me, and never had any dates or telephone callers. Mother felt that she was totally reliable. I knew I had to get along with her. She helped me read *Struwelpeter* but she didn't know that both Johnny and I thought she had table manners just as bad as that horrible little boy in the stories.

Frau Neisser was interested in hearing about the activities of the *Hitler Jugend*; she clearly liked Adolph Hitler and his efforts to build and promote Germany. Every few weeks a bundle of newspapers would arrive from Germany. These she read cover to cover, sometimes conveying tidbits to us when she joined us for tea. She was especially opposed to some people called *Juden*, sometimes she called them "Juice," and was pleased that Hitler was kicking them out of Germany. I didn't bother to ask who they were or what kind of juice was involved.

Now that I was growing older, Mother began taking me on shopping trips to various places around the city when I had time away from school.

One day we visited a silk factory called, Mother said, a "filature," in Chapei, far from the areas that the Japanese had bombed a few years earlier.

A guide showed us the different stages of development of the cloth. In the first room, hundreds of silk worms were squirming around, feasting on leaves.

"What are the worms chewing on?" I asked. Their little mouths kept going up and down on leaves, leaving ragged holes."Those are mulberry leaves. It's the only food that the finicky worms will eat," she replied.

In another room the worms were spinning a fiber into cocoons that they wrapped around their bodies.

"Maybe that fiber is a little like what spiders make for their webs," Mother suggested.

In an area with very moist warm air, young girls were separating the silk threads from the cocoons. Their bare hands turned the cocoons around and around in furiously boiling water. I knew that it was hard, painful work, but they also had to stand for hours every day doing this. I whispered,

"Mom, can't they find another way of turning the cocoons? Can't they use a spoon, or chopsticks? That's just awful." The girls' hands were red. She nodded but couldn't do anything about it.

We were guided to where the threads, separated from the cocoons, were coiled around spindles. Afterwards, it was like a miracle to see the threads being dipped into what seemed to be hundreds of colors before being woven into shimmering bolts of cloth before us. Mother picked out several bolts of silk for our dresses."Tailor will love these."

The girls were about my age, and I wondered about their lives. I wanted to speak to them and saw that they were curious about me, but we didn't know each other's languages and so just smiled at each other.

"Where do these girls come from?" I asked Mother."They're younger than I am. Why aren't they at school, or with their families?"

"The girls are homeless orphans," she explained."Victims of

the wars."

I was worried about those girls. Later, when I asked her about them, my Amah told me that many of the girls had been sold by their impoverished families and brought to Shanghai to work in the filature.

On a different day Mother took me to a convent in an area in southwest Shanghai called Siccawei (Xujiahui). The grounds around the convent were attractive, with a creek running nearby. She planned to order a richly embroidered, monogrammed dinner set.

In the convent, young Chinese girls in neat uniforms were learning to embroider and to create lace. A large bright room with many windows was set up with narrow tables. .At each, one girl was seated before a white linen cloth stretched flat and pinned to the table. A design of grape clusters and bouquets of flowers was drawn onto one cloth with a blue pencil and pinned solidly. On another, the design was squares of lace inserts.

The girls were embroidering the design onto the cloth with tiny stitches. When one was finished, she carefully cut out the unnecessary cloth with fine scissors.

"Gosh," I said."I can't do what they're doing. That is very delicate work. Are they orphans, like the silk worm girls?"

Mother explained."Yes. Like those girls, these have no homes, no families. Here in the convent, while they have long hours and probably hurt their eyes and backs, they can at least have food, friendship, and a safe warm place to sleep." She paused."Patty, it's better, safer, for them than living on the street. You know how little value girl children have in China."

Yes, I knew. The knowledge of the traditional rejection of baby girls was always with me. I was given explanations of why newborn girls were sometimes drowned—not only were they useless, but also, they just cost money, especially a wedding dowry, while boys could make money. This concept did not appeal to this Littie Missie.

Trips and visits came to a halt when we found that I was itching all over, not from prickly heat but from measles. What an unpleasant experience. Father was especially kind to me as Mother was away.

"Oh my little sweetheart," he said one afternoon when he got back from work,"you look miserable! Let's see, maybe I can help make it all better." He went downstairs and returned holding a bowl. Then he sat down beside me on my bed, and peeled and de-seeded cool grapes. He then fed them to me, one juicy grape after another. It felt like Heaven.

Another afternoon he brought up sweet, gritty pears that he peeled down to the thin end."You should hold the pear at the unpeeled thin end. That way, you won't touch the flesh with your hands, and so not get some major disease."

When I had recovered, Father took me with him on little trips that were, to me, adventures, like those with my mother — an escape from Frau Neisser, a look at a different part of Shanghai, something interesting to learn. On one occasion I accompanied him on a mission for a client to Zung Kee's go-down, his warehouse and carpentry shop in Poo Tung. This was a run-down area across the river from The Bund, composed of dilapidated warehouses, slums, swamps, the large ugly British American Tobacco company warehouse, coolie quarters.

But his shop itself was a pleasure. Pale curled shavings of wood lay on the floor by the sawhorses, while the long boards balanced on them were being shaped into chests with fanciful scenes carved in relief. I breathed deeply. The fragrances of sandalwood and of cedar filled the air.

Zung Kee was the person who had built my Teddy Bear house. He greeted me warmly on Father's introduction, then asked: "Missie Patty likee house for doll?"

"Oh my goodness, yes, Mr. Zung Kee!" I exclaimed."I love the house, it is beautiful! Did you really really make it?"

Father laughed."Yes, Patty, this gentleman built the house from Mother's and my design."

He discussed arrangements for shipment to America of a rare collection of rose quartz figures — people, trees, rocks, belonging to Judge Cornell and Dallas Franklin who were moving back to Virginia.

I had first seen their rose quartz displayed in front of windows in the living room of their home, the sunlight through the window turning each piece translucent.

My best adventure with Father was when he was able to take me with him for a dinner party with Chinese friends. That evening he asked Frau Neisser to help me dress in appropriate clothes for a dinner party."You're in for a special treat," he told me."You have been included in an invitation to dinner at the home of one of the most distinguished Chinese scholars and art collectors in the nation."

I didn't like Frau Neisser to touch me, she repelled me and made me very jittery, so I managed to dress myself with help from Amah. Mother was still insisting on my looking like a four-year-old Shirley Temple. Amah and I constantly quarreled about my curls but, tonight, I didn't want to make trouble for Father and just acquiesced. Amah brushed my hair into curls and tied on a ribbon.

This invitation was an unusual honor, since the Chinese elite rarely invited foreigners into their homes, and certainly not their children, for dinner. I appreciated my father's thought in arranging for me to accompany him. His courtesy and intelligence as well as his good looks always gave me a quiet pleasure. I was proud of him.

"Are you going to wear your green jade cufflinks? Please?" I asked. These were his most elegant. He let me push them, deep apple-green jade ovals set in gold, through the little slots on the cuffs of his dress shirt. My fingers enjoyed the smooth texture of the jade, my eyes sinking deep into the color."Have I told you," Father remarked,"that your mother gave these to me as her wedding present?"

Ah Ching drove us past the International Concession into the broad, tree-lined avenues of the French Concession, and from there into the old, Chinese, walled part of Shanghai, Nantao. We entered an area of ancient narrow winding streets. I looked excitedly at the pagoda-shaped buildings and the advertisements showing Chinese characters in red and glittering gold flashing on and off.

Crowds of people jostled each other in the street. The sounds of clashing gongs and sing-song music from night clubs, car horns blasting in every level of sound and tone, cries from peddlers hawking their goods in sing-song from push carts, animated the air. Beggars crowded our car.

"No got mama, no got papa, no got whiskey soda!" cried a haggard Russian lady begging for money. Then a skinny Chinese baby was pushed up against the window, the mother crying "Helpee baby, no got food!" As we slowed for a clutter of farmers leading water buffalo, the crowds of beggars pushing against our car became frightening."Please, Daddy, these people, it's awful that they are so miserable! I'm scared!"

"Just shut your eyes, Patty. Ah Ching is doing the best he can."

There was nothing the chauffeur could do but bellow in his

most frightening Shanghainese for them to get out of his way, honk the horn, and make violent gestures. Slowly he was able to maneuver our car out of that impasse and work his way through the next: vendors with pushcarts laden with dishes of fragrant hot noodles and cups of tea, and pedestrians blocking the road when they stopped for noodles or to tell a joke in the middle of the street.

Finally we turned away from the crowds into an inconspicuous street, the sudden silence startling. We stopped at an almost invisible doorway in a high stone wall. Ah Ching parked and we got out. He pushed a button on the wall. A gate opened, closing behind us. Father and I entered a sheltered well-tended garden. A stone path led to an arched red zigzag bridge across a pond.

The zig-zag shape, I knew, prevented devils from reaching the house. Devils, in China, could not make 90-degree turns.

Willows and chrysanthemums bordered the pond. I walked across the bridge with Father, noticing different reflections on the water's surface as we changed direction. After the bridge, the path continued to a moon gate with red lacquer accents. This opened to the courtyard of a mansion whose eaves were decorated with red and ocher tiles symbolically arching upward. The arching eaves protected the residents of the house against evil spirits, which, much like the devils, could move only in straight lines.

A pair of vivid yellow ceramic Fu dogs--half dog, half lion— guarded the front door. Originally, the fierce-looking animals had "defended" Buddhist temples. I glanced at them: yes, they were placed correctly, the male dog at the left, the female at the right of the person in the house. The people we were visiting were well protected from anyone determined to harm them.

My father and I entered. There was a welcome quiet in the house. The restfulness felt like part of its personality. Father bowed to the elderly host and hostess, and I curtsied when he introduced me.

There were four other guests present. We were ushered into the dining room, the walls decorated with Chinese art. Our host seated us at a large round table in the middle of the dining room.

The centerpiece was a version of a large Lazy Susan that enabled the guests to reach with their ivory chopsticks for whichever tidbit they desired. A dish of sunflower seeds was at the left of each place; on the right, the chopsticks were presented on a small raised porcelain piece, a decorated porcelain spoon beside it. A small teacup with no handle was placed above each setting. The dinner plates were of my favorite Chinese porcelain from the Chien Lung (Emperor Qian Long) dynasty with vividly colored flowers on contrasting backgrounds.

Dish after dish, following a precise pattern of hot and cold, sweet and sour, spicy and bland, were brought from the kitchen by white-robed servants. Jasmine tea, blossoms floating, was poured. The servants came in and out soundlessly, their steps muffled by flat cloth slippers. Our meal was not disturbed by kitchen clatter in this well-disciplined household. Nor did our hosts have to address the servants.

The featured dish was a "One Hundred Year Old Egg." I had heard about these eggs that were buried in a plaster of clay, lime, salt, rice hulls, wood ash and tea that preserved them for many months. Its un-familiar and, to me, unpleasant odor of mixed sulphur and ammonia wafted over to the table when the serving dish was carried out of the kitchen. The Chinese guests gave exuberant exclamations of joy and amazement. I was amused to see that Father joined in their joy. I just sat as still as a flower, an attempt at a smile on my face. Then this rare treat was presented to me. It looked like a large peeled boiled egg that was blue and green and purple with no help from Easter egg dyes.

I looked over at my father, my eyes imploring. I couldn't touch this horrible thing on my plate. But he signaled silently to me that I had to eat it. Our hosts were honoring us by serving it. I recognized the need not to be discourteous and so took several bites of the revolting delicacy. But I loved everything else, especially the dessert: cold creamy almond soup.

After the dessert the houseboy brought in warm, damp, jasmine-scented face cloths with which to refresh ourselves.

Then the host led us into the living room, where he opened a tall sandalwood chest with many narrow shelves. He carefully selected scroll after scroll of Chinese art from the shelves. Each painting was rolled up and tied with a ribbon. He untied each and held it up against the wall so that it could be fully seen. He told us about it and about the artist, in fluent English. He explained about the "chop" or seal that was the sobriquet of the artist, and translated the calligraphic text running down the side. Each painting was bordered with textured silk brocade.

Neither my father nor I wanted to leave, but soon we were walking back across that lovely bridge. I had to look down again at the reflections of the chrysanthemums blurred in the now moonlit water. Somehow they were important to me; they created a mystery, the flowers almost alive, moving and changing with a breeze and with each change of direction.

In spite of the beautiful hidden homes, the Old City had a dark side. There were too many one-legged men pushing themselves along on wheeled boards; too many malformed people, some with large swellings around their necks; too many beggars following our car with outstretched hands; too many hungry children trained to tug at our clothing with piteous cries for help. The wretchedness bothered me greatly. I remembered and understood Mother's telling us that she took us to California to be born because she was afraid that we might pick up one of the diseases if we were born in China.

Some friends had whispered to me that there were opium dens in the Old City. As we drove through the streets I could see the half-dead-looking addicts. The smells, not just of opium or peanut oil or incense, but even more of sewage and unwashed bodies, nauseated me. The odors raised the level of misery — the screaming children, the calling, clutching, skeletal bodies. The open sores on people's faces.

Then as we slowly turned one corner, a creature as thin, flat and lifeless as a fly-swatter pushed his face and hands against the window a foot from my own face. He grinned toothless and grotesque at me. I screamed in fright. Father reached over and pulled me to him, hiding my face in his shoulder.

"Ah Ching, can you go a little faster?" he asked."The opium addicts in this area are frightening Littie Missie."

That man's face bothered me for days after. When I shut my eyes and tried to go to sleep, there he was, despair etched in every line on his face.

My tenth birthday came and went that November in 1936. Father was too worried about the Japanese to remember it, Mother was away, and the governess was worse than no one. No one had planned a birthday party for me. Johnny, now age twelve, spent his free time with his friends. I had no American girlfriends and my German friends began to change toward me. My loneliness increased.

Father gave me a present: the heavy large book of the *Fables de la Fontaine* that had been in their library. It certainly wasn't what I had been hoping for. The book contained a lot of poems with moral lessons. Father liked to quote from it, telling us not to be like the grasshopper that sang while the ant worked, so when bad weather came, the grasshopper had no food and had to beg from the ant. Frau Neisser made me memorize that Fable and several more.

Unfortunately Father chose to lecture us frequently on the value of being a hard-working ant and not a useless, indolent grasshopper. Once at dinner he was so cutting to Johnny that my brother ran from the table crying. I just sat frozen until I was excused.

My favorite room was the sunroom that adjoined my parents' bedroom and the study. Large windows on three walls overlooked the garden and the street. Here I created worlds by writing books—some beautiful, some frightening. My typing and spelling had improved since my first attempts. some were now several chapters long and they looked respectable.

At school we learned another patriotic song: every morning we began the day by singing the Nazi anthem, the *Horst Wessel Lied*, in unison, followed by several *Heil Hitlers*, our arms raised up in the Nazi salute, then *Deutschland Über Alles*, the national anthem. The boys and girls in the Hitler Jugend marched around as before.

I learned long German poems by Göthe and Schiller, and I really worked to learn one Schiller poem,"The Hostage" *(Die Bürgschaft)*, which was dramatic and suspenseful. Two of the lines in particular allowed for dramatic rendition:

"Die Stadt vom Tyrannen befreien!"
"Dass sollst Du am Kreuze bereuen."

"To free the nation from the tyrant!"
"You'll regret that when you're crucified!"

I became a great attraction at my parents' parties when I recited and enacted this poem. In the middle of the living room, my arms waving for effect, I would dramatically tell of the frightful events. No one could turn me off.

Glowing Pearl, Sew Sew Amah Mary's daughter, began to spend more time in Tailor's room, learning the various embroidery stitches. I thought she was very slow in learning the simplest stitches; Tailor kept having to hold her hands to show her how to move the thread with her fingers.

Christmastime came; Mother was back. My parents sent out specially made red cards with a photograph of Johnny and me in Chinese costumes, and good wishes expressed in gold Chinese characters and Western words.

A separate group of people, friends of Father's from when they were all in the Philippines as young men, received a different kind of card. Each one was sent a worthless stock certificate for a share of a played-out gold mine in Baguio, northern Luzon.

"I guess you left school because you wanted to see the world, Dad?" Johnny observed.

"Yes, I was hungry to learn everything I could about the whole wide world. My life at home was restrictive. My grandfather, Rev. Isaiah Potter, was a 'hellfire and damnation' preacher who was highly respected but scared everyone. He scared my father, Rev. Milton George Potter, into drinking too much alcohol and he became unkind."

"I wanted to see the world, and so when the US government asked for young Americans to become teachers at the other end of the world in our new Territory, the Philippines, I grabbed the chance. I was only 18, but I could teach."

"And you went there, and then came here?"

"That's just what I did. The USS *THOMAS* took us adventurous young teachers to the Philippines, where I became a Supervising Teacher and organized schools where there weren't any, or very rudimentary ones.

"I learned the Philippine languages Tagalog and Ilocano as well as Spanish so that I could serenade the ladies as well as teach the children."

"Daddy!"

"Yes, well, it was the custom for the young men to wander the streets singing, attracting girls to come out onto their balconies to talk to us." He grinned, and sang a few lines of a Tagalog love song.

It was now 1937, springtime, and the gardens began blooming again. We could spend more time outside, and the governess became more and more irritating. I felt that her futzing around me was unnecessary to my survival.

One day Johnny and I were in the pantry laughing about something the cook had said. The door swung open, and Frau Neisser appeared.

"Were you at mich laufing?" she said in accusatory tones. "I know you were at mich laufing. I shall tell your Fahzer."

I insisted that we had not been laughing at her, but she wouldn't believe me. Lurching at me suddenly she shrieked: "You vicked girl! You at mich lie! I giff you patch-patch for being so vicked!"

She chased me wildly around a column in the living room, pushing furniture out of the way. I was frightened and raced upstairs, locking myself in the bathroom, the nearest room with a lock. Frau Neisser pounded on the door, demanding to be let in. I was crying desperately from fear and couldn't say a word. Finally she left, hissing under her breath.

After several minutes, Johnny knocked on the door.

"Haggie (our secret name for her) has finally gotten into an awful mess, Sis," he said, laughing. "Dad was there all the time.

Gee, he sure is mad at her for treating you the way she did. And is he telling her off now!"

Johnny and I crept down the stairs until we had a clear view of the living room, Frau Neisser, and my father. Hands on hips, he was berating her in the angriest tones I'd ever heard him use. Not listening to the whimpering sounds she was now making, he observed that a lady doesn't wear a night-cap down to breakfast as she did, and that her sloppy table manners made him feel ill. Then we heard him say,"…and we believe that the children are quite old enough to get along without you." Oh joy!

Mother arranged for Amah to escort me around the city. Calm, resourceful, beloved Amah restored order to our lives.

Soon after Frau Neisser's departure the school year ended. It was summer again, and again time to renew the house to its hot weather attire and pack away the winter needs.

I asked about our summer plans, but my parents avoided the subject with vague words like "Not now, Darling," or "We'll see." They referred to "trouble in the North." Then I read in the newspaper that the Japanese so-called skirmishes had been serious battles and that their army had moved well south of the Great Wall and was nearing Peking. There had been warnings of what was coming, but with of a sense of inevitability, or perhaps exhaustion from the 1932 Japanese attack, we Shanghailanders didn't seem to be doing much about it.

At dinner one night my parents finally began talking about what was happening. Johnny who started the conversation.

"I hear that the sneaky Japs have been building armed strongholds from the Great Wall down to Peking all these past years. This year they attacked and conquered one town after another all the way to Peking."

"But they couldn't take Peking, could they?" I prayed not.

"They did, Patty," Mother said quietly."Just a few days ago.

July the Seventh."

"What! That's awful. I can't imagine the Japanese in Peking! That's scary!"

"None of us believed that they could take Peking, but they rolled over the city with hardly a shot. Now they are marching to Shanghai."

My father angrily stubbed his cigarette out in an ashtray. "They're almost here now," he said bitterly. "I don't think they can take Shanghai, but we need to be prepared." He sighed deeply, then straightened his shoulders. "Ah Kung, please gather all the staff together in the living room after dinner. We must prepare for everyone's safety just in case the Japanese capture the city."

I silently noted that we'd been through this exercise only five years ago.

"Yes, Mister Potter. Thank you, Sir."

A few days later the Japanese Army attacked Shanghai.

It is hard to believe, today, that people back then had to rely on spies to peer around corners and over mountains to seek out enemy troops and weapons massing for combat. No drones, no satellites. Not even a 1950s U-2 spy plane in 1937 China. The Chinese Air Force was limited in its operational capacity and airfields. The government had focused on uniting and strengthening the nation, helping her recover from the devastating effect of the Opium Wars and the Boxer Rebellion. Now she was also fighting both the invading Japanese and a civil war. I believe that, today, no invader could take any part of China by surprise.

On an adventure *Patty & Johnny on verandah swing* *In her German School uniform*

Patty as a rose

The topee is almost too large for Patty's head *Outside Cornell Franklin's house, age about 11*

Johnny with his erhu, Patty looking on, both in Chinese dress

Patty and Johnny as Pirates

Mother and Father are married

Father smiling at his bride

Mother as a 22-year-old reporter

Mother, far right, and Father, 4th from left, meet at a Columbia Country Club "Red Dog" party.

Great-grandfather Rev. Isaiah Potter

*Grandmother Jessie Livingston Booker with
Great-grandfather William Lowry Livingston*

*Father's transportation to classes he
taught, Philippines*

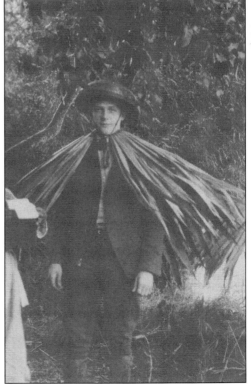

*Mother travelling by sedan chair to get an
interview with the Hakka people*

Father solving a weather problem, Philippines

In Wei Hai Wei, the jalopy with Mafu Jim   *A three-sail junk in the harbor. Courtesy Diana Angulo*

Off to a picnic with boatman Lao Lu

Johnny and Patty in their punt, the "Jitterbug"   *Mother going down the cliff to Half Moon Bay and the cabañas*

Wei Hai, beach by East Cliffe Hotel, Courtesy Diana Angulo

Burning of Chapei 1937.Cred US Army

Credit: Richard Hubert

Mother interviewing Pere Jacquinot at his Refugee Safe Zone

Father in his Volunteer Army uniform

Mother's newspaper office

Credit: Bundesarchiv

The Hitler Jugend on a training trip, October 1933

Prize awarded to Patty "in recognition of hard work and cooperation"
on May 20, 1939

Erika Resek (Meier), Patty's
favorite governess

Chiao Quei, our Amah

Number Two Boy Lin Sing

Ah Ching, Chauffeur

Fo Sun, Lin Sing and Ah Kung

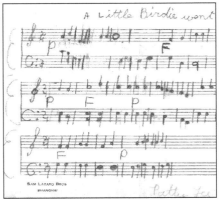

Patty's first song, "The Swing"   *A later song, "A Little Birdie Went to Sleep"*

Father's scrapbook for Patty   *Invitations from German School friends*   *One of Patty's Teddy Bear family*

Jim, the family English Setter   *Patty's drawing of a flood near her home*

XIII

1937-38. JAPAN INVADES SHANGHAI. AGE TEN

THINKING, NOW IN *the heat of August, about that other August when the Japanese invaded Shanghai, I take a sip of iced tea and stare back into those days before we fled from Shanghai. I shudder. The war is now in me again, in my eyes and bones.*

The colors--scarlet skies, black clouds billowing up into the red. Color of blood, color of death.

The sounds--screams, moans echoing across ruins. Deep thuds and concussive blasts and staccato rat-tat-tat. Running feet, creaking wheels. Jim whining in pain. Rattling windows.

The smells--gunpowder. Unwashed rotting bodies. Opium. Burnt flesh.

The feelings--wide-eyed terror, quivering body, stomach cramped by fear, vibrations into my bones. Bewilderment.

Uncontrollable tears now suddenly overtake me. Groping for a box of Kleenex I curl up in my chair, hugging my body, trying to control the hurt.

It was August. Before we knew what was happening, war crashed down on us. From my father's office I could see the Japanese warships in the harbor. There were so many now; the number had grown to twenty-six—an invasion armada. The Japanese

Flagship, the armored cruiser *Idzumo*, was berthed not far from the Cathay Hotel and Nanking Road at The Bund.

Staring out of my bedroom window I watched as the Japanese airplanes, flying from their aircraft carriers in the river, set fire to Chapei with incendiary bombs. My body shuddered from the noise and shock of the explosions.

The red smoke from the fires surged up across the sky like an incandescent sunset. North of us, Chapei, an area where Mother had taken me to the silk-weaving and other handcraft and artisan shops, was turning into blocks on blocks of ruins.

The unwarned and helpless residents, most of whom lived above their shops, could not escape in time and were dying in the flames. The girls at the silk factory — had they gotten away? Had they burned up along with everyone else? I imagined the girls screaming, and hugged my body in horror, choking on heavy gulps of tears.

It was worse for Jim. The noise caused his sensitive ears piercing pain. He whined pitifully and ran frantically from place to place looking for a sanctuary where his ears were protected. Johnny finally bundled him up in his bed under the blankets. Day after day, after his run in the garden, he hid in Johnny's bed.

Over dinner I asked my parents how the war was going.

"The Chinese seem to be losing," Father said. "Because of the 1932 League of Nations Treaty--you won't remember, you were only about six then--Japanese troops were already in the city and the suburbs, and no Chinese soldiers were allowed to be stationed here. Also, sometimes the Chinese troops of the ruling party, the Kuomintang, are forced to fight Russian and Chinese Communist soldiers as well as the Japanese Army. The government's power is split, having to fight two different wars at once." It was confusing to me that Chinese were fighting Chinese while Japanese were invading us.

"I don't know what that League is, but they are on the wrong side," I muttered bitterly.

My parents agreed.

A few minutes later I wailed, "All this is just awful! What's happening to the poor people? Are they all being burned up or something like that?"

The bombing of Chapei continued ferociously, day after day. The newspapers reported that, where two million industrious people had lived and worked, in a few days not one person, not even one mutt or wonk, remained.

"What are the blankety-blank Japs doing! They're ruining our city!" I yelled one day.

"They're bombing and burning Chapei so that they can occupy it with their army, I guess," Johnny replied, hanging out of the same window.

I was terrified. Our house shook with each bomb and so did I. Sometimes the explosion was near enough to hurt my ears. I could feel the vibrations in my bones and smell the gunpowder.

"Daddy, what will happen to us if the Japs win?" I asked one day when the bombardment seemed exceptionally heavy. "I'm frightened! I don't want us to be bombed!"

"I don't think that they will dare harm the people in the international sections," he replied, patting my shoulder to reassure me. "I believe that they will respect the international treaties."

But we were not allowed to go far from our home, only to the Country Club for cooling swims.

Tens of thousands of Japanese soldiers stormed into Shanghai that August. The outnumbered and outgunned Chinese Army fought as well as it could, but Shanghai was lost, a little more every day. The smell of gunpowder, the burnt buildings, the destitute refugees, were everywhere.

It was clear that we children had to be gotten to safety until things settled down. Our parents discussed the future with Johnny and me over a family dinner.

"Shanghai won't be able to hold out much longer," Mother observed."We don't know what will happen when the Japanese occupy the city; they may respect the treaties, but what if they don't? I don't have any faith in their respecting international laws; they haven't kept their word at any time in their drive to conquer China."

"You're right. Edna Lee," Father said."Children, it looks as though you have to go back to California. You'll leave on whatever ship is available."

Mother's eyes were worried and sorrowful."It just makes me sick that Daddy has to stay behind again because of business. But he has to look after the interests of his clients."

She went on a furious shopping binge on Nanking Road. It was no longer possible to go to the silk filature or other fine artisan stores in Chapei that she preferred because of her many friendships among the creative Chinese workers. All areas of Shanghai not under the protection of the international treaties were either destroyed or too dangerous for us to enter. But the Japanese had not yet invaded our sectors.

Mother and Ah Ching returned with bolts of brocades, silks, cottons and linens. Tailor turned these into "used" furnishings to be stored at Zung Kee's so that, if we lost our home to the Japanese, they could be shipped to us as duty-free "used personal effects" and in America we could still have some of the familiar elegant things that we lived with every day.

The room next to mine became crowded. Tailor hemmed fictitious curtains and drapes and spreads. Multicolored weavings were couched as pillowcases; fine silks and linens became sheets. Extra large coats were made of doubled-over heavy Harris Tweed and camel's hair fabrics, and lined with double layers of English flannel. Yards of nubby Shantung silk and luminous *pongee* were converted into voluminous kimonos and robes lined with layers of silk gauze hidden beneath more silk.

With mixed feelings I helped pack the boxes to go to Zung Kee's go-down. I wanted us to have these lovely things in whatever new home we might have to go to; but I didn't want to leave our home in Shanghai and our life here when there wasn't a war at our front door.

The preparations continued in a frantic rush until we ran out of time; we had berths on a ship. There were last-minute details at home; phone calls to friends. Our heavy trunks with clothing for a year had been sent ahead and were already in the hold of the liner.

Our departure was more dramatic than usual because of Mother's eternal problem with being late for everything except her newspaper's deadlines. Halfway to the dock we had to turn around and drive back to our house for a forgotten item.

Ah Ching and Father in two cars drove us back to the dock as quickly as possible now, horns tooting frantically to clear the road.

When we finally arrived and unloaded the cars we were very late. Mother, Father, Johnny, Amah, the two coolies and I ran along the long pier to reach the tender before it left. Boxes, suitcases and hatboxes swung from hands, fingers, arms. I was gasping from the strain and the stress but made my legs keep pushing me and my duffle bag forward.

The pier was made of slats of wood about one inch apart.

Mother caught her heel between slats, lost her balance, tripped, and dropped her purse. It flew open. The contents scattered over several of the slats. Many items fell through the cracks into the

Whang Poo. Everything stopped. We couldn't breathe.

Mother's lipstick disappeared between the slats. Her compact disappeared. Keys disappeared.

I spied the passports lying where they had fallen across a couple of slats."Mummy, here are the passports!" I cried.

"I've got the tickets!" Johnny shouted, picking them up where they had landed, a few slats away.

The precious envelope of money, enough to last us for several months, was retrieved by Amah.

"Whew!" Mother sighed, fanning herself with the envelope. With great relief we scrambled aboard the tender. I turned to wave and blow kisses at Father and Amah, but we were too hurried for long goodbyes. Mother and Father hugged each other; Father's eyes were moist as they pulled apart."It'll be a long lonely time without you, my sweetheart," I heard him say. His face looked grim.

"Take care of yourself, John, darling, keep safe, and let me hear from you! I'll miss you every minute!" she called back to him. The tender began to chug out to the liner."Keep safe darling!" she shouted across the waves.

The tender had to weave among the many Japanese warships now filling the harbor. How my beloved Bund had changed! It was horrid, now. The loathsome red and white Japanese flags flew everywhere. Our liner looked vulnerable, alone among the many Japanese warships. I was relieved to board it and escape from those menacing ships that had taken over my Bund.

Once on board, looking back at The Bund, we could see our family as little spots on the pier. We stood silently at the railing, each deep in our own thoughts, knowing that we had to leave Shanghai until the Japanese invasion had settled. We also knew we would return as soon as it was safe.

I watched the ship pull slowly away from familiar scenes

along the Whang Poo. The noise of the ongoing destruction of Chapei shocked me. On this sunny day where the skies should have been blue, I saw red and black clouds created by the bombs and the burning city. I wanted to cry, but controlled it; crying couldn't mend my anguish. My family wouldn't be any consolation; Mother and Johnny were as miserable as I was. I tried to put thoughts of the suffering people, especially of those girls of my own age, out of my mind and just manage one task and then the next, one foot after another, in order to hold onto myself. I couldn't think about the burning people, or about my father and our household. It cut too deeply.

Our ship turned slowly into the Yangtze River, and finally entered the China Sea.

I was soon mesmerized by the action of the ocean as I stood at the stern, especially by the shapes and colors of the wake. The ocean always gave me strength. Johnny came up; he had been looking for flying fish but we hadn't gone far enough yet for them to appear.

"The Captain has called for a gathering of all the passengers," he told me."We have to find Mom and locate the major dining room for the meeting."

At the meeting we received instructions about fire alarms, lifeboats, and an outline of life aboard the ship, one of the Dollar Liners with years of experience of traversing the Pacific. We were served tea and biscuits and, after the session, went down one hallway after another until we found our cabin. It held two beds and an upper berth, a small desk and chair, and a washstand and clothes closet. Johnny settled on the upper berth. I grabbed for the bed by the porthole and, almost squealing with joy, unscrewed it and opened it to the sea air. There was pleasure in the tingle of an occasional splash of salty water on my face. Mother joined me at the open porthole, breathing deeply, also enjoying the carefree ocean breezes.

Over the days that passed we saw flying fish, sometimes porpoises, leaping about the bow of our ship as though they were guiding us; and sometimes a bird would break across the sky. I absorbed the smell of the ocean, the colors at the wake curling behind the ship, the occasional phosphorescence. I stood at the rail for long stretches, looking at the water changing like an oceanic kaleidoscope.

We stayed for about a year with our Booker grandparents in Rialto, California. Mother entered us again at the local public school and set up an office in her bedroom at the end of the house on the second floor. A sturdy bridge table held her Remington typewriter, pads of paper, paste pot and scissors, and other needs just as though she were at home in Shanghai. Her main project was to get going on a book called *News is My Job*.

I helped with the typing, and cutting and pasting of corrections.

When I wasn't doing that or going to school I liked disappearing into the huge storehouse at the end of the garden. It was my escape from duties and from people. Here I looked at the collection of *Saturday Evening Post* magazines with covers by Norman Rockwell, and wrote letters to Father as well as some poetry. There were strange objects lying around — metal wheels with sharp points on them, axes and wheelbarrows and mysterious bags. There was also a smell of garage oil, and dark spots on the cement floor. I liked sitting very, very still, balanced on a wooden sawhorse, observing the colors of dust specks floating in rays of sunlight.

I also explored the storm shelter under the house. A large wide plank with a rounded handle angled down away from the wall of the house.

"The slant lets debris blow away and not block the door, and also makes it easier to open from inside if rubble has built up on top," Grandfather explained in answer to my question. "We have our share of troubles with Santa Ana winds and other violent storms."

A ladder led me into the darkness; I felt around until I found the light switch at the bottom. After a couple of visits it became less interesting. There were an equal number of spiders as of Mason jars of fruits and vegetables that Grandmother put up. I helped her a few times in the kitchen pour the steaming hot tomatoes or peaches into the sterilized jars, then coat them with paraffin to keep out any air, and seal them. She kept bags of root vegetables too and I ate my share of parsnips and turnips.

One day, as she was peeling a green apple, Grandma asked me, "Patty, would you like me to tell your fortune?"

"My goodness, yes, Grandma. I didn't know you were a fortune-teller! Where is your turban and glass ball?"

She laughed. "Here", she said, pointing at the apple. "I'll tell you the initial of the man you will marry one day." She continued peeling the apple in one long curl, then let the skin fall to the ground. "The letter it forms will be the initial of your future husband. Let's see," she said, looking at the peel on the floor. "It seems to be an 'S'. Do you know anyone named Steve? Sam? Sylvester? Snoopy?" I started laughing. "Squeaker?" I added.

We did it a few times with different apples and a different initial appeared each time. We didn't take that too seriously.

She played the piano and sang around the house, teaching me songs like *"Old Zip Coon"* who *"drank all night by the light of the moon,"* *"Little Brown Jug,"* *"The Trail of the Lonesome Pine,"* *"The Isle of Capri"*. *"The Old Spinning Wheel in the Parlor"* was one of our favorite songs. She also made my dresses on the sewing machine in her bedroom; there was rick-rack on many of them. Her feet see-sawed back and forth as she worked the treadle, often humming one of the songs she loved.

When Mother was in Los Angeles dealing with her book and renewing her publishing and newspaper contacts, Grandmother took me to various events. Once we went to a Methodist taffy pull where I learned that I would never make taffy—too hot on the taffy-pulling fingers.

I learned that Grandmother had taught mathematics as a young woman. To me, her greatest claim to fame was that, in addition to her girl detective mystery stories, she invented a great board game similar to Monopoly. We often played it, especially when the Craig cousins were visiting.

Grandfather wouldn't let me have a cat but he did take me with him once to see his date grove. It was lovely to walk under the tall straight palms, and I enjoyed the dates. Another time he took me to inspect some houses that he owned. On this expedition I learned that nettles, which were growing in the nearby field, hurt if you touch one. I learned the verb "to nettle" that day.

We lived for news from home. Father, free from worry over us, focused on keeping business going despite the destruction and danger. He wrote long letters on what was happening in Shanghai; these were smuggled out by his network of Chinese friends. When a letter arrived, Mother called us all together in the living room to read his news. In the first letter that arrived, written in November, he wrote:

The Chinese Army fought the invading Japanese from August until this month, when it could no longer hold out. Some 50,000 refugees have fled to the safety of the international settlements. In these treaty areas, the Chinese are safe from the Japanese. But those in all Chinese-administered districts of Shanghai are in peril. They can't stay in their homes. In addition to the bombing, torching, and strafing by the Japanese airplanes, the two armies are fighting in the streets with every weapon they have. The Japanese soldiers, many drunk, enter people's homes to rape and rob the Chinese at will. The civilians have to escape into the countryside or into the international areas.

Hordes of Chinese civilians push and shove as they shuffle across the Garden Bridge to safety, and over the Soochow Creek.

Mother stopped to explain to her parents that Soochow Creek was a little river that meanders through Shanghai, roughly separating north from south.

"Grandma, that's near our house! Oh, do you suppose they've bombed our house?" I wailed.

Mother continued reading:

Others row across. Some have to make the dangerous swim across the Whang Poo crowded with Japanese ships coming in and sampans, junks and liners fleeing out.

After the Imperial Japanese Army finally broke through the Chinese defenses and Shanghai surrendered, tens of thousands of Japanese soldiers took over the streets. Warplanes bombed all Chinese parts of the city.

Grandmother asked me to help her bring in glasses of iced tea for everyone. The news was truly dreadful. Scary. Mother just sat, shaken. I knew she wanted to be there where not only her husband but also the news was.

In December he wrote:

New hardships include the arbitrary Japanese shooting and beheading of the citizens, the rape of young girls. New Japan-imposed laws force increasing hardships that make life both extremely dangerous and intolerable to the Chinese. And Japanese soldiers threaten Westerners from behind barbed wire defenses and sand bags at critical intersections in the city.

Johnny and I exclaimed over this news."If one of them threatens us I'll punch him in the nose!"

Johnny's anger was catching."I'll jump on him and squash him!"

Letters from friends in both Shanghai and Nanking told about the Japanese invasion of Nanking, the Capital, with an army 50,000 strong, and the subsequent "Nanking Massacre" in December. We found it hard to hold back tears as Mom read parts of several to us:

December 15, 1937: Never have I read or heard of such brutality... The whole Japanese army seems free to go anywhere it pleases and do anything it pleases. There is no discipline whatever, and many of them are drunk...

December 18, 1937: Today marks the sixth day of Dante's Inferno. Murder wholesale and rape by the thousands...One of my patients, admitted this afternoon, represents the last word in fiendish brutality. He is the sole survivor of 20 who were led from one of the refugee camps to the hills. They were first sprayed with gasoline, then set afire. His eyes are burned out...

February 18, 1938: we hear that as many as 300,000 of 600,000 people in the city have been murdered...Now the Japs are bringing in opium and heroin to sap the strength of the remaining people.

We all were silent for a few minutes after she read these paragraphs. The news was so horrible that it was hard to absorb.

In January 1938 Father wrote that Japanese naval aircraft had attacked the American river patrol boat the *U.S.S. Panay. The boat, hit by two bombs and strafed by nine fighters, sank in the river in two and a half hours. In the attack three U.S. sailors were killed, with 3 sailors and five civilian passengers wounded. The Japanese claimed that they could not tell the American from the Chinese flag.*

This attack on an American ship caused us in America shivers of insecurity. Americans were supposed to be safe in China. Mother didn't want to frighten us so we didn't discuss this with her, but we heard more about it through the newspapers.

Then Johnny received a letter from one of his friends with news that Father had not shared with us. I guess he knew it would scare us.

Do you know that your father was nearly killed by a bomb that fell next to the Chocolate Shop when he was there with my father?

We stared at each other, wondering what could happen next. Would there be another bombing in Shanghai, would our father be killed?

"Land sakes, Edna Lee, do you think you should go back?" Grandmother worried.

"Of course, Mama. That's our home, that's where we live."

"Perhaps you should leave the children here? They have made friends and have adjusted well to life here. And I know it's not as glamorous as China, but the bombs aren't falling here."

"Mama, the children will return with me. I'm not going to leave them behind even if they love being with you and of course are safe here. We won't leave until it's safe there.

"Oh, dearie, you're right. But I do worry about you way off there in a war in China!"

Finally Father wrote that it was safe for us to return. We left for home in time for Johnny and me to enter the 1938 fall terms in our respective schools.

We didn't know what to expect. We knew that there had been fierce fighting in and around Shanghai, and that buildings had been destroyed. We knew that our home in the International Settlement was safe, but that Chinese Shanghai was now Japanese.

We knew, but couldn't absorb, that we would now live surrounded by the Japanese Army.

I learned self-control during this period. When I feel threatened, my feelings shut down. Somehow I build an inner wall that protects me, or so my system thinks, and enables me to corral my thoughts. On the other hand, in a crowd I have no self-control, I need to get away, almost to escape. This is true at a garden party at the British Embassy and equally true in a mob of people at a Fourth of July celebration at the Washington, DC Mall. I attribute both responses to a childhood living in a war zone. My feelings about war itself: well, when it's necessary to save the soul or the defenseless, yes.

XIV

1938. OCCUPIED SHANGHAI.
AGE ELEVEN

THERE'S AN ARTICLE *in a newspaper: a school official is complaining that they haven't enough money, their science lab isn't modern enough, they need a new gym. I set the paper down, irritated.*

How spoiled you are. You should give thanks every day for your blessings, and go do something for some people who really need help, people who have no place to live, no floor on which to uncurl a bamboo mat to sleep on, much less a science lab. My mind skips to the hundreds of refugees who had suddenly appeared in what had been a quiet little village a few blocks from our home in Shanghai.

I hear again their tears in the night. The repeated monotone Buddhist Mantra "O Me Doh Veh" (a mi tuo fo) that echoed across the streets and up into my window. A rush of pain grabs my solar plexus; and suddenly I start to cry.

Writing this book is good exercise for my tear ducts.

Mother, Johnny and I returned to a dramatically changed Shanghai in the summer of 1938.

In our absence, rudimentary guardhouses had sprung up like toadstools at international intersections. I had to accept barbed wire and sandbag barricades when we drove beyond the concession boundaries. Mounted machine guns pointed toward us. Bared bayonets gleamed. I hated seeing and hearing the Japanese soldiers who stood outside the barricades. They were slovenly, malodorous, staring at us with brutish eyes. Rude invasive eyes.

Thirteen-year-old Johnny immediately got into trouble. On one of our first days back, when Ah Ching was forced to stop the car and get out to bow down at the international barrier leading into a formerly Chinese, now Japanese, part of the city, Johnny baited the soldiers behind the barricades.

"You dirty pigs!" he yelled, jumping out of the car."You no make my chauffeur bow down, no *kowtow* (ketou), no knock head on street!"

A tirade in Japanese came in reply. The second Japanese spat and scratched his crotch, while his comrade jabbed his bared bayonet at Johnny aggressively.

Johnny cursed at them in Chinese, shaking his fist at them. The first one stepped forward, stabbing his bayonet in front of him.

"*Noong ze iguh tzu loh*!" Johnny shouted."You are a pig!"

I cowered in the back seat, crouching as low as I could get."Johnny, quit it! Get back in!" I whispered."We'll all be killed!"

Ah Ching murmured,"Please, Littie Master, you no make trouble. Maybe angry Jap-man take you sister for play-play or push long knife in you! You no savvy Jap-man number one bad man."

Johnny knew that Ah Ching was right; he might have started an international 'incident.' He could have had Ah Ching captured, tortured and killed. Resentfully, reluctantly, he stamped back into the car. From then on he restrained expressions of his anger at the intersections. My own emotions jumped from anger to heartbreak to a sense of futility, of inevitability. I realized that there was nothing I could do to punish the Japanese.

Near our house soon after our return we saw a street fight between Japanese and Chinese patriots that turned into a battle with bullets flying. Suddenly two Chinese lay dead. I took off running as fast as I could, hoping I wouldn't feel a bullet going through me; wondering how that would be. Did the air rush through the hole it left behind?

Our dinner conversations began to take on a sober tone. My parents now usually spoke about how the Japanese presence was beginning to affect not just the Chinese but the entire foreign population of Shanghai.

"John, my friends are talking about shortages of supplies," Mother said one evening."Is this going to continue?"

"I'm afraid so, so long as the Japs retain control," he replied."The whole international community is getting jittery. And it's only going to get worse. Fewer international ships are bringing goods or visitors, and business is beginning to suffer."

"I'm beginning to feel shut in," she said.

"I understand, darling. So do I. Shanghai was built on trade and needs international trade to survive. I don't know how this is going to end up."

I was now eleven, and began to join in the conversation with some of my own worries."There are so many miserable people," I said one evening. We had that afternoon driven past streets where Chinese refugees had laid down bamboo mats or bits of cloth to rest in any doorway or empty space or windowsill; clutters of graying people without food, water, shelter just sat, like fallen leaves swept into crevices, and began the process of dying.

"Isn't there anything we can do to help them?" But I knew there were too many tens of thousands of people just like them who had been forced to leave their homes with nothing but their clothes, and who had nowhere to go.

Johnny joined in."One family can't do much to help. I wish we could. I have to bike past them every day going to and from school. It hurts like heck to see. And smell."

Still I protested. I saw the dying. I could smell the dying. I could hear the dying.

I could hear the voices of the dying. In my bedroom when I went to bed, my warm soft bed, I could hear tears in the night, and it hurt me that I couldn't help. My own tears often joined theirs.

"*Ai-yah, ai-yah!*" they cried; and there was soft moaning from the suffering. Some nights the repeated monotone Buddhist Mantra *O Me Doh Veh O Me Doh Veh* murmured me to sleep.

At the dinner table I insisted on being heard."Daddy, they are like my own family! There must be some place they can go!"

Father patiently replied,"There just isn't anywhere for them to go. These people don't have any way of getting to a safe interior area of China. Their only escape from the Japs is here in our protected international areas. Once they work their way here they move into any empty space they can find but where they have no clean water, no food, no sanitation, no heat. It is a massive tragedy."

I began to look on death as part of daily life; death was not surprising or shocking. Death in the streets never made the news. Yet the piles of dead bodies were everywhere; and the stench.

Another evening over dinner I complained again about the bodies lying in the streets. Mother said that she had just learned about a charity organization, the "*Tongren fuyuantang*" that was created in 1913 by the Tongren and Fuyuantang families to take care of abandoned coffins or corpses in Shanghai.

"I've just done some research about it because I'm writing

a feature story about the human disaster here," she said."The Shanghai officials, in the great confusion caused by the Japanese invasion and the bombings and looting, can't provide many services for the people. No one knows who to turn to. This *Tongren fuyuantang* is stepping in where the government can't, and gives out food, clothing, and sometimes even shelter. The *Tongren* also has taken on the dreadful task of collecting dead bodies when no one else does or can."

"That's very interesting. I don't know about it," Father said.

"This private organization, sort of a Red Cross and Salvation Army combined," she stopped to reach for a pad with notes she had scribbled, then read: "collected 24,119 corpses from the streets last year and this year the number is around 41,000 and counting. They put them into coffins and bury them; the organization maintains 13 cemeteries.

"You like lions at doors, Patty," she added, gently reminding me of the brass lions at The Bund."There is a round stone carving of two lion heads at the organization's front door; people who walk past sometimes caress the heads in appreciation."

She paused."John, you've heard of Père Jacquinot, haven't you? I had the privilege of meeting him today at the Jacquinot Refugee Zone Shanghai. He has created this safe area for the homeless children, in an ancient temple in the Old City. He is saving the lives of many thousands of children."

The cold November air was exacerbating the suffering around us. On a especially wintry day, when Amah and I were walking in our neighborhood, we had to step off the sidewalk into the road because there was a boy lying dead in the middle of the sidewalk. A handkerchief lay over his face. Flies crawled over his body. Gaunt toes protruded from his loose cotton trousers. One stiff arm clutched his jacket around him as though he were trying to find warmth even in death. A flurry of cold wind caught his trousers, ruffled them up and down, giving them a look of life. His skin was the color of a wash of pale blue watercolor. The boy had frozen during the night.

A woman sat beside him, wailing *Ai-yah, Ai-yah*! Her body rocked back and forth. Amah rushed me away.

"No fear, Littie Missie, never mind," she said."He no-count." At first this attitude shocked me; then, as death in the streets became customary, I almost grew accustomed to it.

It wasn't just the cold, food, a roof. Cholera, ever-present, was a now growing disease. Inadequate sanitary and waste treatment facilities were contaminating the water. We all had to have anti-cholera shots, all except for my mother, who was scared of needles and refused to have the shot. She accepted a few pills instead.

A quarter of a mile down the road from our house, which was at the outskirts of the city, a little native village had always existed. Now it became a village of refugees.

Amah and I, on our walks in our neighborhood, watched groups of families trudge past our house on their way to the village where they hoped to find a blessed yard or two of empty space in which to forge a life. They pushed and pulled what possessions they could bring, miles and miles from the Chinese sectors across the city and over the river into the International Settlement and safety. Chairs, trunks, birdcages, mattresses, stoves—all were piled dangerously high onto handcarts, wheelbarrows, rickshaws, whatever conveyance could be found. Elderly people who couldn't walk the distances balanced on top of the load, rigidly holding on to their precarious positions.

One day when Amah and I were watching a group file toward the village, I asked her why they looked so fat if they were starving.

"He takee too muchee pants, dress, coat, on top, put more on top, takee away from Jap-man, have plenty for cold time," she replied. I realized that, on their journey from their homes to their unknown destinations, the refugees wore all of their clothing, one cotton padded jacket and pants over another, to transport it as well as to have the warmth when necessary. And they could thus prevent the Japanese from having the benefit of that warmth.

Sometimes we walked to the village, where Amah had friends. She and I carried bamboo baskets of hot food to give to them. The refugees had created makeshift huts of whatever materials they could find. Boxes. Newspapers. Tin roofs that had survived the bombs and fires. The smell of peanut oil burning on rudimentary outdoor stoves almost nauseated me. However, the smell of incense from their good-luck joss sticks was pleasant. Many of these joss sticks were thin, long, and colorful. Some spirals hung from roofs. The refugees' music, squeaking *erhus* and clanging cymbals, and their sing-song language—all floated across to us.

One wintry day my father got more frustrated than usual by what was happening to the bamboo fence around our garden. The fence poles were disappearing.

The city turned extremely cold and damp that winter, and people had to bundle up to keep warm. The refugees, with no heat in their makeshift lean-tos, were freezing. We found that our fence was being burned stake by stake in the village as firewood for cooking and also to provide a little flame of warmth. A few villagers would creep up to our garden at night and steal poles. In the morning, there would be gaps in the fence that would have to be repaired immediately to protect our home from thieves.

Bamboo for fence poles was hard to replace at a time when China was at war. The wood was needed by the troops. It was a serious problem.

One day I saw Father so angry over the theft of the chunks of fence that he got out a rifle from a hidden safe and headed downstairs.

"Daddy!" I cried."Daddy, what are you doing with that gun!"

He didn't answer, just stamped down the stairs and out the verandah door to the garden.

"Daddy, please, don't shoot them!" I screamed.

"Of course I'm not going to shoot anyone," he answered testily."But I am going to scare the thieves from stealing our fence. We have to help them find some other way of staying warm in this cold."

My parents regularly provided the village with staples of rice and vegetables, as well as boxes of our leftover food. Together with American neighbors they collected and turned over to the village chief outgrown or outworn clothing to be distributed to the needy. Especially welcomed were winter coats and blankets, without which the refugees could not survive the long, cold nights.

In turn they helped us however they could. Once, when my brother was ill with pneumonia, they conducted a 24-hour Chinese village doctor treatment with reverberating gongs, clashing cymbals, and screeching *erhus* accompanying exploding fire-crackers and wailing in Chinese. Fragrant sandalwood joss sticks were waved around. All this was to chase away the evil spirits that were harming Littie Master. The cacophony was continuous, day and night.

At the same time Johnny was yelling with pain from the hot viscous mustard plaster applications that had been boiled and slathered steaming on his chest. White flannel cloth was then wrapped tightly around his chest, trapping the heat against his thin body.

"Ah Kung, you think so village doctor fixee Johnny?" I asked Number One Boy, praying that someone somehow could heal him. Johnny's screams from the hot plaster applications made me cover my ears."More better makee *chop-chop*, makee more big *walla-walla* talk talk noise for joss God hear you, please makee too muchee talkee-talkee to joss God." I was frantic.

"Plenty soon Littie Master number one goodee," Ah Kung intoned gravely as the noise became particularly penetrating."My savvy how fashion village doctor fixee he. All village-man love Littie Master, help chase bad joss."

Sure enough, Johnny recovered. The staff was convinced that the village magic had chased away the evil spirits. The noise of banging cymbals and exploding firecrackers were, I thought, probably more helpful than the painful mustard plasters. And I believed that my prayers also contributed.

That village has always lived vividly in my memory. Political refugees, such as these Chinese, have particular poignancy for me. My first awareness of the courage and tenacity that political refugees must find within themselves to survive, arose with observing the Chinese refugees in that village in 1938.

My awareness and understanding of the problems faced by political refugees deepened after my mother and I were refugees from the Japanese in 1940; and then observing my father after he was evacuated from a Japanese prison camp in 1943 and then from the Communists in 1950. My Austrian Jewish governess Erika Resek Meier was a refugee from the Nazis in 1938 and from the Japanese in 1945. My second husband István Botond was a refugee from the Hungarian Communists in 1956. I taught English as a Second Language to refugees from Communist countries in New York in 1956 and 1957. I know a lot about how totalitarian governments harm their citizens and also, about how they take power.

Refugees from natural disasters such as floods and hurricanes have no choice but to leave for safety. Political refugees, however, have to make a choice, they have to take a chance: to adapt to the dictator's laws and to stay, perhaps to survive, perhaps not; or, to escape to what they hope will be freedom, from a life that has become intolerable.

Whether coming from privilege or poverty, all political refugees have to have guts and brains to build new lives and to meet and overcome extraordinary problems in an unfamiliar environment.

XV
1938. LEARNING ABOUT REFUGEES NOW FROM NAZIS. AGE ELEVEN

THE CHANGES TAKING *place in my German school reflected in miniature what was happening in Europe. Hitler's National Socialist — Nazi — party policies rolled like a tsunami from Germany across the oceans, splashing upon the shore in China.*

Hitler had worked out his takeover carefully. His campaign began with his book, Mein Kampf, *in which he spelled out clearly what he was going to do, but no one took him seriously. Then he took over the military; he also made himself into an idol* (Hail Hitler!), *to replace Jesus and Christianity.*

He charmed the youth through the Hitler Jugend; *he took over the parliament, strong-arming any opposition and establishing himself as the government. He created an enemy, the Jews, against which he could rally people. He wooed and won over the newspapers and the elite intelligentsia, so there would be no criticisms of his policies. Massive anti-Jewish rallies, repetitions of the "big lie," and false promises, were staged to accent the program.*

By the time the basic good German citizens realized what had happened to them, how the Austrian evil genius Hitler had twisted their thinking, it was too late to change. Catastrophe followed.

Funny how the word "program" becomes "pogrom" so easily.

With variations, the same technique worked for the Communists in

Russia. The Communists used the aristocracy and the wealthy as their propaganda enemy. It works every time. Just replace God with yourself, control the media and the military, establish yourself as the one-party government, seduce the youth, build an enemy, and you've got fascism.

Brilliant Thomas Jefferson broke ground in giving sovereignty – the power to rule--to "We the People," not to the government. Lincoln buttressed the concept with his "of the people, by the people, for the people." He did not say "of the government, by the government, for the government" at Gettysburg. John F. Kennedy joins them in greatness in his Inaugural Address when he called out: "Ask not what your country can do for you; ask what you can do for your country." Those leaders understood that the strength, the heart, of America, the quality that brought millions of independent, creative people suffering or strong to our shores, came from non-government people ruling the government, not from government ruling everybody but itself.

Summer, 1938, sneaked up on us while we were preoccupied with adjusting to the Japanese around us. We were glad to be back home. But one day my parents realized that, while I was no longer a little child, the changed circumstances of our lives required me to be accompanied by a governess when driving around the city. When he drove me around Ah Ching, a Chinese, or equally our Amah, would be vulnerable and powerless to help if there were difficulties with the Japanese. There would be no repercussions if one ran a bayonet through them. It was safer for me to be accompanied by a white non-Chinese woman.

Father had Jewish friends, Eduard and Margaret Kann, who were well established in Shanghai in the construction business. One day Mr. Kann sought Father out to brief him on recent events in Europe, telling him that Nazis ordered the Austrian Jews, including his cousins, to leave Austria; those who remained would be sent to concentration camps.

"My cousins," said Mr. Kann, "weren't able to obtain permits to enter Australia or the United States without waiting years for a visa. But they learned that China would accept paperless Jews."

"That's a blessing for them, isn't it," said my father.

"Yes," said Mr. Kann. "They were deeply relieved to realize that they had a cousin established in a vibrant Jewish business world here in Shanghai.

"Anyway, they, the Reseks, have just arrived. We're grateful that they don't have to be crowded together with the many Russian and other Jewish refugees in Hong Kew; we found an apartment for them in the French Concession.

"They are highly educated, delightful people. And," he paused, "their 19-year-old daughter Erika is looking for work." He paused again. "John, she would make an excellent governess for Patricia."

And so Erika moved into our lives and our hearts.

I didn't know anything about contemporary Jews or Judaism when I met her. I had only heard about Frau Neisser's "juice" and her delight that these juices were being expelled from Germany. One day, while she was still with us, I asked Johnny if he knew what kind of juice she was talking about.

"The Frau keeps talking about some kind of awful juice that the Germans don't like, and they are getting rid of it," I said. "Do you know what she's talking about?"

"It's her accent. She says 'Jews" but it sounds like "juice."

We were American Christians, and while I had read the Old Testament as well as the New, and learned about Moses, Abraham, David and the Queen of Sheba, about the parting of the Red Sea and Salome's Dance of the Seven Veils, these were ancient history and I didn't know that the stories were about Jews. The Old Testament's Ten Commandments to me were current in the sense that the New Testament's Beatitudes and the Lord's Prayer also were current; I just thought that these were living guides to behavior and thought in my daily life. I was taught the Old as well as the New in church.

It was only months later, after Fräulein Erika took me to have tea with her family, that I learned more about Hitler and the Jewish people, about the Nazi persecution of the Jewish people and their desperate urgency to flee from their homes.

At first glance, the lives of the Reseks seemed to me like anybody else's who was accustomed to good things. Their apartment was furnished with drapes and comfortable furniture. Family photographs and professional certificates crowded the walls.

Mrs. Resek served me dark bread slathered with butter, and homemade yogurt in which she put crunchy brown sugar. Opera music played on the Victrola. Mrs. Resek spoke in correct but heavily accented English, breaking occasionally into Yiddish or German phrases.

I had asked a question about one of the photographs.

"That was our home," Mrs. Resek said.

"But it looks lovely! Why did you leave?"

After a pause, Mrs. Resek answered."Of course, how could you know. Well, one night only a few months ago, there was a loud, frightening rapping at the door. It was an unexpected visit from Austrian Nazi officers. They ordered us to leave our home with 24 hours' notice.

I was shocked."What? How could they!"

"Oh, we were so scared! Can you imagine packing up your whole life, to go you don't know where, overnight? Well, of course we took what we thought we might need—for survival, for family memory—and that's how we happen to have these photographs, and my music, and my husband's diplomas. *Gott sei dank.* So we moved to Vienna temporarily, crowding into the home of friends while we tried to decide what to do. It was impossible to stay, it was dangerous to leave."

I didn't understand."Weren't they satisfied when you moved to Vienna?"

Fräulein Erika explained: "Patty, under the Nazis, just being Jewish is a crime. In Vienna a lot of trucks drove about the streets hunting us. Hunting for Jews. Every time they found one they took him or her in the wagon to a concentration camp. Some of my friends, my age and younger, were taken, along with older people." She paused."Patty, they are today still looking for Jews to be taken away."

"Wart' a bissl'," Mrs. Resek said, getting up and walking to the kitchen."Wait till I bring some tea and biscuits." On returning with the teapot and a plate of biscuits she poured our tea."We tried to get visas to go to America, to Australia, to other countries, but they didn't want Jewish refugees. We grew frightened. What if we couldn't find a place to go, and were taken to a concentration camp? Then we remembered Shanghai."

Erika broke in excitedly."Patty, we had such adventures getting here! Many people were kind to us. So kind." She blinked, her eyes suddenly bright with unshed tears."By a miracle, Papa was able to get three tickets on an Italian luxury liner, the *Conte Verde.*" She smiled."So the three of us refugees left Europe in great style. We took the train from Vienna to Trieste where we boarded the ship.

"From then on, we were free from fear. You can't imagine how this feels, after so much terror. Most of the passengers were making a pleasure trip around the world. Can you picture it? And here we were on a one-way trip to freedom."

"That is a feeling that my family and I do understand, Mrs. Resek. We had to escape to America when the Japanese invaded

Shanghai. But of course our situation was less frightening."

"I am glad that you can understand how we felt," Mrs. Resek continued,"when finally we entered the Yangtze River and Shanghai, *Gott sei dank,* after three weeks on the *Conte Verde.*"

She paused to sip her tea, and passed me the biscuits.

"You probably know that there are established Jewish businessmen in Shanghai," she said."When they heard that a great many stateless, homeless, and almost penniless Jewish refugees like us were coming to China, Jewish merchants and bankers such as the Sassoons and the Hardoons organized food, shelter and clothing for us. *Ach, Gott sei dank!*

"Our cousin found this apartment for us in the French Concession. It had belonged to a French officer. We moved in on the day we arrived to Shanghai, a few weeks ago."

"My goodness, what luck!" I said.

"Can you imagine the joy of finally having a safe home again? My husband, who had been an architect and civil engineer in Vienna, was able to join his cousin's construction firm, and now I am again in my own profession, teaching classical voice to young singers at the McTyeire School."

It was time to leave."I've a little present for you," Mrs. Resek said, handing me a brooch of a tiny brown leather suitcase that could be opened and shut."Now open it."

Inside it I found delicate quarter-inch leather flowers."Erika and I have made this for you. It is our It is our—what is the word in English? Hobby. Our hobby, to make these."

"It is beautiful," I said."Thank you."

With the opening of the September 1938 school year, it was noticeable that there were fewer foreign students. I was now the only American. Most other foreign students had been withdrawn after Austria, now renamed Ostmark, was annexed by the Germans in March. We were soon drawing new maps showing the larger Germany. The absence of fellow Americans didn't bother me, but one day I mentioned it to my parents.

"Daddy," I asked,"Why aren't there any other American kids at my school now?"

"Is that so?" he mused."I guess their parents were reassigned to go to a different city, or perhaps back to America, because of the war in Europe. How do you feel about it?"

"All right, I guess," I said. I had good friends among the students.

There was a great celebration of the *Sudetenland Anschluss* in September. The student body assembled to hear of Hitler's triumphal entry into that northern part of Czechoslovakia. We sang a litany of songs glorifying Hitler, the Third Reich, and the German people.

Ever larger wall maps showed us the amount of land now incorporated into Germany, and our classroom geography drawings began to reflect this even larger German area."*Heil Hitler!*" we all shouted, saluting with our arms raised high.

New young German teachers with cold eyes began to arrive. They spoke of themselves as "Aryans", members of the Master Race.

Later that year, there was a class discussion about America. The teacher told us about the mid-term elections to be held in November, and told us about the American president, Franklin Roosevelt. Roosevelt, a Dutch name, was Jewish to the Nazis.

Once when I was out of the room, one of the students drew a large picture on the blackboard of a head with a gigantic nose, labeling it *"Rosenvelt, der grosse Amerikanische Jude."* (Rosenvelt, the great American Jew.)

Some of the students looked at me somewhat sideways and others giggled nervously when I came back into the room. After

I saw the blackboard I paused for a minute, then pretended to laugh, covering up my anger for having the American president so denigrated. I was slowly learning to hide my real feelings among the Germans. My apparent indifference was a survival reaction, like a clown laughing to hide his hurt. I took the chalk and added other horrid featuresa mole with hair sprouting out of it, crossed eyes.

My twelfth birthday, on November 9th, 1938 arrived. Mother had arranged for a few friends to come over for tea and cake. But as the afternoon progressed, I couldn't help noticing that, while Erika tried to be celebratory, she was unusually quiet. Something was wrong. She received frequent phone calls from her family, and they weren't about my birthday. Finally I pulled her aside and asked her what was the matter.

She hesitated. She was having trouble speaking.

"There has been a Nazi nightmare," she said."This day will now forever be remembered as the night when hundreds of thousands of Jews were expelled from their homes and from their jobs."

She stopped, seemed to gasp for air. She reached for the back of a chair to steady herself.

"All over Germany last night, all over Germany, Jews were sought out by official thugs. Their homes were looted. Their shops and synagogues and belongings were smashed. Smashed. Broken glass everywhere. Broken lives everywhere."

She stopped again, and shuddered."They are calling it *Kristallnacht*, the night of the smashed crystal."

"Oh, Erika," I whispered."This is terrible. I'm so sorry."

She nodded, speechless.

"You must go home to your parents. Ah Ching will drive you."

"Thank you, *Liebchen*," she whispered.

I asked my parents to excuse her for I knew she needed to be in the comfort and solace of her parents.

My parents learned more about *Kristallnacht* during the next few days. From Mother's sources at the *China Daily News* and the International News Service, and Father's contacts from all over the world, we leaned that the Nazi attackers were armed with axes and sledgehammers as they rampaged through any Jewish property that they could find, even desecrating Jewish cemeteries. Daddy was told that some 30,000 Jewish men disappeared on *Kristallnacht*.

There is in me a fathomless distrust of big government balanced by an equal trust in the innate good of the human spirit. This personal credo is derived directly from my first-hand experiences in China. I witnessed, I lived with, the destruction of people's lives caused by Japanese and Nazi dictatorships. Later I learned that the same holds true for other dictatorships, even today.

The human mind, this gift of God, can soar to infinite heights of beauty and of courage and of faith and of goodness. The power of excessive government crushes this spirit with its regulations, restrictions, barriers; enforcers, and worse, when it threatens an opposition with force, it effectively chills the people's voices and spirit.

XVI
1939. The end of The German School for Me. Age Twelve

Reading what I've just written, I realize that I grew up well ahead of my age in today's terms. It wasn't that I was precocious or exceptionally smart; it was a combination of excellent schooling, educated parents who conveyed knowledge through books and music and conversation, and the circumstances of my life. I learned, very young, that life and people weren't perfect.

I learned about brutality and distrust from the Nazis and from the Japanese. By the end of the summer of 1939 I had learned to avoid body contact with people I hadn't come to trust. I am a failure at Baptist church gatherings where I am unable to tolerate the body hugs that these nice strangers wish to greet me with.

Fortunately I am blessed to have been born with my glass half full and always expect wondrous things to happen and people to be kind while, nevertheless, watching my back.

My last days at the German school were exceptionally educational.

By the next term, in January 1939, there were substantive changes at school. On some evenings, there were events at which I was not included, but which all the German students attended. One day a classmate whom I'll call David came to school with a bandage around his head. He avoided speaking to anyone, just went to and from the classrooms.

"What happened to David?" I asked a friend.

She shook her head, unwilling to tell me, and sidled away.

Later in the day I asked another friend. Very quietly she pulled me aside to the playground. In a secluded corner she whispered,"He was hurt at the rally last night."

"What rally? Was I supposed to be there too?"

"No. It was an anti-Jewish rally, just for Germans."

"Why was David hurt?"

"Patty, he is half-Jewish."

I knew what a Jewish person was. I knew that my precious Erika was Jewish, and that her family had fled to escape from being killed. But we were in China, not in Nazi Germany.

"Why should he be hurt because he is half-Jewish?"

"They were showing anti-Jewish movies and giving anti-Jewish speeches." She paused, tears welling in her eyes."They got some of the kids so upset that they ganged up on David. Patty, they tore his ear half off."

I gasped, then silently reached into my pocket for a hankie and handed it to her.

She continued."You mustn't tell anyone at the school that I told you. All this anti-Jewish stuff is supposed to be secret."

"Poor David," I whispered, shaken."How awful." I was deeply shocked and frightened. And bewildered.

She wiped her teary face, and said to me quietly,"There was blood all over his face. I'm so scared. I don't know how our own classmates could do that to one of us. What will they do next?"

I was stunned. How could such a thing happen at my school? How could my German friends become monsters overnight? I thanked her for telling me and promised my silence at school.

For several days afterward I held within me what she had told me, feeling frozen. Externally I continued with my life as though nothing had happened. Inside, however, I was processing the events at the school, trying to decide what, if anything, I should or could do. I knew that I shouldn't create some big scene, especially as I was the only American there and therefore already at a disadvantage. I decided that it would be pointless to ask my parents about it; they were preoccupied with managing our lives under the Japanese occupation, and I didn't want to cause them more trouble.

Finally I told Johnny about David, and asked if he knew any Jewish people.

"Sure," he replied."Mom and Dad's friends Florence and Julius Reese, and our dermatologist Dr. Frederick Reisz, and the Kanns, and Sir Victor Sassoon. All are Jewish, like Fräulein Erika and her family."

"But those are all wonderful people! Why would anyone want to hurt them?"

"I don't know," he said. 'We have Jewish kids at my American school, but there's no problem about them. Jewish people worship a different way, and so do the Chinese, and nobody cares. It's their own business how they worship." He thought about it for a few moments."I think you should just shut up about it because there's nothing you can do to help David and you'll just make trouble for our family."

I took Johnny's practical advice and adjusted to the changed circumstances. I did want to continue my education. However, I became careful not to express myself to my schoolmates, even to those who had been my close friends. The Nazis, I now knew at first hand, were people to be scared of. I began to evaluate the teachers newly sent from Germany. How could they wish so much harm to innocent people just because they were part of a different race?

I was honored for scholarship at school that May. At a

ceremony in the auditorium I was awarded a book, *Abenteuer um Saratow* (Adventure in Saratov) inscribed *"An Patty Potter als Anerkennung für Fleiss und gute Mitarbeit"* ("To Patty Potter in recognition of diligence and good cooperation.")

The book had a Nazi swastika stamped in it, the date, May 20, 1939, and a book plate. This showed a spread-winged eagle roosting on a swastika and the words,*"Gabe des Deutchen Reichs"* (Gift from the German Reich). I pasted in a clipping about Hitler's birthday celebration.

A few weeks later an event occurred that got me into serious trouble. I had an autograph album, a little book 4" by 6". All the girls were using these to collect signatures, sayings, and drawings from their friends. I took mine to school and collected a few pages of signatures and various good wishes and drawings. But the center spread was saved for my adorable friend Wilhelm, now the head of the younger boys' *Hitler Jugend.*

When I gave the album to Wilhelm for his signature and remarks, I didn't know that my brother had already gotten his hands on it.

Early the next morning the Headmaster telephoned Father. Would he and his wife and daughter please come in to see him immediately. Father called Mother and me into his study for a discussion. What had I done? he asked. I told him that I didn't know.

Ah Ching drove us off to the school.

In his office, the Nazi Headmaster displayed my autograph album on his desk. It was open to the centerfold. He pointed angrily to the two-page drawing.

Wilhelm had indeed found something inappropriate in my album and had turned it over to the Nazi Headmaster. Now I saw my brother's artwork of the previous day. I almost burst out laughing. There was a drawing of Hitler, little moustache and all, sitting on a pile of garbage surrounded by boxes labeled TNT. Fuses were sparking, about to blow up the TNT and Hitler. Johnny's name was clearly signed: John S. Potter. The Headmaster showed the book to my parents, shouted at them, shook his fist in the air and then pointed angrily to me.

Not knowing that I had a brother also named John S. Potter, the Headmaster thought that Father had drawn the insulting cartoon. My father began to get riled. Soon both men were shouting. Mother turned on the Southern Belle charm that had won over fierce warlords, and both men quieted down.

But Father made it clear that my parents did not want me to continue in a school that had turned Nazi. The Headmaster made it clear that I was no longer welcome. I was shocked that my friend would turn me in. And I was upset and angered that this laughable little incident was being made so much of by the Germans. It was ridiculous.

Fortunately the school term was nearly over. My parents enrolled me in the Shanghai American School for the fall of 1939. I was saddened at being forced to leave the German school, but the atmosphere had become frightening.

What had been an open, innocent, happy school had become a place of whispers and hard eyes.

Despite increasing difficulties and shortages, Shanghai held to its traditions as best it could. My parents and their friends continued to host and attend sumptuous parties. At most of the ones that I was permitted to attend, Mother's friend Marlys Calcina was one of the most elegant guests. On one memorable occasion she was radiant in a sleeveless full-length yellow satin gown, its low-cut décolletage adorned by a weighty jeweled necklace and pendant earrings—maybe they were large topazes set in gold. She nodded to me across the room. Then she strolled tall, slender, and shapely toward me, the golden satin moving subtly and gracefully with her.

"Patty dear, I hoped that I would see you here."

"It's wonderful to see you again, Auntie Marlys," I said shyly. Her rich dark hair set off the porcelain quality of her skin. She was just simply glorious, glowing like a jewel.

"Do you remember, a year or so ago, that I said I would teach you how to make a Court Curtsey?"

"Oh, yes, of course I do."

"Well, let's step into the Powder Room, and I'll show you how."

I was almost trembling with fear that I would fail and with gratitude for her interest in me. We walked into the mirrored room. She stepped back from me to demonstrate.

"You must make a deep curtsey down almost to the floor without losing your balance. To maintain balance on your perilous journey down to the floor," she said, laughingly emphasizing the word "perilous," "you must cross your right leg over your left, and as you begin to move down into the curtsey, interlock your knees for reinforcement. Both feet flat on the floor. Let's see you do it."

I wobbled half-way to the floor. Marlys moved one leg into the back of the knee of the other. "There. Now, straighten your back. Hold your arms about a foot away from your body. Good!"

She then took my hands, curving them into a graceful arch. "Now, bring your arms toward but not touching your body." To my surprise, and perhaps to hers, I moved slowly down to the floor, arms held as she requested, my back straight. "Now come back up again. Great!" Marlys hugged me. She added, "You'll never forget how to make a Court Curtsey, no matter what the circumstances. Oh — and, wear a full skirt. It would be helpful in hiding a potential catastrophe."

Another time, at a party at our house, she coached me on beauty.

Once again we were looking into a mirror together, her eyes appraising me."You have fine skin, you must take care of it so that you will still be lovely when you are an old lady."

I looked at myself, and didn't like what I saw. Mother had finally given up on forcing me to have Shirley Temple curls--maybe she finally saw that I was too old for them--and my hair just hung there. I didn't see any kind of beauty. I had wanted to wear stockings to the party, and Mother had made me wear socks. I was feeling ugly and discouraged.

Marlys gave me instruction on creaming my face and protecting myself against the sun. I knew she cared about me and felt that I could trust her with my feelings of inadequacy.

"But Auntie Marlys," I stammered,"just look at me. I'll never be lovely. I'm shaped like a potato and have awful hair. Mother makes me stick a ribbon in it, and makes me wear socks to a party like this. I look just awful."

"Oh, my dear," Marlys hugged me."You are in what is called the "awkward age", when you are no longer a little girl, yet not a young woman. But in one year you will indeed be lovely. You have a beautiful smile and most expressive eyes, and very attractive parents. You can't miss." She hesitated."You are understandably annoyed by your mother, but I wonder if you fully appreciate what an outstanding person she is."

"I guess not," I grumbled.

"Has anyone ever told you about her exploits as a journalist?" she asked."Your mother gave up a brilliant career to be the best mother she knows how to be to you and your brother. She scooped the world with her stories about President Sun Yat Sen, and the Tokyo earthquake, in addition to her write-ups about the battles between the warlords.

'She's had to give up so much excitement to stay home and take care of you both. There must be times when she's frantic to have the freedom she had before, when she was free to follow a lead to a story. Maybe you could see if there are times when you could be a little more understanding of her, and perhaps in turn she would be more understanding of you and your needs. You aren't a little girl any longer and perhaps she doesn't recognize that yet."

"I'll try, Auntie Marlys. Thanks. I promise that I'll try."

I guessed that Marlys didn't know how frequently Mother was away because she could leave me with the governess.

But there were times of fun and sweetness between us. When we were travelling together, we often played card games in the evenings. One was a competitive game of double solitaire that had us laughing until tears ran down our cheeks.

Mother also taught me a lullaby sung to her by her mother that had come down from my great-grandmother Mary Catherine Moore Livingston:

"Little birdie in the tree, in the tree, in the tree
"Little birdie in the tree, sing a song for Patty
"Sing about the birdie in the treetop tall
"Sing about the roses on the garden wall
"Little birdie in the tree, in the tree, in the tree
"Little birdie in the tree, sing a song for Patty Lee."

I felt safe and cherished when she held me and sang this to me.

Marlys' words stayed with me, and I began to think about my mother as a person, about her life before she had us children. I knew that she, then Edna Lee Booker, had come to Shanghai in 1918 when she was a 22-year-old graduate of Scarritt College for Christian Workers in Kansas City, Missouri. I had helped her type parts of her book, *News Is My Job*, and so learned about some of her work.

Sometimes our family didn't know what was legend and what had actually happened.

It is fact that she scooped the world with her interview with President Sun Yat Sen. Once when we were lounging on deck chairs on a ship she talked a little about this episode.

"He was in hiding on his gunboat on the Pearl River near Canton, during a civil war," she said. "I had negotiated secretly for an invitation to interview him on his ship. The speedboat I had hired was caught in a crossfire. Bullets hit my helmsman, so I had to take the helm for the first time in my life, bullets whizzing overhead, while the guide and a Cantonese officer halted the flow of blood and roughly bandaged him. I was scared to death."

I was mesmerized. "Oh golly, Mom, what did you do?"

"I couldn't stop even if I wanted to. I bumped my boat into the warship." She giggled. "I was welcomed to the warship, but, well, I had to climb up the side of the boat clinging onto iron ring handholds, my camera and notebook flapping from their straps with every step. After I got my interview I returned to Canton by the same rented boat, with the same now bandaged helmsman."

The legend went that her hired coolies smuggled her onto the ship hidden in a bag of potatoes, like Cleopatra in her rug when she met Julius Caesar.

Another major international scoop was her coverage of Japan's 1923 earthquake that demolished Yokohama and led to the construction of earthquake-proof buildings. 100,000 people were killed; at least 40,000 were missing. Mother had the contacts, skills, and determination to arrange for transportation from Shanghai to Yokohama before any of the other correspondents could get there.

She told us once about her coverage of the battles between Chinese warlords, especially the one where she was on a train carrying dead and wounded Chinese soldiers."One of the soldiers had lost his mind, others were moaning, and as the train went "clickety-clack" I kept hearing the sound as a dirge:

"A crazy man and a corpse.
"A crazy man and a corpse.
"A crazy man and a corpse. "

On another assignment, she ventured into the interior of China to write about the Hakka people. She broke up laughing in telling us about it."No train or car or even rickshaw could manage the mountains, and I needed more protection than I'd have on a horse. So I hired teams of men to carry me by what is called 'sedan chair', that is, a chair in a sort of box with a window, carried on poles. Changing teams of two men carried me up and down mountains and across streams. It was a hilarious experience for all of us, since my chair lurched over cliffs and I was nearly dumped into a river. But I got the story."

When I thought about my father, I thought about music.

He sang and whistled around the house."*Going Home"* and *"Santa Lucia," "My Sweet Hawaiian Maiden"* and the *"Lorelei"* and *"Barcarole"* floated up from his study. He would get out his guitar and play songs from all over the world. He especially loved Spanish flamenco music. But his favorite was *Carmen*. A smile always broke over my face when I heard the *Seguedilla,* or my own favorite, *Michaela's Aria*. He sang in Spanish, French, German, some Italian. Sometimes he would sneak in a love song in Tagalog, a Philippine dialect, and tease mother about how he used to serenade the ladies in north Luzon when he was a young teacher there.

But now he had tired lines around his eyes and mouth, and hadn't sung or whistled in a while. I hadn't really thought about those lines on his face before; I talked to Johnny about this.

"Johnny," I asked one day,"Why can't Daddy come with us on vacations? You and Mom and the servants and I have had many vacations, at the beach or in the US. Why can't he come with us?"

"You're right, he's always working." Johnny paused."I don't really understand what he does, but no wonder he looks tired. I've never thought about it."

"Why won't he come with us? I miss him on our trips."

"I think he has to work all the time to keep us safe and have enough money for us. Daddy goes to the office every day, through humidity and heat and Japanese occupation and—what's that word when someone steals our money---embezzlement, to keep us comfortable. I think most of the fathers of our friends also work through the summers, not wanting to be away from their offices when there's trouble."

A friend of Father's, Charles Ferguson, summarized for us what Father actually did at work. We were on the verandah. He and his wife Isobel were sitting on the swing, moving gently; their children Joan and Peter, and Johnny and I, were at the glass lunch table, waiting for my parents to join us all.

"Your father is the foremost property appraiser in Shanghai," Mr. Ferguson said,"on the Board of several U.S. companies like Motorola and Philco. He's a 33rd Degree Mason, and a Trust Officer of the Bank of China. Being a Trust Officer," he explained,"shows the complete trust and tremendous respect the Chinese have for him. In this important position he has the authority, called the Power of Attorney, to sign papers dealing with the immense amounts of property owned by the Bank of China."

"That sounds very important," Johnny observed. I didn't know if he understood any better than I did or was just showing off as he liked to do, pretending to be oh so grown up.

I thanked Uncle Charlie for explaining this to us.

"You're welcome, Patty. You and your brother need to know that your father is very valuable to the Chinese," Mr. Ferguson continued. "After Shanghai surrendered to the Japs, he was ordered by the Japs to turn over to them all the Bank of China property documents. But he was too smart for them, and, maneuvering out of doing this, he has managed to protect the documents safely for the future post-Japan China. You can see, children, how his honesty, combined with his brains, has led to the rare trust in which he is held."

In addition to all that, which I didn't really understand, Father was the most courteous person in the world, it seemed to me. I never heard him curse; if he did, I wasn't around to hear it. And I never saw him drink too much. Some of his lessons to us at dinner:

"In offering a second helping, never ask if they want more. It makes them sound like greedy pigs." He chuckled. "Say instead, 'Would you like the other half?'"

And, in spooning up soup from a soup dish, "Always tilt the bowl away from you. If you tilt it toward you the soup may land in your lap."

I did learn to tilt the bowl away from me, but didn't do so well with the "other half." Instead I said, "Would you like some," omitting the word "more."

He liked to serve sherry or martinis to our guests on small silver trays that he called "salvers," in pyramid-shaped glasses for the martinis, and small engraved glasses for the sherry.

The most beautiful of our parties was an indoor-outdoor event early in July to honor incoming and outgoing U.S. Admirals Thomas C. Hart and Harry E. Yarnell. Some two hundred guests, the élite of the diplomatic, military and business circles in Shanghai, strolled through the garden and our formal rooms.

For days beforehand, Number One and Number Two Gardeners, who came over to work regularly, brought in teams of women in black jackets and trousers to join them. These women crawled — I thought they looked like a line of black watermelon seeds — from one end of the garden to the other plucking weeds from the grass and placing them in bamboo baskets. I watched the gardeners and coolies push floral arrangements of orchids and gingers around to create outdoor sitting, dining and dancing areas. Just before the party they lit red and gold Chinese lanterns hanging in the branches of the willow trees. The garden was transformed into a fairyland with magical lights.

Ah Kung's resourcefulness, intelligence, and problem-solving skills were frequently demonstrated at parties.

On the night of this party, there was an incident involving the wives of two of the high-ranking American guests. One of the women, who felt that she out-ranked the other in going through a door, nudged the other aside. The latter, insulted, stepped deliberately on the short train of the first woman's dress, ripping it. She then strode triumphantly through the door.

Ah Kung immediately informed Mother and sent for Tailor, then escorted the first woman to the powder room. The dress was repaired on the body of the lady right there. Mother sent Ah Kung to bring to her the wife who had stepped on the train, and she soon majestically re-entered the room with one wife on each arm. Between them, Ah Kung and Tailor had saved my parents' face.

Cook's greatest achievement was the dessert created in honor of the two admirals. He outdid himself, gaining great face for himself and for my parents. First he carved a block of ice into a battleship two and a half feet long. Each detail correct, it was displayed on rolling spun sugar waves over blocks of ice, a dramatic centerpiece for the table. Balls of various ice creams, meringue kisses and liqueur-laden fruits were tucked among the waves.

Cook had created the spun sugar with his chopsticks. I had hung around to see how he made this amazing sugar lace.

"Littie Missie," he had said."Please, more better you go to door, too muchee trouble you stay this side."

After I had stepped out of the way, he covered the floor with Chinese newspapers, then dipped his chopsticks into the sugar syrup that he'd prepared. In one fluid motion he flung the golden liquid high above him. The strands floated down onto the heavy black ink characters and advertisements of the paper. I wondered briefly if the ink would stain the sugar strands. But he knew what he was doing. When done, he tenderly gathered the fragile glistening strands and arranged them into waves around the ice battleship.

Those months, I recall, those months felt like the lull before a storm when the air is suddenly still, the birds disappear, the sky turns metallic.

The Shanghailanders' glamorous lives went on but with a difference; holding on now as long as possible to the aura of their make-believe world, knowing that the beauty and laughter were destined to disappear, to slide into a cultural sinkhole, champagne bubbling all the way down to nevermore.

A new China, a different Shanghai, would eventually be reborn, but not before the anguish of the Japanese occupation ended with the arrival of the American military in 1945; not before the painful Civil War brought power to the Chinese Communists and exiled the Kuomintang government to Taiwan, in 1949; and not before the Cultural Revolution tore families apart and sent artists and intellectuals to farms where they were forced to dig up stones with their delicate hands, fine brains wasted.

It was after the excesses of the Red Guards that the new China began to emerge. A September 2013 issue of the South China Daily Post *reports on the remorse felt by many of the former Maoist leaders. In a monthly magazine,* Yanghuang Chunqiu, *a former cultural-relics official from Shandong province is quoted by the writer as saying that* "This is how deeply I feel the sorrow as I grow old - I cannot forget the evil things I should be held responsible for, that I was somehow coerced into doing during the Cultural Revolution."

The article further states that Mao launched the Cultural Revolution to purge dissent within the party, but the movement spiraled out of control, plunging the country into anarchy.

I had a personal experience with the terror inspired by the Maoists. At the time, I lived in Washington, DC, a few blocks from the Chinese Embassy. During the 1989 Tiananmen Square protests, Chinese-Americans had built, in a small park directly facing the embassy, a smaller version of the 10-meter-tall statue of the "Goddess of Democracy" that students had built in the Beijing square. We pointed this out to a visitor from China as we drove past it. I have never seen anyone move more quickly: in one second the visitor was hiding flat on the floor of the car until we had driven well past the embassy and the statue. The visitor did not want to be seen by any Chinese Embassy official.

During the following years a new form of governance evolved in China that, while still Communist in name, has encouraged the extraordinary economic growth of today. China, 25 years after that Tiananmen Square event, has become a superstar among nations, overcoming the destruction caused by the Opium Wars, the Boxer Rebellion, the Japanese invasion. It's hard to believe the terms imposed on the Chinese by the foreigners during those wars.

From my perspective, the opium dens are gone, the frightful walking dead addicts are gone, the wretched rickshaw coolies padding wheezing and hawking up and down the streets are gone. I read that there is still poverty but it is nothing compared to the poverty in filth and utter hopelessness that I witnessed.

I am so proud of the Chinese people.

XVII
1939. LOVELY PEKING.
AGE TWELVE

*LOVELY PEKING, now Beijing, shimmers and sparkles in my memory like
a cascade of jewels in a computer game. Gold and red buildings, white
marble buildings, against blue waters and skies, the greens of willows
and pines. Intricate shapes, fanciful yet thought-provoking names of
buildings. The use of reflections in water and placement of opposites
for dramatic effect. Ancient and less ancient events among these
buildings — Kublai Khan and Marco Polo contrast with the Boxers and
the British, French, Japanese occupations; Tiananmen demonstrations
with the Marble Boat. My father was in Beijing in 1917; I have his
photograph of a ruined building in the Old Summer Palace,* Yuan
Ming Yuan, *trashed by British and French looters in 1860 and on
which Father wrote the date in white ink.*

*I read that Beijing today is horrible to live in because of smog; but
I'll bet it still shimmers and sparkles.*

The Japanese now controlled much of eastern China—all of the
north-east, including Shantung Peninsula where Wei Hai Wai
was located. But it was now again summer. Something had to be
done with us children.

Friends advised my parents against Wei Hai Wei.

"Too many Japs there," they cautioned. "Jap officials and

soldiers have overrun the place. There are only vestiges of the British navy there; the Jap Navy has taken over. It's unpleasant and unsafe."

"And Shanhaiguan is interesting, and with fewer Japs," another said."Beautiful and historic. The name means mountain—*shan*, ocean—*hai*, pass—*guan*. Mountain ocean pass. It's where the Great Wall enters the ocean, and there's a pass between the mountains and the ocean controlling Manchus from the north."

My parents decided to take their advice and go to Shanhaiguan. In July mother galvanized the staff into getting us packed up.

Our train would go first to Peking, where we would change to the local train to Shanhaiguan. But Mother wanted to stay in Peking for a few days in connection with an article she was writing. She was troubled by the conflict between her newspaperwoman mission and her mother instinct. Peking was occupied by the Japanese now, and our only protection was our passport. She wasn't worried for herself, but could she subject her children to possible Japanese maltreatment?

The four of us discussed the problems that could arise if we children were rude to the Japanese, as we often were at home. But Johnny and I wanted to go to Peking, too. We'd been there once when we were too little to remember much, and wanted to return.

Johnny pointed out,"We'll be all right—after all, America isn't at war with Japan. And Patty and I know what awful things the Japanese can do to people."

I added, smiling as sweetly as I could: "I promise to be careful and behave perfectly. After all, we aren't little children any longer. We do have some common sense."

So in July we—mother, two children, Amah, cook, and the coolie Fo Sun—set off to Peking and Shanhaiguan and the Great

Wall for the summer. Father drove us to the North Station, Ah Ching following in a second car loaded with the servants and baggage.

As we drove toward the station we saw piles of rubble, broken bricks and chunks of cement lying on the sidewalks. It was a shock; we hadn't been in this part of Shanghai since the occupation. Shops were missing their roofs; windows were still blown out. Burned buildings bore two years of debris; rubble, broken bricks and chunks of cement lay on the sidewalks.

"How terrible this place looks." Johnny observed."Why haven't the Japs fixed it up yet!"

"This looks just awful!" I agreed."I'm so glad we missed most of the bombing of Shanghai."

"Yeah. I thought the bombing was mainly in the outskirts of the city," he replied."I guess the Japs were targeting the railway station."

The six of us boarded the train to Peking. We three would stay there, going on to Shanhaiguan a few days later. The servants would continue on to Shanhaiguan. Arrangements had been made for the local agent to meet them at the station and to drive them on to the house that Father had rented for us. Amah would see to organizing it.

Mother's eyes sparkled.

"We'll soon be there!" she said. Her smile dimpled her cheeks as we chugged along mile after mile; occasionally she would squeeze my hand. Her excitement was contagious. We were on an Adventure!

The train trip itself was an adventure. We first took the Shanghai-Nanking train, getting off in Nanking to board a ferry across the Yangtze. Mother was turning around in every direction; I wondered why, then remembered the Massacre of Nanking. She was looking for signs of that nightmare two years earlier.

The ferry took us to Pukow (Pukou) where we boarded another train, now on the Tientsin-Pukow Line, that went to Tientsin North Station. We, with all our household and luggage, now once again had to change trains, taking taxis to Tientsin Station East. Here we boarded the PMR (Peking Mukden Railway) train that stopped in Peking, and would drop us off on its way to Manchuria. The servants would stay on the train until it reached Shanhaiguan, the last stop before Manchuria.

All the trains were crowded with Japanese soldiers. We had our own compartment on one side of the aisle for most of the long trip. Otherwise, we would have been overwhelmed by our fellow passengers. Japanese officers carrying swords, pistols, heavy cases, field glasses, peered out the open windows, exclaiming over the sights. Avoiding them were garlic-smelling Chinese families, their squawking chickens and ducks tied up by the feet. Babies were alternatively screaming or suckling, sleeping or laughing. Older children chased each other up and down the cluttered aisles.

The windows of the warped wooden carriage sidings were open, allowing sooty air to flow in as our train rattled and lurched north. Cinder and yellow-orange dust settled everywhere, onto everything. The heavy charcoal smell stayed with me for a few days after we arrived, even after washing.

Johnny began drawing intersecting lines in the dust on the seat between us. "Want to play tic-tac-toe?" he asked.

"Sure," I replied. "I'll be the X and you be the O."

After several games we became irritable, so Mother stepped in. "Who can see the most buffalo?"

"I see two!" Johnny shouted. Then I began counting, and the day passed.

As our journey progressed, the coolie Fo Sun and Amah found

boiled clean water in which they soaked face cloths. It was a relief to be able to refresh and clean ourselves. Vendors and passengers crowded around the train at the many stops along the way north. At these, the coolies got off to buy "crispy sugar-coated fruit on a stick," *tang hulu*, made of jujubes, a kind of fruit-flavored candy. These we sucked and ate a bit like lollipops. They also bought fresh oranges and brought hot tea that Amah served us.

As night approached, our servants converted the compartment into sleeping areas.

The views from the train made up for any discomfort. Along one stretch we rode past rows upon tidy rows of vineyards. Soon thereafter blue-jacketed men wearing wide straw hats were threshing wheat in large flat fields. Shadowy mountains rose to the west and occasional hills with multi-storied pagodas; we wondered about their names and history. Ancient villages with temples appeared and disappeared. Occasionally rice shoots poked up through large paddies. At other times when we rode through villages, scrawny water buffalo, scruffy yellow *wonks* (mutts) and children splashed in puddles or ran alongside our train, calling to us.

When we reached Peking, Japanese soldiers with guns and bayonets were standing around in the station, but they didn't bother us. Loading our luggage onto one of the old Model-T Ford taxis was a complex game of squeezing soft bodies and hard luggage into too small a space. I suggested that we tie Johnny onto the roof but he didn't like that idea. Finally we strapped some pieces onto the roof, others to the running boards, sat on some and stuffed small bags around us. Then, after bidding farewell to Amah and the servants who were continuing on to Shanhaiguan, we drove off.

"Grand Hotel de Pékin, please," Mother instructed the driver. I peered happily out of the windows to see what Peking looked like. I saw immediately that it was different from Shanghai. There were fewer modern office buildings and many more decorative and ancient structures. Peking looked more Chinese than Shanghai. Additionally, there were fewer people and no clumps of miserable families; I couldn't see any refugees dying in doorways. There seemed to be more laughter, more bicycles, water buffalo and camels on the streets. But fewer cars.

Now I realized that something else, something important, was missing.

" Do you notice anything funny about this city?" I said slowly.

"I don't know," Johnny said." What."

"The buildings don't look bombed."

He studied the buildings that we were passing."You're right, Sis. I guess the Japs didn't think they needed to."

Mother answered us, explaining that, unlike Shanghai or Nanking, Peking had not been bombed by the Japanese in 1937 because the battle for the capital took place outside the city.

"The Japanese," she amplified,"used a classic strategy: they made impossible demands on the Chinese which, if they were not met, would result in war."

"Like what?" I broke in.

"Well, because of the Boxer Rebellion, the Japs had permission to station troops near Peking. Now, as part of their overall plan to conquer China, they conducted military training exercises near the walled town of Wanping. It happens that Wanping controls entry to Peking from the southwest. Claiming that one of their soldiers was missing, they demanded permission to enter the town. The Chinese refused, and so Japanese aircraft bombed Wanping and the Japs occupied it and then took Peking anyway.

"It was like one of your games of chess with Daddy," she continued,"where by taking one pawn you checkmate the King, in this case, Peking. They took the capital without firing a shot."

"But they bombed everything else," Johnny muttered.

We walked into the lobby, to see that our hotel was the equal of any of the great Shanghai hotels. Its design combined Chinese and French architecture."Isn't it lovely?" Mother sighed."Oh, my. I'm so happy to be here!"

We were taken up to our suite overlooking the embassy area, known as Legation Quarter, and the Forbidden City. As we settled in Johnny found a pamphlet about the hotel."It says here that the international press, business people, diplomats, presidents, and government officials stay here. Well, I know one member of the press who does. Right Mom?" He gave her a teasing look.

I could hardly wait to explore. Mother was ecstatic. On the phone within minutes of entering our suite, she ordered pots of tea while setting up her typewriter, paper, pencils and pens, camera, and address book. Soon key people were briefing her on the phone and arranging for interviews for our three days there, while the hotel boy in his immaculate white robe poured our tea, presented us with jasmine-scented hot damp face cloths, and served finger sandwiches.

After a meeting with U.S. Ambassador Nelson T. Johnson was confirmed, Mother contacted friends for help with Johnny and me. They put her in touch with a newly-arrived young college girl, Helene, who was visiting her family for the summer vacation. She was to take us sight-seeing for the next two days.

Mother was not the only ecstatic person who wanted to get out into the city. I loved Peking on sight. Guidebook in hand, the three of us walked along the broad, tree-lined Chang'an Avenue. The grandeur of the architecture along the avenue contrasted with the camels, water buffalo, peddlers and rickshaws on the road. After a few blocks we reached the Beihai (North Sea) ancient classical imperial Park. There, zig-zag bridges across islets in the lake linked palatial halls, colonnades and pavilions, reminding me of the pond and zig-zag bridge in the garden in the Old City of Shanghai.

"Let's rent a boat and guide," Mother said. "The park's pretty large to walk around in."

So we were guided around the large North Lake. Gliding under the Bridge of Everlasting Peace I could see the Jade Flowery Islet in the middle of the lake. On it rose the Beihai Dagoba, a graceful tall white pagoda.

"Mummy, it's so beautiful!"

"Wait till you've seen more of it," Mother laughed.

The guide first took us to the Marco Polo sites. It was extraordinary to be in exactly the places where Marco Polo and Kublai Khan had truly walked, where I was walking seven hundred years later.

I now stood at the Palace of the Moon, the site where Kublai Khan had received Marco Polo. Even if it was in ruins, it was still exciting. Johnny and I got out of the boat to explore it.

"Can you believe, it, Sis, I'm standing where Marco Polo actually stood!" cried Johnny, acting out a grand imperial pose.

The guide became uneasy and Mother began tut-tutting as I mimicked him. We quickly quieted down. She began reading from her guidebook when we reached the nearby Urn of Dark Jade. "This Urn is ten feet wide, about 3 feet high and 16 feet around, said to be carved of one piece of dark green jade. According to legend, it had held Kublai Khan's wine bottles," she read. On the urn was carved a dragon in clouds and a seahorse on waves. "He must have drunk a lot of wine," she said under her breath.

Our sightseeing tour led us to the Seventeen-Arch Bridge. This low white marble bridge had, indeed, seventeen beautifully proportioned arches spanning a short distance to a little island. The driver told us that along its sides were 554 stone lions, each with a different expression.

"This bridge long long time copy eleven-arch stone Marco Polo Bridge, the *Lugou Bridge*," our guide told us."Very beautiful, have lion all side. Number One very important bridge. Japanese begin fight at Marco Polo Bridge July 7, 1937. In Chinese call *qi qi shibian*, Seven Seven Incident."

Johnny was almost twitching with excitement. I knew he was thinking of maybe finding some spent bullets from the site of the battle that had happened only two years earlier.

"That's the official start of our Chinese war against the Japanese invaders," he said excitedly."Hey, I'd really like to see that. Can we visit it? Where is it?"

"We'll try to get there," Mother assured him.

The guide led us past the Painted Boat Studio and the Quiet Heart Garden. My imagination and love of words and sounds and beautiful things came alive with the names, the shapes and colors.

"Imagine, a 'quiet heart garden'," I murmured, wanting to get out and sit there just to enjoy my heart being quiet. Then we were rowed to an immense, colorful screen sculpted in relief: the Nine Dragon Screen (jiulong pingfeng). We got out to look at it. I walked up close. Separated from it only by a narrow moat, I felt like a toy person.

"Just look at this magnificent work!" Mother turned to the page in her guidebook."It features, sculpted in relief, nine coiling and flying dragons playing with pearls." The dragons still held the brightness of the glazed tiles of which they had been made centuries earlier.

"Tiles made in Peking place call Liuli Chang," our boatman said."Ceramic man make now all same like old time, same place."

"That's something I'd like to see on another visit," Mother said,"and pick up some tiles for our garden."

A breeze ruffled the water in the moat. The dragons reflected there appeared to move.

"Look," I said, pulling Johnny over."Look how the Chinese used water as a part of the design. The dragons in the water are moving, but those in the screen, aren't."

The dragons were moving in the water, but were static in the air. This fascinated me. Again, like the water under the zig-zag bridge in the Old City in Shanghai, what I saw was, and was not.

Back in the boat, the guide took us to an extraordinary feature of the park, the White Jade Buddhas. The figure, a whole piece of white jade one and a half meters high, and decorated with a gold crown and jewels, seemed to glow. The guide pointed out slash marks on the Buddhas' left arm."Long time gone," he explained."English soldier-man cut Buddhas arm, fight China-man, fight Peking, from the Eight Power Allied Force." Mother reminded us again about the destruction caused by the Alliance when they occupied Peking for a year after the signing of the Boxer Protocol of 1901.

She looked up at the Buddhas raised high on a pedestal."He has the sweetest calmest face I've ever seen."

The next day we met Helene, our temporary escort. Mother gave her some money and instructions, then we three took a taxi to the Summer Palace, the summer home of the Dowager Empress Cixi. This complex was on the Kunming Lake, about nine miles from the Forbidden City.

Again the names of buildings captivated me. Each evoked a different image: surrounding the lake were the Spring Heralding Pavilion. Jade-like Firmament in Bright Clouds. Dragon King's Temple. Longevity Hill with the Cloud-Dispelling Hall.

"Well," Helene said after a bit,"Ready for the Marble Boat?"

"Yay!" Johnny almost jumped into our boat."You're great!"

We boated over to an amazing sight: a marble boat with paddlewheels apparently floating in the water. Our guide explained to us that the strong-willed and imaginative Dowager Empress Cixi had diverted 30 million *taels* of silver, which had been provided to her to build the Chinese navy, for improvements to her Summer Palace. She had the Marble Boat built as the flagship of the non-existent Navy. She had paddlewheels carved on each side, like a Mississippi River paddlewheel steamboat, to give the illusion of motion.

There were little tables and chairs on the upper deck of the Marble Boat, and we needed a rest and a snack after walking all over the Summer Palace and grounds. No time for a real lunch. Helene found waiters to bring us tea and cookies.

I was amused and amazed by the idea of a Marble Boat. "Johnny, do you believe this? Just look at this boat!"

"This is really OK," he said, grinning. "It's really something to tell the Gunpowder Gang about. A marble boat in the water. Guess I won't tell them that it doesn't float. We'll see how long it takes them to figure it out."

"I'm taking tea on the Dowager Empress Cixi's Marble Boat!" I cried, putting on Grand Duchess airs. "My dear, do join me!" I laughed. "Isn't this something! Johnny, don't you wish that Mom were here, she'd love it too, wouldn't she."

"She certainly would."

From the vantage of the upper deck, I looked down into the water and became aware of the moving reflections of the boat and admired again the Chinese use of water as part of the design.

Helene and the guidebook gave us some facts. This 118' long boat, she read, rested on a platform intended for a monastery. However, the platform was ideal for the marble boat that had been designed to resemble a Mississippi River steam paddlewheel steamboat at the specific request of the Dowager Empress.

The boatman took us back to the entrance. We hailed a taxi, and headed south toward the Yongding River and the Marco Polo Bridge. Our guidebook quoted Marco Polo's Diary:

*"Over this river there is a very fine stone bridge,
so fine indeed, that it has very few equals in the world."*

The bridge indeed resembled the Seventeen-Arch Bridge. It was low, with eleven graceful arches. Made of granite, it had artistically unique stone lions lining the sides.

Johnny and I got out and began counting the lions — he down one side, I down the other. The long-ago carvers were clever in creating and also in hiding the lions. Each one was different, and among the hundreds were baby lions, lions hidden beneath paws or on paws, more lions hiding on the head, back or under the belly of each of the big lions. It was like a Hidden Objects puzzle. We'd counted around 100 before we got tired of that game. John began taking pictures of one lion after another.

Helen read from our guidebook that the bridge originally had 627 lions.

"And you only found 100 of them?" she teased.

On one end there was a stele with calligraphy by Emperor Qianlong (1711-1799) that read:

"Morning moon over Lugou."

We read about a modern song called "New Moon over Marco Polo Bridge." It was about Chinese bravery against the Japanese troops during the "Seven Seven Battle."

"They were fighting here to save China only two years ago," Johnny said to himself.

He was impressed. Then he became rapturous when he

found what he swore were bullet holes from the shelling by the Japanese invaders. However, he could find no spent shells.

As we walked away the three of us became quiet, looking back at that bridge. I was thinking of what it represented in my own life. Brave Chinese soldiers had died there trying to save me, save us all, from the Japanese. I said a prayer to them and was sure that my brother had similar unspoken thoughts.

We climbed back into our tour boat, exhausted. Now the sun was moving toward the west, beginning to cast shadows. The guide took us back to the entrance. It was time to leave for our hotel.

Mother had organized a full day of interviews at the American and British Embassies, and with Chinese officials, for the next day. Now she gave Helene money to cover transportation, guide, and lunch, for a visit to the Forbidden City.

What an exciting name. Who was forbidden, and why?

The Forbidden City was near enough to our hotel for us to walk. The streets were exciting, crowded with people, cars, rickshaws, and peddlers. We stopped to admire the massive Front Gate (Tiananmen) that had walls about 60 feet high and an immense gate that we were told clanged shut at dusk. There was a group of peddlers, pushcarts and stalls selling goods in front of and inside that gate. I decided that Chinese certainly knew how to create impressive gates when they wanted to keep people controlled. They knew how to make a point.

A caravan unfamiliar to me was passing slowly through the Front Gate: men leading a camel train that was bringing in supplies from the Western Provinces along the ancient Silk Road. I had seen single hump dromedaries on a trip to Egypt when I was little, but never a two-humped Bactrian camel. The ones coming along, swaying awkwardly under the burdens strapped on between their humps, had reddish brown hair, relatively thin short legs, and heavy bodies.

Helene told me that these camels, referred to as "boats of the desert" on the Silk Road, transported tea, silk, pottery and lacquer ware from China to the western regions and pearls, medicines and perfume from Central and West Asia and Europe back to China. The lead camel carried practical goods to meet the needs of the grooms: bags of grain, tents, kitchen utensils, water. The last camel wore a bell with a pleasant, cheerful sound that helped the grooms keep track of the whole caravan and scare away small animals.

In the long caravan of around twenty-six camels and four grooms, the camels were linked by ropes. As ugly as they were with their floppy lips and heavy eyelids, I decided that they were cute. One turned his head, looked at me, and sort of winked.

I giggled and said, "Well, hello!" He lifted his lip into a sneer and screeched. I decided that I didn't want to know him any better.

We followed the camel train through the gate into the Tiananmen Square. Some children were flying kites, and we stopped while Helene bought a dragon kite for each of us. It was somehow unearthly to see our dragon kites fluttering above such a magnificent square. Our guidebook said that the Tiananmen was nearly a mile square, the largest such square on earth.

Happily flying our kites in a nice breeze, we came to the Forbidden City. We stopped and stared, stunned into silence. Quietly we put away our kites. Then Helene read again:

"Within this huge compound—the size of 80 football fields—there were 980 buildings still standing after over 500 years."

The sun lit up each building's glazed tile roof, each one golden yellow, the color of the Imperial Family. Equally brilliant red pillars and walls added vibrancy and drama. And again, there was the use of water inherent to a design, enhancing and deepening the meaning of its beauty. What could be lovelier than an Inner Golden Water Bridge made of white marble?

Helene turned to the guidebook again, paraphrasing: "The Forbidden City was isolated from the rest of the world not only by 32' high walls but also by a moat 17' wide and 20' deep."

"Why is it called Forbidden? Who was forbidden?" Johnny asked.

Helene read that the City was originally forbidden to all but the Celestial Emperor, his family and his household staff, with no men, except for eunuchs, allowed to enter.

When Helene told me what eunuchs were, I was less enchanted. Still, how irresistible are the Gate of Moon's Radiance opposite the Gate of the Sun's Shine.

Helene got a taxi for us, and we drove back toward our hotel. We were quiet, thinking over what we had seen.

As we neared the hotel, I noticed an area where people were sitting at little tables, nibbling at interesting tidbits. A vendor came by, offering hot snacks, cold drinks, fruit and candy. The lusty smells floated over to us.

"Helene," I somewhat timidly suggested, "do you have any money left?"

"Yeah," John added. "We don't have any, and wouldn't you like to have something cool to drink?"

Helene gladly agreed. She asked the taxi to stop, paid him, then found a table for us and hailed a waiter. Soon we were enjoying refreshing iced tea and a tray of Beijing-style pot stickers, shrimp dumplings, and pork dumplings that in Shanghai we called *jiao-dze* but the waiter called them *jiao-zi*.

At a table near us some Chinese men were excitedly playing a rousing game of checkers. They were chewing on sunflower seeds and spitting out the hulls, laughing loudly when they jumped over the opponent's piece. Nearby, a little festival was being celebrated. On the sidewalk, young boy tumblers in bright clothing were doing acrobatic feats; one round-faced tumbler turned somersaults with a live goldfish in a little bowl of water on his head. We noticed a group of men hunkered down over a game of old blue and red "Bicycle" cards. I guessed that they were gambling, as some coins changed hands.

A lively game of stone-paper-scissors was going on in another group, while a few feet away conjurors were pulling chickens out of hats and making other things appear and disappear. Across the way jugglers were throwing different objects up and back and forth.

Soon a beautiful woman in a tight red *cheongsam* slit up her left leg started singing in a high sing-song voice as cymbals clashed and the audience yelled its appreciation. Then a very, very tall thin man on stilts came tottering along and began throwing out one-liners that made the audience scream with laughter. I was so frustrated that I couldn't understand their jokes as I didn't speak Chinese of any dialect.

My goodness, I thought. This city is fun. These Beijing people aren't shy about expressing their sense of fun.

Back in the hotel, as we were packing to leave, I began musing over the differences between Shanghai and Peking. It seemed to me that, in Shanghai, the foreigners had the money. In Peking, the Chinese had it. Also, I felt that Shanghai was focused on money and progress whereas Peking cared more about beauty and the quality of life.

Mother interrupted these musings, calling Johnny and me to bring our bags downstairs. It was time to go on to Shanhaiguan.

All three of us were quiet as our train chugged along past villages and farming scenes, each of us in our worlds. I thought about what we had seen in Peking. It seemed, in the quiet of my own mind — my mental "quiet heart garden" — that there had been almost too much. So many colors, so many shapes, so many ideas. The simplicity now outside the window contrasted with what we had seen in the city. The richness of those sights had been like sugar icing; and now we were in a landscape with no icing. I concluded that the icing had to be balanced by the relative dryness of the cake. Cake by itself might be dull; icing by itself too sweet. Well, of course I liked cake with icing too, too much.

Extraordinary, to think that Beijing today will have an office building taller than the Empire State Building! According to the newspapers, the "China Zun" would be a super skyscraper of 108 floors, 528 meters high. Construction, which was undertaken in 2011, is expected to be complete by 2016. An amazing building underway is the asymmetrical 51-story CCTV Headquarters building that consists of a continuous loop of five horizontal and vertical sections, creating an irregular grid on the building's façade with an open center — a balancing feat affectionately known as "Big Pants." It will become the second-largest office building in the world, after the Pentagon, according to Chinese sources, with millions of square feet of office space.

A look at a photograph of the skyline shows a city of skyscrapers. I hope that, squashed in beside these huge business structures, there will remain the essence of Beijing, that vibrant beauty, the parks, the artisan sectors. But then I'm thinking as a romantic, perhaps somewhat arrogant, outsider. From inside, I am sure that the Chinese are very proud to have achieved so much in so little time; rising from wretchedness to superstardom.

And they have reason to be.

XVIII
1939. Tea on the Great Wall.
Age Twelve

I am at my desk, musing about the chapter about Shanhaiguan that I am about to write. There is so much emotion, so much sudden growing-up of the young girl that I was, such a richness of history and architecture. I look up and see the 15-inch gilt bronze statue standing alone on an illuminated shelf, and remember my younger daughter Tina's questions about it. A visiting friend of hers, Laura, had noticed it.

"This is so unusual," she said. "What is it?"

"My mother told me that it's a 16th century figure of a Judge in the Court of an Emperor," I replied.

Tina reached up and held it carefully in both hands, passing it to her friend. "It's very heavy." She added: "I've always loved it. Mom, where did it come from?"

"It came from Shanhaiguan when we were there. In 1939."

And now a little shiver moves through me. Is it possibly one of the treasures looted from the Old Summer Palace after the Boxer Rebellion?

Our train was noisy with clusters of peasants and squawking ducks and chickens. We passed villages and glimpsed mountains, and sometimes the Great Wall in the distance. Local servants met us at the little station and drove us in a horse-drawn carriage the three miles along the road beside the Great Wall to our house at the beach. I was too tired to pay much attention but did sit up when I realized that that high gray wall along the road right beside me was the Great Wall. I greeted that old friend with a huge smile.

"Mommy, look, there's the Great Wall, here at the ocean!" I was bouncing in the car.

"Sit still, Patty," Mother said."Yes, this is where the Wall begins. From here it travels to just above Peking, and on and on west across China."

Finally we jerked to a stop. Dusty and hungry, I raced up the steps of the villa shouting,"We're here! We're here!" Johnny raced me up to the front door as the Houseman opened it. We ran across the entrance hall and out onto the terrace.

And then I stopped."Oh my, look at that."

The clear, clean, blue Bohai Sea and the wide beach lay in front of me. To the left the Lao Long Tou or Old Dragon's Head temple and fortress, though damaged still a fantasy, stretched into the ocean, its two-story "head" dominantly leading the Great Wall of China. To the right were the ruins of the delicate Sea God Pavilion.

"I wish I could show those kids in America how beautiful this is," I sighed."They wouldn't believe it." I still resented their laughing at my accent."There's so much that they don't know."

Mother had never been here before and was exclaiming about the architecture, the originality, the philosophy, the vision."Just think of the skill it takes to create buildings like this, to turn a vision into a reality! To create an Old Dragon's Head and a Sea God Pavilion introducing the Great Wall to the ocean! Lovely, lovely."

Behind us rose the Han mountains (Hanshan), and then the mysterious purple and dark green Jiao mountains (Jiaoshan). The Great Wall snaked sharply to the right and up Jiaoshan.

Johnny pointed out that the height gave defenders on the Wall a strategic advantage over any invaders. The Wall then seemed to grow smaller until it disappeared behind the mountain.

It was a perfect day. Shanhaiguan was warm with cooling ocean breezes. Mother and Amah organized our unpacking, Mother checking over the arrangements that the servants had made for our arrival. Fo Sun was sent off to get more supplies. Johnny and I ran down to the beach, staring in wonder at the ruins of the rugged Old Dragon's Head.

There was a letter from Father. He was miserable in Shanghai's stagnant wet heat, and glad that we were not there with him. He would join us in August if the Japanese occupation did not interfere, or if the Chinese anti-Japanese guerillas did not start a battle.

Cook prepared a simple dinner of local seafood, and afterward we chose our bedrooms and settled in for the night.

"Mom, where are the bathrooms?" I asked after checking the entire house. "I can't find a bathroom."

"Well," she stumbled around, "you'll find sinks to wash in. In your bedrooms."

"But how about our more serious bathroom stuff? You know, the toilets?"

"Sorry, there aren't any." She had apparently asked the houseman about this on arriving. "Here what we call doo doo and what the locals call 'night soil' gets picked up in the morning."

"Yuck."

"Well, at least it's not a smelly outhouse like in Wei Hai Wei," she snapped back. "I don't like it any better than you do."

We looked for the chamber pots and found them under the beds, then went to sleep.

At around 10 in the morning, the *mudong* (toilet) coolie came to collect the "night soil." He dumped the contests of our chamber pots into larger wooden buckets that were hung, one at each end, from a thick long swaying bamboo carrying-pole. As the coolie jogged off to fertilize the peanut or wheat fields with our deposits, he chanted *hai-ah hou-ah, hai-ah hou-ah*, keeping a steady rhythm.

Later we could see him at a distance, a tiny figure tending nearby fields, carefully applying the valuable contents of the pots with a long wooden ladle. It pleased me to see how our natural products were being used to benefit the soil that would grow fresh crops.

After breakfast Johnny and I raced out to the beach. There were exhilarating smells of ocean and salt and fish. The sand was disappointingly pebbly, not powdery as at Wei Hai Wei, but the blue transparency of the ocean and the waves lapping up to the shore called to us to play.

There were interesting nooks among the rocks where sea creatures became trapped. Near us, the wide Dashi River meandered.

The harbor was active. Many fishing sampans and junks were bobbing in the water, and motorboats crossing the harbor left bubbly white wakes. A former British naval base, the British Naval authorities in Shanhaiguan retained several war ships in the harbor to protect Britain's interests.

We settled in as the days passed. Mother helped us create aquariums with a collection of hermit crabs, sea anemones, and other little marine creatures. We built complicated sand castles, hurrying to finish them before the tide came in and washed them away. Mother found friends from Shanghai, and there were some children for Johnny and me to play with.

Sometimes peddlers, carrying on their backs small chests with shallow trays, came to the house. They squatted down and showed Mother one tray after another. Arrayed were carved earrings of green jade, white jade, rose quartz, carnelian, filigree of gold and silver. Some were shaped like little Chinese lanterns. Silver brooches with enamel flowers; ivory and silver letter openers, carved ivory or *blanc de Chine* fat laughing Buddhas, sets of matching necklaces, bracelets and earrings, nestled in perfectly shaped silk-lined boxes.

One peddler held out to me an especially beautiful small white porcelain Kwan Yin (*Guanyin*) figure.

"Littie Missie likee? Bring too muchee very goodee joss."

Mother had a *blanc de Chine Guanyin* similar to this one, about 15" high, that I loved. Now, as I carefully cradled the graceful, delicate figure in my two hands, she explained to us that *Guanyin* is a shortened form of a name in Chinese that means "One Who Sees and Hears the Cry from the Human World."

"Oh, how beautiful!" I said.

"She is also called the Bodhisatta of Compassion by Buddhists." She paused, looking at me thoughtfully, "Perhaps you are old enough now to care for so valuable a figure."

"Oh, I need lots of good joss! I need good luck especially at a new school!" I pleaded.

Mother and the peddler bargained back and forth and finally settled on a price. He placed the *Guanyin* in a padded container molded to protect the figure and her pedestal, the interior lined in red silk woven with traditional Chinese symbols. Holding this carefully with both hands, I thanked Mother with words and expressive eyes.

Other peddlers brought linens and laces — luncheon sets for eight with rich lace and embroidery; damask or lace tablecloths; dinner sets for twelve of heavy linen with deeply embroidered hems and corners.

One day two young conjurers came to our villa with a bag of tricks. One of them picked up one ball, waved his arms and hands around, and turned it into three balls. Then the three balls turned into four and then five; then back into one.

The second conjurer pulled stick after stick, each about three inches long, from his nose until he had nine sticks. I didn't like that trick, it mildly disgusted me. The first one next took a red bag, turned it inside out, and hit it a few times to prove that it was empty. To our surprise, with great flair and a Chinese form of "presto!" he took five eggs out of it. The other one did balancing tricks with jade-green bowls whirling on chopsticks, and turning blue handkerchiefs into red ones.

It was a fine show and mother thanked them appropriately with gifts of rice and money. We practiced magic tricks for days afterward. Johnny and I noted that the conjurors' jackets had unusually wide sleeves.

Then one day a peddler arrived at the door with something rare. After an elaborate, almost fawning greeting to Mother, he slowly, carefully, unwrapped a heavy 15" gilt bronze statue.

"What is it?" I asked.

She was quiet for a moment, turning the figure around and around and upended, feeling it, studying it from top to bottom.

"He bring number one goodee joss," the peddler said, breaking the silence.

"I think he was a Judge in the Court of an Emperor," Mother finally said. "It's a really heavy bronze. Must be about 16th century." I don't remember her asking the peddler how he happened to have this piece; it became one of her treasures.

Mother organized our days with her usual energy. It was a relief that there didn't seem to be many Japanese around. It was totally relaxing for us, after Shanghai. Yet we knew that this part of China was occupied by Japan.

"How would you like to go exploring today?" she suggested one morning over breakfast.

"Great. Where are we going?"

"To the fortress town of Shanhaiguan and then up a mountain to a temple. A British group is organizing the expedition. Want to go?"

"Yes, of course!"

Soon twelve of us summer people clambered into a British trolley drawn by two horses; this served as our transportation for the first leg of the trip.

Riding beside the Great Wall, we reached the fortress town itself.

Mother pulled out the guidebook. "Long ago, invading armies from up north above the Great Wall could be prevented from entering China. They had to pass through the gate of this city so strategically situated between the mountain to their right and the ocean to their left, on their way south."

She put the book back in her purse. "It was the first place, the first pass, where invading soldiers, cavalry, military equipment, could enter easternmost China," she explained.

We changed to burros, riding in a long cavalcade under and through the East Gate — the first and most important of the Great Wall forts and passes: the First Pass Under Heaven. Northern invaders had to go through this very gate.

A massive grey stone building 45 feet high, the First Pass gate straddled the road under its arched entrance gate. Its red upper story and blue eaves caught my breath. A huge white plaque with strong black Chinese characters inscribed by the Ming dynasty scholar Xiao Xian proclaimed its name: *tian xia di yi guan*. The plaque was placed conspicuously in the center of the second floor of the tower.

Clattering across a drawbridge, we crossed a deep, wide moat that protected the city on all sides. Solid grey stone walls surrounding the heart of the city reached up 44 feet and 22 feet across.

We jogged on our burros into its narrow streets. The Temple of the Drum and the Bell Tower stood at one end of the fortress.

"In the olden days, it sounded the hours," one of the group noted.

The surrounding people's homes depressed me; they were the poorest that I had ever seen. The guidebook said that the town had been created in 583, and then rebuilt into a fortress in 1381.

"I'm not surprised to find most of the houses falling apart, considering their age." Mother said."The beauty of the First Pass Under Heaven emphasizes the poverty of the surrounding crumbling, ancient, houses."

We knew that Japanese soldiers were stationed at the fortress. Some looked us over, but no one disturbed us.

We rode out of town on our burros and headed toward the hills, passing fields of drying sorghum and peanuts. It was a hot day, and the steep trail in the foothills was long, dusty and covered with loose rocks. We rode as far as it was safe, then scrambled on feet, hands and knees up the rest of the way. I was annoyed that my brother could wear pants, whereas I had to wear a skirt that made climbing much more difficult.

"Johnny," I called,"Wait! I can't go as quickly as you!" But my dratted brother paid no attention and clambered eagerly ahead.

Finally I could see a pagoda rising through the cypress trees.

"This pagoda with seven eaves," Mother read from a sign written in English,"was built around 1330 AD and later rebuilt to include the Ten Thousand Buddha Hall named for the 10,000 plus gold-plated Buddha statues it houses."

We reached a grove of ancient cypresses that enclosed the Bailin Zen Temple. Under a shady ancient pine in the courtyard of the temple we were served lunch. Then Johnny and I explored the temple, delighted to find hundreds of what seemed to us to be truly hideous Buddhas. When we began making faces and gestures to match those of the Buddhas, Mother ordered us to stop.

Buddhist priests, called Lamas, wearing long yellow robes, served as guards of the Temple. Mother interviewed several about damage done by Japanese invaders in 1933 and 1937, while Johnny and I chased each other around the trees. Then, after a short rest, we started down the mountain. This was harder than climbing up because of the rocks. I slid and slithered down, trying not to lose my balance, until we reached our burros. Then, exhausted and dusty, we rode back to the trolley, and home.

For our next expedition we didn't go very far, exploring Old Dragon's Head, the *Lao Long Tou,* a short distance down the beach. It stretched sixty feet out into the ocean at the very end of the Great Wall. The heavy stone structure appeared to be dipping its head in the ocean for a drink. Two windows formed its nostrils. Johnny and I loved playing on the sand on our side of the structure; on the other side the beach was piled with rocks and chunks of cement, making it impassable.

We climbed up to its long flat top, looked around at the view and down into the water. Then we walked to an ornate two-story building, the Chenghai Pavilion (chenghai lou), and saw that visiting emperors traveling north had left poems and inscriptions.

But the building was damaged; it showed burn marks, and some of the delicate wooden lattice-work was broken. A reproduction of an ancient inscribed stone tablet stood in front. Its original had been set there by the Lord White Tiger, Xue Ren Gui, a famous Chinese general who had conquered Korea.

"He was here over a thousand years ago," Mother said, reading the inscription."It says that he lived from 614 to 683 AD. .

A man in our group said that the original tablet had been

torn down by British Forces in the Boxer Rebellion in 1900. "The Brits used the pavilion as part of an ammunition warehouse," he said. "The building was burned during the fighting."

I didn't believe him, and turned to my mother.

"That can't be true! The British are friends of China!" I exclaimed. "They wouldn't do anything like that!"

"Sorry, but it's true," said a British member of our group. "Shantung Province and this northern area, including Peking, was the scene of battles and bombings some, um, well, only forty years ago. The fanatically anti-foreigner Chinese peasants, called 'Boxers,' were fighting to drive out an 'Eight Power Alliance' of 20,000 soldiers that included five European nations—Britain, France, Italy, Austria-Hungary, and Germany, plus America, Japan, and Russia."

"But why!" I asked.

"I'll tell you another time," Mother replied. "It's too long and too sad for today. But briefly, those are the same soldiers who looted Peking and slashed the arm of the White Jade Buddha. "

Some of my joy in the beauty of Shanhaiguan was diminished. I kept visualizing the army of invaders—not Mongol hordes but Western hordes this time—pouring down from the north, bombing the Lao Long Tou and the Sea God Pavilion, burning the historic Chenghai Pavilion, breaking into pieces the precious ancient stele with its inscription by the Lord White Tiger. They were ignorant brutes, with no appreciation for the treasures they were destroying.

The days passed peacefully. Johnny did a lot of fishing. He told us he was sure there were big fish in the river, and one morning coaxed Mother into hiring a sampan. The boatman *yulohed* us out to the middle of the river where we dropped anchor. Johnny baited four hooks and cast his line overboard. After a few minutes he pulled it up only to find his bait gone. He did this three or four times with the same result.

After a long wait there was a strong tug on his line. When he pulled it up there at last was a fish. At the same moment a friend on the boat with us, John Bonnet, yelled excitedly,"I've got a fish!"

A few minutes later mother pulled up her line—with a big crab wiggling on it.

Johnny didn't catch the *Bai-Yan-Yu*—a delicious fish with white eyes —that he was hoping for, but at least he caught a fish. I was the only one of us who didn't catch one but I didn't really care because the boys' fish and Mother's crab, cooked by the boatman and devoured by us on the beach, made a delicious snack.

With the coming of the tide, fish began swimming up the river, not knowing that they would bump into the net placed earlier by the fishermen. Now from the beach we could see their silvery scales flashing in the sunlight. The fishermen worked quickly to get the fish into their junks.

"Wouldn't it be great if I could catch one of those big four-pounders!" Johnny said. He went home to get his fishing rod ready for the big catch he was sure of the next day.

At about five a.m. he and the coolie were down at the beach digging for worms for bait. Then he went down to the Point.

"I was amazed to see that the same fishermen were still there, now dragging in their last net of fish," he reported later."They began celebrating their squirming catch, they said it was about a thousand pounds of fish during the night. Next they divided up their tasks: some of them sorted out the fish, and others had the job of loading the nets and poles on the junks. Some of the guys waded across the river, their loose cotton pants rolled high above their knees, carrying bamboo baskets of fish hanging from poles on their shoulders to sell. It was quite a sight."

On another fishing excursion Johnny caught a rock trout nearly a foot long. We were obliged to congratulate him on his catch for days.

Sometimes life was so peaceful that I forgot the war. But one morning it landed on us. I was wakened by a noise that sounded like the pop - pop - pop - pop - pop - pop - pop of machine guns. Were we going to be bombed? Were we being attacked? I was suddenly emotionally back in Shanghai, trying to stay calm. The sounds were not heavy, like the morning mortar shelling that we had lived with, but I knew they came from guns. Almost crying with fear I ran to Johnny to ask him what was going on. "I can't stand it again!"

"It's OK," he calmed me, patting my shoulder and disengaging himself from my arms. "It's only the British machine gunners practicing their shelling."

We threw on our kimonos and raced out to the verandah. Red danger flags were flying. I saw targets at the Point. The water around them splashed high in the air like fountains. I began to breathe again.

Pop - pop - pop - pop - pop - pop. The noise was unpleasant. I looked at the British fort but couldn't see the guns. After two hours the soldiers on guard took away the red flags and so, at last, we could go swimming in safety.

Johnny had a love of hunting that I did not share. He was always writing Father asking him to send slingshots from the Japanese bazaar and lead BBs for his BB gun. The area was rich with snipe and quail in addition to hawks and woodchucks. The birds flew so low that they were in his range. We benefited from his hunting skills with some delicious meals.

I was spending time on the verandah painting, designing paper doll's dresses, beginning to dream about boys, and writing poetry. I tried to paint the colors of a sunrise — pink and orange with red ocean and red sky—but it didn't look natural.

Mom had us both learning about great art. She had subscribed to an American museum program-by-mail that sent albums with places marked for specific pictures of paintings, like a stamp album. There were photographs of the paintings to be pasted above the right artist's name and biography. We had to accomplish some pages every day or not go swimming. So Johnny and I had learned about many artists.

The beach was less and less attractive to me as the weeks passed. While it was a good three miles from the fortress city of Shanhaiguan itself, there was sometimes an oppressive presence of the Japanese soldiers prowling, or perhaps just patrolling, the beach and the Wall.

They began to look at me in a way that made me uncomfortable. I would turn thirteen in a few months, was developing a girlish figure, and I felt they were appraising me. Sometimes they made weird gestures and giggling noises as they walked by. They didn't harm me, and I hoped that I was protected by the presence of the British Navy, but having to live around the invaders with no barricade or wall to separate myself from them made me uneasy. I was grateful that they generally left our residential beach area alone. On the occasions when they did appear, however, they frightened me, and I sidled rapidly out of sight.

I didn't mention this to anyone; it embarrassed me.

In August, Mother organized a tea party with some friends up on Old Dragon's Head. Our procession of British and American parents, children, nannies and amahs carrying babies, ambled up the beach. Coolies carrying folding tables and chairs, trays of food and ice chests, followed us. We climbed up the side of the Wall on a narrow uneven stone stairway. The coolies opened up the chairs and set up the tables while the amahs arranged the food and iced tea.

Comfortable in a long beach chair, I began to relax into our surroundings. What a totally nice thing to be doing. Tea on the Great Wall. A pleasant breeze coming in from the ocean caressed me. The ocean was on three sides of me; on the fourth, the Great Wall stretched into the mountains. From the height of the Wall I felt as though I were up on a narrow peninsula, sitting on top of the ocean itself, the waves rolling up toward me. There was a tinkling of long iced-tea spoons in the tea glasses, and a murmur of interest in the cakes and sandwiches. The lapping sound of the surf, the calls of birds, the quiet contentment in the voices of the people around me, led me to shut my eyes and begin to doze.

After a short time I sensed a restlessness in the voices of the Chinese servants. My eyes still shut, I listened to their mutterings, then half-opened my eyes to peek around. A group of Japanese men had climbed up on the Great Wall. They were standing provocatively close to us, many of them staring at us and at our food. At me. I was the only young girl present.

The local Chinese servants began to disappear down the side of the Wall.

Fo Sun was standing near me."What thing?" I asked out of the side of my mouth."What happen?"

"Jap-man makee too muchee trouble for Shanhaiguan Chinee-man," he whispered. The Japanese were threatening the local Chinese."Jap man takee man for fight war, takee wife for play-play, kill he baby. More better go way."

"How fashion you no trouble?"

"No trouble Shanghai Chinee man. He all same you American man." The Chinese from far away down in Shanghai were like foreigners to the Japanese soldiers in the north, and they were left alone.

I began to feel extremely uneasy. One of the Japanese men

kept smiling at me; it caused unpleasant prickles to tease along my spine. Our friend Major Bonnet spoke up with forced heartiness."Well, what a nice time we have had, haven't we! Now it's time to pack up and go home. Right away." We'd been there only about twenty minutes.

"Jolly good," another answered, getting up and folding his chair.

The Japanese approached our group. One, a short bulky man with an arrogant swagger, reached out and picked up a whole chocolate cake. Johnny made a grab for it. He pushed him away."My like," he said.

"My like too, and it's my cake," Johnny replied angrily."You no take my cake." Johnny raised a fist. Another Japanese pushed over the table, the array of foods spilling onto the dusty surface of the Wall. The first advanced toward Johnny, who was cursing at him.

"Noong ze iguh tzu loh!"

I was horrified. The Japanese wouldn't understand the Shanghainese insult, but he would understand Johnny's raised fist.

Mother hurried over and wrapped her arms around Johnny lovingly but tightly."No matter, he just boy, cake no matter, *maskee.*" She had had too much experience with the Japanese occupiers' arrogance and cruelty to bother trying to negotiate with them; and, we were vulnerable. Major Bonnet hustled Johnny, yelling all the way, off the Wall.

The man who had been leering at me stepped a few feet forward, pointing to me."My like."

"My no like," I said as calmly as I could."You go way." I made a brushing gesture with my hand.

He reached a heavily muscled arm out and grabbed me, yanking me hard against his body."My like."

I screamed, pulling away from him as hard as I could. "Leave me alone!"

One of the English men drew out a weapon. "Let go of her or I kill you!"

I didn't know which was worse, my fear of what the man might do to me or my disgust at the feel and smell of his body against me. Another Japanese muttered to my attacker, who suddenly let go of me. I fell to the stone surface. Mother and the English man got me to my feet and helped me away and down the steps.

Everyone else followed quickly. The servants hastily bundled up the dishes, folded chairs and tables, and got everything off the wall

I was shaking. "I want to go home," I cried. "I can't stay here. I can't stay here!"

Johnny echoed me. "Yes, we have to go home."

My experiences with Japanese men, in Shanhaiguan, later in Wei Hai, and finally most brutally in Shanghai, have scarred me forever. World War II didn't improve my opinion of them. I have stood on the beach at Tarawa where incredibly brave U.S. Marines waded ashore under machine gun fire to liberate the people of Kiribati; I've seen the beaches and Bloody Nose Ridge at Peleliu in Palau; I have many friends among the Micronesians and Marshallese, Guamanians and people of Saipan and the Philippines who were subjected to Japanese occupation.

The only Japanese products that I can tolerate are Japanese food, and my car that I love, a yellow Suzuki that I call Suzy Sunshine.

The depth of my hatred was vividly exposed at an awkward moment. Some years ago in Washington, DC I attended a dinner hosted by the local Harvard Club honoring the Japanese ambassador to the United States. My former husband István Botond, who had graduated from the Harvard Graduate School of Architecture (after escaping from

Hungary) while on the I.M. Pei team of architects, enjoyed the Club events. Pleasant background chatter warmed the room; I was glad to be there, and looked forward to the ambassador's talk on Japanese relations with the Atlantic nations. I was at the time CEO of an organization (Association to Unite the Democracies) created to build lasting ties among democratic nations.

I looked around at the other tables. There was a huge flag on a wall behind the speaker's dais: it was white, with an enormous red circle in the middle. Suddenly I heard myself cry out angrily:

"What is the Japanese flag doing here in America!"

People turned around to hush me. Of course I was embarrassed by my bad manners. The guest beside me quieted me. After learning about my past in China, my emotions further affected by Pearl Harbor and the Japanese torture of prisoners, the guest said that he could understand how deeply and how lastingly a horrible childhood experience can live in the soul. Members of his family had been killed in the Holocaust.

I was shocked to find that, decades later, I still harbor hatred so profound that it blurts unexpectedly out of my mouth. I think of myself as a forgiving, loving person with good manners and self-control. Is this hatred to live in me forever?

XIX

1939-40. JOHNNY LEAVES FOR AMERICA; I LEARN ABOUT THE GOVERNANCE OF SHANGHAI. AGE THIRTEEN

I'VE BEEN SHOPPING for presents for my grandchildren, blessed to have three grandsons and one granddaughter. Idly a thought creeps in: how easy it is in America to shop for clothing! One of my grandsons, Will, is the age Johnny was when he went off to America to school, with knickers, shorts, Harris Tweed jackets and monogrammed underwear. And not one pair of long pants like what the other boys were wearing. I had a similar problem, wearing Madame Garnet-type dresses in my first months of the Shanghai American School. In the German school, we had worn uniforms.

Eventually, to our great relief, both of us got properly outfitted, dressed like the other children. But I'll always remember the embarrassment.

A few days after we returned to Shanghai, thankful for the safety of home, Johnny ran into my room with news.

" Guess what!"

"What."

"I'm going away to school in America! I've been accepted at St. George's in Rhode Island!"

"Oh my gosh. That's really something!" I yelled."Gee, that's really something!"

"Yeah. Daddy just showed me a letter from the school accepting me. You know, that's the school near where Admiral Yarnell lives. He'll be nearby to help me. But I won't need any help of course," he teased, putting on an air of bravado.

"We don't know what school there in America will be like. All we know about schools in America is the little Rialto public school."

We were quiet for a moment, wondering about the future.

"When are you leaving?'

"As soon as Dad can find a berth for us. Mom is coming with me to help me get settled in, and also to talk to her publishers about her book."

Now fifteen years old, he needed to be schooled in America. But I overheard my parents saying that they had to get him out of China especially because he got into trouble with the Japanese soldiers. He might have been killed in Shanhaiguan, and my parents feared for his life. With me they had no such problem; I stayed out of the way of the Japanese and also of the Nazis from my former school. The Japanese nauseated me and the Nazis scared me.

Johnny was worried about missing the opening day of the school because the ship couldn't get him there in time.

"Mom, Dad, the other guys will have taken the best places, and they'll have made friends already," Johnny complained.

"Can't help it, Johnny," Father said."I'm working to find a cabin for you and Mother on the next boat. But as you know, war conditions in Shanghai make it hard to get a boat. Europe is at war, the great European liners aren't coming here, and few ships are travelling to the States. It's not as it was before the Japanese occupation."

He smiled wryly."I know that that's little comfort and that

it will initially make problems for you. But you've always been able to conquer your problems, now haven't you!"

Overnight Tailor made Harris Tweed jackets, woolen shorts, flannel and plaid sport jackets for Johnny; his fine linen underwear was monogrammed. Johnny showed me where he had packed his Chapei bullets in some socks.

In September a cabin was found on a Dollar Liner, and son and mother left for the month-long voyage. We tearfully saw them off.

Father and I returned to a quiet house."It'll be strange not to have Johnny around, won't it, Daddy. He's always been here."

"We'll be lonesome, but we'll manage, won't we. Maybe you and I can do some interesting things together. I'm glad that Fraulein Erika is with us." He gave me a hug."And I'm especially glad that you're here with me."

I trudged up to the third floor of our house, paused at the top of the stairs, then turned left into my brother's room. It was so empty. His personality had given life to every piece of furniture. Jim was lying on top of the bed, looking just as forlorn as I suddenly felt. He thumped his tail a couple of times to greet me and looked at me with doleful eyes. I cuddled up with him on the bed, stroking his sleek white and black fur.

"We're going to miss him, aren't we, Jim." He licked my hand.

Amah joined us, her cheeks wet with tears."What we do, Littie Master go America! When my Johnnie come back, Littie Missie?"

"I don't know, Chiao Kuei. I don't know." I reached up to hug her."But we'll manage."

Father had entered me into my new school, the Shanghai American School, the SAS, after the drama at the German school.

The school was not completely unfamiliar, but most of

Johnny's classmates had returned to America, and I knew only two girls at the school.

The SAS was a large three-story brick building on Avenue Pétain in the French Concession. It looked a lot like photographs of Independence Hall in Philadelphia, with a little white bell tower on top. Colonnades linked the main building to dormitories and the gym. We were classes one through twelve. My schoolmates were the children of American businessmen, diplomats, and North China missionaries whose Missions had been overrun by the Japanese.

The classes were about the same size as in my former school, with a similar mixture of boys and girls. But after a few weeks it seemed to me that the teachers didn't control the students; rather, the students controlled them. The kids threw spitballs around the room at each other. And they talked while the teacher was talking. They got up and walked out of the room without permission. I didn't like this absence of order.

It bothered me even more that there was an emphasis on boy-girl romances. Love notes were passed around the classroom. Girls were constantly primping and fluffing their hair. It was also a bother that there were no uniforms, as there had been at the German school, so there was competition in dress. And my clothing was a disaster.

Coincidentally, a cable came from Mother. Johnny was having similar problems.

"Please arrange some money soonest. Johnny wardrobe wrong. Must buy long pants.

I understood his dilemma perfectly. In November I would become a thirteen-year-old. Both my school and my body had changed. I was faced with the need for a going-to-school wardrobe for a young teenager, often wishing that I were back in the German school where everyone wore the same uniform and no one cared whether my dress fit my body perfectly. Father was useless in this area, so Fräulein Erika and I selected from fashion magazines the dresses for Tailor to copy for me. It didn't help that I didn't care about style, the way the other girls seemed to. They gossiped about who was better dressed, who had the most expensive clothing, what so-and-so was wearing. I hated this.

Miss Erika was my best friend during the school year. She was fun. The girls razzed me about still having a governess, but I didn't care. I would have been very lonely without her, especially with Johnny away. We went to movies like *The Wizard of Oz* and *Alice in Wonderland*. The *Blue Bird* was especially beautiful. Of course I loved *Gone with the Wind*. After seeing it I practiced smiling in the mirror, trying to look like Vivien Leigh. That didn't work, and I'd break up giggling at my silly faces in the mirror. Erika and I played cards and dominoes and Concentration, and she helped me get my schoolwork done.

One afternoon I escaped Erika and, with some of my new girlfriends, went to see Hedy Lamarr in *Ecstasy*, a movie in which she was seen in the distance swimming with no clothes on in a lake. We giggled nervously the whole time. I don't know how we got away with it.

A good friend was Mary Jo Buchan, the daughter of U.S. banking friends of my parents, and several years older than I. She and I spent many afternoons on our horses riding into the countryside west of the city toward the relatively safe Hung Jiao (Hongqiao, Rainbow Bridge) area. As Americans we were protected from any lurking Japanese soldiers, for Japan and America were not at war. Still, we didn't venture too far from home. We almost got into trouble once, when we encountered three Japanese soldiers sitting on the grass, taking tea under a willow tree by a stream.

My Arabian, Mona, loved to canter and so did I, the steady smooth rising and falling motions both fun and soothing. The wind blowing through my hair, I imagined myself a warrior woman on a Quest as I cantered along, aware of but paying no attention to the soldiers. Mary Jo glanced over at them and quickly looked back at our path.

"Beware the Mystic Warriors!" I shouted into the air. The three soldiers put down their tea and stared at us. I sensed their interest and became nervous, remembering Shanhaiguan. But I was determined not to let them spoil our afternoon.

"Fear the Wondrous Adventurers!" Mary Jo yelled, laughing partly in defiance of the danger we knew we were in. What if one of our horses stepped hard into a hole, breaking its ankle and leaving us at the mercy of the Japanese soldiers? Our escort from the stable had more sense than we did, and immediately got us headed home, loudly praying in Russian that we wouldn't fall off. *Bozhe moi!*

Otherwise I had few friends to play with. An American girl, Fanny Jo Sheridan, and I liked to sing a hilarious "Three Little Fishies," the newest music hit:

Down in the meadow in a little bitty pool
Swam three little fishies and a mama fishy too
"Swim," said the mama fishie, "Swim if you can"
And they swam and they swam all over the dam.
Boop boop did-tem dat-tem what-tem Chu!
Boop boop did-tem dat-tem what-tem Chu!
Boop boop did-tem dat-tem what-tem Chu!
And they swam and they swam all over the dam.

Mother wrote that her book was to be published by The MacMillan Company in February 1940 and that she needed to stay in New York for a full schedule of newspaper interviews, magazine articles, and radio programs before returning to China.

She stayed away for half the year. While she was away I had the fun of being Father's hostess, greeting his guests and helping to plan dinner parties. He included me in his activities when possible, but he was preoccupied with the real estate investing and banking that, he said, the Japanese were not making any easier. The ever-present soldiers with their coarseness and pretentiousness were a deterrent to simple enjoyment. The arrogant flags could not be avoided. And I could feel in my body the humiliation that the Chinese of every rank were forced to endure.

On New Year's Day Father took me to a brunch at the home of a Chinese friend in the Old City. We were obliged to stop at the border between the French Concession and the Old City so that the Japanese soldiers could look us over. How I hated this. I especially resented seeing Ah Ching again being forced to kowtow almost to street level, low enough to suit the Japanese. My hands fisted in anger. I wanted to strike the soldiers. How dare they deliberately humiliate the Chinese! But there were mounted machine guns pointing right at me.

Finally we were waved through and drove slowly past the checkpoint, through the crowded streets and finally to the secluded home of our host.

When we entered this traditional garden with its own zig-zag bridge over water I smiled with pleasure, remembering my first zig-zag bridge several years ago in a different home, and then the zig-zag bridges in Peking palace parks. To show deference on being introduced to our host I automatically curtsied, despite being older now; Father bowed his head to the old man and congratulated him on reaching the august age of 80. His natural courtesy was one of the many reasons I loved my father.

"Aren't you being rude to say how old he is?" I whispered.

"Reaching the age of 80, in the Asian world," he explained to me, "is a distinction and suggests great wisdom." Indeed, the celebrant had a long white beard and looked extremely wise. He even had a mole with a long hair poking out of it.

Father flourished when presiding over an elegant table, and he had fun with me serving as his hostess. Every few weeks he would permit me to sit at my mother's place. Now he planned our Sunday dinners with my education in mind. He had Cook prepare a series of birds, one kind at a time, graduating upward in size.

"The tiniest bird is the 'rice bird,'" he said on introducing the series of birds. It was small enough to be served whole on one piece of toast. I found it very hard to eat as it seemed to be mostly bones and skin. I wasn't allowed to pick it up and eat it with my fingers.

A few Sundays later dove was featured, then pigeon, quail, squab, partridge, the birds growing larger each time. "With partridge," Father told me, "the traditional accompaniment is quince. With pheasant, the next specialty, it is bread sauce." Then came duck, chicken, goose, and finally turkey. With each, he gave a little exposition about the bird and its proper presentation and sauces: orange or cherry with duck, bread stuffing and gravy with chicken, spiced peach with goose, cranberry with turkey.

My life during Mother's absence was simple. Ah Ching and the governess or Amah or Father took me places and drove me home.

But, now older, I began to wonder about things that seemed incongruous. Why were there streets named after French military heroes like Avenue Joffre and Avenue Pétain? Did the Chinese so love the French? There were avenues named King Edward VII or Edouard VII depending on which part of the city we were in. And it occurred to me that our summers were spent in a Chinese town where the British flag flew; our home was in an area of a Chinese city that flew the British or American flag and we visited areas that flew only the French flag. The German Corner flew the Swastika and German friends referred to German summer activities in Tsingtao (Qingdao) and Tientsin.

I once asked my father for an explanation as we drove through the city. We had gone from where signs were in French to where they were British.

"Daddy," I asked him, "Why aren't the signs in Chinese? We're in China. Why are the road names in French or English? Why are they named for foreign generals? It doesn't make sense."

He summarized the governing arrangements of Shanghai.

"Simply put," he said, "Shanghai was divided into three parts in the last century by trade treaties between foreign governments and businessmen, and the Chinese government and businessmen. The British, and later the Americans, took over an area of Shanghai that became the International Settlement. It is operated generally according to British or U.S. law. Today, there are Japanese and Chinese as well as British and Americans on the governing Council."

"What about the French?" I asked.

"The French wanted to have their own separate French Concession organized and run by the French according to French law, and it remains generally independent."

"Isn't that unusual? I've been learning about history and don't remember any arrangement like it."

"I believe it's the only place like it in the world," Father replied.

He paused, choosing his words. "In some ways the separation

between the International and the French sections is a nuisance —
for instance, in the French section the electricity runs on 110 volts,
but in ours, it is 220 volts. Also, there's the matter of driving
licenses that vary according to the section. Also the guns, and
the military."

"I guess that's why the police are different in different
parts of the city?" I asked. In the parts of the city with French
street names, the policemen wore French uniforms, and were
Vietnamese rather than Chinese.

"The French," Father said, "can trust the Vietnamese to police
the French part of Shanghai, whereas they fear that Chinese
policemen might not always be so responsive to French interests."

He lit a cigarette. "In the International Settlement, you don't
see Vietnamese policemen, but rather, Punjabi Sikhs. You know,
the ones with bushy black beards and brightly colored turbans
who patrol the streets on horseback. As Britain had colonized
India, these British-oriented Sikhs came to Shanghai about a
half-century ago to protect British interests, and then took over
the protection of all of the International Settlement.

"The foreigners, people like you and me who came from
other countries but have made our homes here, we are called
'Shanghailanders.'"

I thought about this as we drove along, dodging rickshaws,
peddlers, bicyclists, water buffalo. Finally I asked, "Do the
Chinese like this? Do they like Shanghailanders?" I had heard
the phrase, *gui luo*, "foreign devils", applied to us.

"Well, here's the short version of a long tragic story. A
hundred years ago the Europeans took shameful advantage of
the Chinese, who had been isolated for centuries. The Chinese
Emperors weren't familiar with warships other than their junks,
or with international laws. They thought that China was the
center of the universe. The British invaded Chinese ports to force

trade in the devastating drug 'opium.' I think you've probably heard about it and the harm it does to people who use it. The Chinese tried to prevent the British from selling it because it was sapping the energy of the people and bankrupting the nation, but they lost, and had to make important concessions first to the British, then to France, America and other nations. The Shanghai Concessions are part of those treaties.

"There have been protests and shootings and even battles from time to time; you know about the Boxer Rebellion around 1900. That was very unpleasant on both sides. But today's Chinese rulers want the business that is brought in by these international trade concessions. And, many Chinese have moved into the International Settlement where there are good living conditions and business environments. Most Chinese leaders see it to their advantage to keep the concessions in place. Some people, however, resent the foreigners, and battles can start very quickly."

Another day, when we crossed over the river into Poo Tung, I wondered about the Chinese parts of the city—about the Old City, and Hong Kew, Poo Tung, Chapei.

"What about the parts of the city not run by foreigners?" I asked.

Chinese Shanghai, Father explained, had been run by the Chinese government according to Chinese law."You've been in all the major sectors—you've visited shops in Chapei, that was the handcraft and artisan area that's now destroyed; you've been to Poo Tung and the Old City with me; I believe you've been in Hong Kew where the poorest of the Russian and Jewish refugees have congregated. These areas were run by the Chinese, but are now administered by the Japanese occupiers."

He continued."There are other cities in China, mostly the major port cities, over 20 of them, that have various forms of privileged trading relationship with China. These are called 'Treaty Ports.'"

He stopped at a red light, beside a huge bearded Sikh police officer on a horse. I looked up at the fierce-looking policeman with new interest and understanding."You and Johnny and Mother have spent summers in the British Treaty Port Wei Hai Wei, which was the Summer Station of the British Naval China Station. Its Winter Station is Hong Kong. Tientsin is German oriented; Tsingtao was the base of the Far Eastern Squadron of the Imperial German Navy."

I broke in."Some of my German school friends were always talking about Tsingtao."

"You'll find more Germans in Tientsin, which has some lovely German architecture. Canton also is a major Treaty Port. In these ports the foreign business communities have special trading arrangements with the Chinese, enabling goods and money to move in and out under the protection of the foreign flags. Usually there'll be a foreign warship in the harbor to help keep order. This is felt to be to everyone's advantage."

He paused to reconsider what he'd just said."Well, in this wartime, I'm afraid that the foreign warships will have been replaced by Japanese.

"But unoccupied China, which is huge, is still run by the Chinese." He patted my hand."I hope that one day you will read the Treaties; they will give you a better understanding of China. But for now, that's about enough of a history lesson for today, young lady. Would you like to come with me to the Chocolate Shop in the International Settlement? Maybe a butterscotch sundae?"

Mother returned in the spring, bubbling with news about the success of her book.

"It's an alternative Book-of-the-Month Club selection!" she exclaimed. She brought news of Johnny, too, who was enjoying his beautiful school; every morning before classes he and some friends went swimming in the Atlantic Ocean. And, he now had long pants to wear, like the other American boys.

"Well, now I need some normal American clothes, too, for the American school," I said. "I don't have clothes that fit me and look normal, like the other kids."

Mother soon had Tailor making some dresses for me. Unfortunately she wasn't current with what teen-age American girls were wearing any more than Erika or I were. Her elegant formal Madame Garnet-type dresses weren't right, nor was wearing socks to a dance.

"Mother, the other girls laugh at me because of my clothes. I've got to have American school clothes, like skirts and shirts and sweaters. And I need normal party dresses, not Madame Garnet dresses but just nice modern dresses. Maybe you could visit the school to see what I'm talking about."

After visiting the school, she realized that my problem was real. Soon Tailor had Glowing Pearl at his side helping with basting or embroidery. With more appropriate clothing I was more relaxed and could fit in better with the other students.

Springtime brought thoughts of summer. I needed a new bathing suit to fit my new girly body. Tailor went to work on a suit for me. Pink of course. He was also at work on something else. I pretended not to notice that he was making a pink silk *cheongsam*, too, and that Glowing Pearl was upstairs in his workroom a lot to try it on when Amah and Sew Sew Amah Mary, her mother, weren't around. Once when I peeked in I saw her fluttering her fan at him and looking directly into his eyes. And he spent a lot of time measuring her body with his tape measure.

School was over; it was June 1940 and long empty hot and humid days were ahead. In the absence of school I was at home more, and so began to learn that Japanese harassment was becoming more frequent and arbitrary. In Father's accounting sessions with me I noticed that he was greatly increasing the *cumshaws* given to one or another of our servants with their regular salaries.

"What's wrong, Daddy?" I asked him."Who's in trouble?"

He looked up at me from where he was writing in his ledger, and sat back, smiling wryly at me as he adjusted his glasses. "The family of Fo Sun," he said,"has had their water buffalo stolen by Japanese soldiers and now they have no transportation until they can get another. And the buffalo are hard to obtain these days."

Another time, when I asked about an especially large *cumshaw,* he answered: "Japanese soldiers have appropriated all the grain from Lin Sing's family farm, and now they have to buy more food. They look to Lin Sing to provide this." There was story after story of the deliberate harm done to the Chinese by the Japanese occupiers.

Many of my parents' friends were packing up to leave not only Shanghai but China herself; they were not willing to wait to see what would happen to them if the Japanese did not honor the Treaty Port and other international agreements.

We talked about it over dinner one night.

"I don't want to leave China," Mother said."I've only just gotten back from America, and I love the Chinese people. I've lived here since 1918. It's my home. And I don't want to desert our Chinese friends now in their time of trouble."

"I know, Edna Lee. So do I," Father replied."So do I. I've been here longer — since 1915. That's, let's see, over twenty-five years."

"To me China is the only home I've ever had," I said."I've lived here all my life."

My parents agreed. The Chinese were family; the bonds were firm. Mother and Father had come to China not to make fortunes on opium or to exploit the Chinese people. China was our home and our life. Further, America was not at war with Japan, and, if we stayed away from them, the Japanese did not harm us.

"If we go back to the States," Father mused,"What kind of work could I find? I'm now almost sixty. Maybe I could work as a consultant on business in China? We might find it hard to have enough money for a decent life, Edna Lee, until I find work with adequate compensation. We'd have to sell our investments to find a new home, to take care of the children's schools, get a car, manage our basic needs. We might be dependent on income from your new book for some months while I'd be looking for employment."

Here, he continued, he was on the Board of Directors of several prominent American companies and was a valued appraiser of real estate and consultant on land matters. He would not have comparable experience and contacts in America.

"You might be able to serve as an officer of the Bank of China in New York," Mother suggested."The Directors all know you."

"That might be possible, good idea."

It was nothing I'd ever thought about. Father went to work and found money for the bills and the servants. It was a bit strange to think about not having money. And Father would go crazy if he didn't have an office to go to which somehow made money appear.

The decision was made that, for now, we were staying in China.

The summer was well underway. Something had to be done about me in the long months ahead without school or my brother to play with. Mother began to think about light-hearted summers past in Wei Hai Wei; the familiar houseboys, our *mafu* and boatman; the parties with the international community also vacationing in Wei Hai Wei; the elegance of the men from the British Royal Navy. Our experience with the Japanese in Shanhaiguan cancelled any resort far from international protection again. She began concocting reasons for us to go to Wei Hai Wei.

"The Japanese there can't be worse than the Japanese here," she said, trying to justify her decision, "and they aren't the same kind of Japanese as up in Shanhaiguan at the Mongolian border. We can't stay in Shanghai through the summer. And we have many Chinese friends there who will help us if there's any trouble."

She bustled around getting the house ready for summer as though nothing had changed — replacing the thick carpets with bamboo mats, having the living room chairs covered with summer slipcovers, storing winter clothing in the camphor closet; making sure that fine bamboo sheets were placed over the mattresses to help keep the beds cool. Then she took care of planning for Father's needs with a reduced staff for the two months of our absence. Finally the fun part — packing our summer clothing, games, bicycles, dishes, medicines, batteries, utensils, utilitarian household needs like flashlights. Her typewriter and stacks of typewriter ribbons and paper. She oversaw what the servants were bringing, making sure that their summer needs, too, were met.

Father made arrangements about tickets for our British coastal steamer and the money we would need. Agents in Wei Hai Wei were contacted to prepare the villa we had rented, to have our boatman Lao Lu and the sampan ready to meet the boat we would be traveling on, and to have two jalopies and drivers ready to take us, and our luggage, from the dock to our house.

Troubling us all were the events in Europe. We heard about Dunkirk, where thousands of British, French and Belgian soldiers had been slaughtered on the beach. Hitler had marched into Paris. Our European friends were living in shock, unable to care for relatives and friends in Europe, getting only snippets of news on the radio.

Miss Erika was affected because, with a German passport— although it was stamped with a large "J" — the British authorities in charge of British and American travel in China did not permit her to travel. So my parents invited Mary Jo in her place.

Our Chinese servants warned us not to go. "My think so Missie jump in wolf mouth," muttered Ah Kung.

And jump in the wolf's mouth we did. Mother had made up her mind. She was desperate to get away. The new Japanese Shanghai had become abhorrent to her. We were going to Wei Hai Wei.

Thinking back now, seventy years later, on that summer, looking through the photographs and writings that have survived, recovering the memories, I still don't know if we should have gone that year--if she was right in forcing the excursion to Wei Hai Wei. Some instinct drove her to go north against all reason and advice. Did she sense that there was a tragic story to be told? Did she feel that she and I would never again see our beautiful summer playground? On returning to Shanghai, I would have only four weeks left of my life in China.

XX
1940, WEI HAI WEI UNDER JAPANESE BOOTS. AGE THIRTEEN

As AWFUL AS the Japanese made life for everyone, they could starve and beat down the people, but they could not kill the Chinese heart or the beauty of the land.

Beauty, this gift of God, remains. Lovely things disappear, other lovely things take their place. Beauty is limitless; like the stars, like love, there is always room for more.

The trip up from Shanghai should have been as delightful as it had always been, steaming up the China coast by boat, nothing to do but bask in the sun, enjoy being brushed by the light wind and looking at the horizon. But that's not how it went. At first it was lovely to be once again on a steamer on the ocean. The fresh breeze, the hum of the motors, the sound of the waves, all led us to relax for the first time in many weeks.

Mother dozed in a long steamer chair once we were underway, missing the treat served to us by a steward: tea and toast with orange marmalade, and rich pound cake with currants. Mary Jo and I feasted on them. As evening approached we noticed that the ship was being blacked out. This was definitely not good. I ran down to my room where someone was fussing with the porthole.

"Hey, don't cover my porthole, please!" I said. "I need to see the ocean!" But the man installed curtains so heavy that no light could escape from the cabin. Then he shut and bolted the portholes.

"What's going on?" I asked angrily.

"We're sailing under a British flag, Miss," he said. "Remember that we are at war with Germany and are vulnerable to German raiders rumored to be in the area. If they can't see us, Miss, we've a better chance of not being torpedoed."

That silenced me.

Overnight the easy atmosphere on the boat changed. We remembered that Germany was at war with Britain and that we were going to a Japan-occupied part of China. Japan, Germany and Italy had formed an alliance called the Axis. Americans were not at war with the Axis powers, but still we were entering an uncertain area. I began to wonder if there were to be other unpleasant surprises.

Yes, there were. The night before we reached Wei Hai Wei, we were each given a glass test tube with the instruction that we were each to supply a "specimen" for the authorities. The issue was, they said, prevention of cholera. The specimens would be tested for cholera in the morning by the Japanese port doctors.

"Japanese port doctors? Not Chinese or British?" Mother stumbled over words, trying to keep her anger in check. All of us had been inoculated for cholera before sailing, and had been given sailing permits by Japanese medical authorities certifying that we were cleared to go.

We were angry but had to accept the inevitable. "More Japanese cheek," someone muttered. That night we dropped anchor, and at dawn, Mary Jo and I went on the deck to watch the docking. I was ecstatic to see Wei Hai Wei again. A loving feeling embraced me, as though the harbor were welcoming me as one of its own.

Japanese officials boarded the ship. As we waited to disembark there was another surprise. Cook came up to Mother, his face twisted with consternation.

"Missie, what thing?" He was wringing his hands. "Jap-man say no Chinese-man can go off boat. What thing can do, Missie?"

Mother went immediately to the ship Captain and other officers to insist that our servants be permitted to land. They had had a multitude of shots and Japanese medical approvals and certificates so that this problem would not arise.

"It's part of the Japanese war of nerves with Britons and Americans. They want to make us feel unwelcome so that we'll leave China to them," the Captain told her.

Mother began arguing with the Japanese officials. Meanwhile, sampans began to surround the steamer to carry passengers and cargo ashore. I saw our boatman.

"*Hao*, Lao Lu!" I called down. He heard me, looked up and smiled broadly. I noticed that the sampan flew a Japanese flag. So did they all. Even here? On the lowly sampans?

We were finally forced to leave without our servants, climbing carefully down a swaying ladder, then jumping from it to the sampan that was bouncing on the waves. Our Chinese servants and those of other families, standing forlornly at the ship's rail, watched our sampan leave, uncertain of their future. We sat, stunned into silence, as the boatman steered our sampan through the clutter of boats toward the jetty. I was very upset.

"Lao Lu," I asked, "You boys, they no come helpee you? How fashion?" His sons always came with him to help us unload and carry luggage into our summer house.

He didn't answer. Instead, "Where blong Master Johnny? He no come?"

Lao Lu was dodging the question. I didn't pursue it. "Johnny go big school America," I replied.

"My sorry Johnny no come, he all same one my boy. Too muchee man likee he." He paused, stroking the *yuloh* carefully as he dodged sampan traffic. His body, always taut and muscled, looked too thin, on the edge of emaciation. Then I noticed that his baggy cotton trousers were tied on by a piece of thick rope. He had no belt.

When he'd steered us away from the pack of boats he said quietly,"My lose plenty face, Littie Missie," Then he looked around to see who might hear him."My no-good sons go up mountains. Jap dwarf man come, want makee he work, carry stone, my no have sons to send. *Ai-yah!*"

Then he broke up laughing. He was telling me that his sons were soldiers in the guerilla army who lived in the neighboring hills, and he was rightly proud of them.

We were nearing the jetty.

Suddenly Mary Jo cried out,"Oh my God, there are Japanese soldiers with bayonets pointing at us! Let's go back to the boat!"

But we couldn't avoid what was ahead. Not just bayonets, but savage German Shepherd police dogs pulled at their chains and snarled at the women and children arriving for the summer. A less friendly welcome could hardly be imagined.

One of the soldiers struck Lao Lu across the face when he presented our luggage for customs inspection. His kowtow to the Japanese had not been satisfactory.

Lu now made another kowtow, this time with a sweep of his straw sun hat and bowing insultingly low before each of the soldiers. Everyone pretended that they hadn't seen anything.

I couldn't take it. I was trembling with rage. Lu was my friend. I began uttering some of my brother's Shanghainese oaths and imprecations of the foulest, not understanding what I was saying. Lu, terrified, whispered,

"*An jing, An jing.* Quiet, quiet."

The soldier calmed down, and soon our baggage was being inspected. Our suitcases and trunks were thrown onto the dock and carelessly shoved open. They pulled out every personal item, turned items over and over. Then they pawed through all of our dishes and linens, books, provisions.

Mother presented a pass giving us permission to unload our personal effects to an official-looking soldier. Obtaining that permit had taken hours and hours in Shanghai. But he took the permit, peered at it closely, turned it over several times.

"Ah-h-h, so-o, Shanghai pass, ah-h-h, so-o. Sorry, unsatisfactory." He put it in a drawer.

A British ship's officer told Mother quietly on the side: "There is a conflict between the Japanese military in the Shanghai area, and the Japanese in North China. Bloody difficult problem. I don't know how we are to solve it."

Mother was worried about our servants. She decided to rely on her experience in dealing with Japanese. First she left Mary Jo and me in the care of Lao Lu with our luggage. Then she found the driver of the horse and carriage we had rented, an old friend named *Mafu* Jim, who greeted her effusively.

"Good day Missie Potter. *Hao Bu Hao?*" A broad smile broke across his pock-marked face.

I was shocked to see how Jim had changed; his body was gaunt, as though his bones were held together by skin.

She replied that she was well and asked him if his rice bowl was full. He replied, "Oh, yes, Missie, plenty food."

"*Mafu* Jim, we have a problem." She explained what was happening and asked him to drive her to Japanese headquarters. Although he was distinctly not pleased about going, he understood the situation, and took her there.

On her return Mother described what had taken place. She

looked exhausted.

"When I went in, there were three Japanese sitting around with their jackets unbuttoned. I explained my visit. The inspectors ignored me. I became more insistent, but they just eyed me coldly, picked at their teeth in front of me, and began reading their newspapers. I lost my temper and began pounding on the desk.

"What? You lost your temper? Oh Mom."

"Well, it was all so unfair." She paused, brushed a fly off her shoulder."Finally a soldier spoke, rudely demanding my address."

We had not been able to stay at our former Half Moon Bay cottage; it had been closed by the Japanese. Too isolated and far from the port, they'd said. But my parents had been able to rent a villa belonging to Italian friends, still near a good beach, and in a neighborhood near friends."I gave the address, glad that I could remember it, as upset as I was.

"The response was astonishing. They almost jumped to attention. A chair was offered to me; the Japanese soldiers bowed very politely. You see, Patty, Japan and Italy have signed a World War II friendship pact."

She giggled."The leader slapped me on the back so strongly that it nearly knocked me down. I knew it was a slap of camaraderie and equality.

"Then he said, 'Japan, Itary, sisters.' He smiled broadly, breathing into my face. 'So happy you sister.' Immediately my passport was approved. He ordered our bags to be repacked and our servants to be disembarked. 'S-o sorry, so happy you sister.'"

Hours of waiting with our bags in the hot sun followed. At last another sampan appeared with the servants and the heavy luggage. We learned that the delay was due to the fact that a customs officer hoped to appropriate a large flashlight from our luggage. "Ah, hand grenade," he had said as he took it. Amah took him on and, after much talk, we got it back. Our flashlight was valuable; the electric current was unreliable and flashlights were not available in town.

Finally we could leave the horrid Japanese and their bayonets and their snarling dogs at the dock. But as we rode along I felt that something was wrong.

"Mom," I asked slowly, "why is it so quiet?"

She didn't say anything, just looked around as we drove. Then I went on: "There isn't any chatter. Where are the children? And there should have been crowds at the dock meeting the boat, peddlers and beggars. They should have been selling live ducks and chickens and goats. I remember them very well. Why do you suppose they weren't there? Did you notice? I know you were busy with the soldiers."

"You're right," she said slowly. "There isn't any chatter, and no one is laughing." Mother paused to think. "I can't imagine Wei Hai Wei without laughing crowds. It must be because of the Japanese. Maybe the people are being made to work harder than usual. Our welcome certainly was very strange. Well, I'll find out what's wrong as soon as I can."

We drove thankfully out of town and away from the Japanese. The road with the simple countryside on one side, the ocean on the other, began to calm us. Then, finally, around a curve we arrived at our rented "Italian" villa. "We're here at last!" cried out Mary Jo, the first to hop out. She grabbed her bag and hat and ran to the door.

As she arrived it opened, a caretaker greeting us with a broad smile.

"Welcome, Littie Missie," he said. "My blong Houseman, makee house nice you, Missie, other Littie Missie. You likee my bring lemonade?" He produced cool drinks and a tray of sliced fruit. The second jalopy with our servants and luggage soon arrived. Mother, Mary Jo and I ran with our snacks through the house to the open verandah.

"Oh, Mom, Wei Hai Wei is still here!" I cried. "Just look at that view."

The great blue sky welcomed us. Red roses lit by sunshine climbed a pillar. Amah and the coolies took care of the unpacking while the Houseman and Cook rummaged around in the kitchen and discussed the foods that were needed. Mother stretched out on a chaise and we girls perched on the terrace stairs, content. A welcome peace embraced us all.

Suddenly the noise of approaching airplanes broke into the serenity.

Mother disappeared behind a chair.

Mary Jo and I ran into the house; we had experienced the attacks on Shanghai. I was panicking, my heart beating furiously. Our servants stood stiffly in place, waiting. They too had experienced the bombing of Shanghai three years earlier.

Amah was on the terrace trying to calm Mother. "No fear, Missie. No fear, Missie."

The planes, four bombers, circled lower and disappeared behind the island, presumably to land there. Mother crawled out from behind the chair and apologized.

"Sorry, girls," she said weakly. She was trembling. "Ever since being strafed, you know, Patty, when I was hiding in a rice paddy being shot at. I can't stand the sound of approaching planes. Mary Jo, you don't know the story, but the Japanese were shooting down people hiding in the water of a paddy. People were dying and screaming and the water was getting bloody. I hid in part of a bombed grave. It was awful! I'm always there in my mind when I hear a plane coming."

"It's OK, Mom," I said, my voice wobbly."We got out of the way too. Don't forget that we were in Shanghai when Chapei was burned up by the Japanese bombs." I too was trembling.

The day had lost its joy. I'd almost forgotten. The odious Japanese were here, too. I reminded myself again that the Japanese had conquered this part of China.

We settled in for the night. In this house, we were glad to find working indoor bathroom plumbing.

The next morning I sat at a table on the verandah overlooking the ocean, and yielded to the luxury of the view. Way off, over sapphire water, past all signs of the town, was the other curve of the mainland—hazy greens, purples and yellows, with the mountain ranges—lavenders, violets, yellows, flowing together—faintly visible. To the left, the Island rose abruptly, its cliffs topped by pines and firs. Here and there indistinct beaches could just be seen, and the waves, hitting rocks, splashed white. Turning to the opposite direction, blue sea became blue sky, the horizon barely visible as a tiny warp in the expanse of blue. Nearer, a three-sailed junk quietly moved toward the harbor. Smaller junks and sampans looked like amber jewels on a blue glass sea in a world silent but for the ripples, in uneven rhythms, of the waves on the beach below me.

Later we all went down to the beach. Mary Jo and I swam to one of the boats anchored near the shore and swung around on the anchor line. The water was exceptionally clear—as it had been when Lao Lu first taught me to fish; I could see the marine life below me. It was hard to separate me from the anchor line, my face in swimming goggles peering into the water.

One morning when Mother came down to the East Cliffe beach and settled under an umbrella, she found herself beside a Danish diplomat and his family. This family included a young Danish man, Rolf Eskelund, about 18 years old, perfect for Mary Jo. Mother said that he was an exceptionally nice young man. The Eskelunds and my family became good friends over the summer.

Rolf was the most courteous and thoughtful boy I'd met in my limited exposure to boys. Johnny's friends were horrid to me and the boys at school uninteresting compared to this Adonis. He was educated, he was funny, he could dance, he could sail. He was perfect. We saw the Eskelunds almost every day, on the beach or at different homes or parties. I believe that Mr. Eskelund was a Danish diplomat stationed in Shanghai.

Sailing with Rolf was a special pleasure. I had never been on a sailboat before, and I loved it. Rolf taught me how to be useful.

"If your head is in the way when the boom swings around it will toss you into the ocean with the other little fish," he said.

I screwed up my face at him.

"Now don't make a face at me. I'm serious. Always pay attention to what the skipper says. Sailing is fun but it can be dangerous."

A week later we were becalmed in a fog near Liu Gong Island. The ocean was slick, the gentle waves rounded; the only sounds were the occasional splashes and the muffled shushing of the now gray water. We crept along, Rolf calling out now and then in different accents, and occasionally we heard a ghostly "Hallooooo" back through the wet gray mist.

He began singing a sailing song in Danish:

Sejle op ad åen – Sailing up the river,
Sejle ned igen – Sailing down again
Det er vel nok en dejlig sang – That is such a lovely song
Den må vi ha' endnu en gang – We must have it one more time

The melody was simple enough for me to pick up. So we sat out the fog happily singing rounds of a Danish sailing song.

World War II was tearing Europe apart, but we in Wei Hai Wei in 1940 were dancing, singing, swimming, sailing. The radio occasionally broadcast bits of news about the war. There was an unreality about it. It didn't seem possible that the Nazis were conquering those countries. Blitzkrieg—lightning war—after Blitzkrieg, Hitler had invaded one nation after another.

Our European friends kept us informed about how the war, now in the second half of 1940, was going. Half of France had been occupied; Denmark, Holland, Luxembourg, Belgium, Norway had fallen to the Nazis. Britain was being bombed daily in what was called the Battle of Britain. The Soviet Union had taken Estonia, Latvia and part of Finland. Other radio news was that the Italians had taken parts of northern Africa, from Eritrea to Ethopia to Somalia.

"Golly," I said when we heard this. "That's just awfully sad." I paused, thinking about the Italians in Ethiopia. "Mom, do you remember, when we travelled through the Red Sea, the ship carrying the troops of Italian soldiers who waved and shouted at us?" I remembered the faces of those soldiers and was saddened to think that Italy had now joined Hitler, and that those soldiers were at war with our friends.

A few days later at a dance it was announced that all the British troops were to be withdrawn from Shanghai and North China. It felt wrong to be dancing when millions of people were suffering. Yet we were dancing. I held my tongue. What would it matter to the war effort if we, here, danced or didn't dance? I didn't want to ruin the evening for everyone.

After dinner we went to our house, turned on the gramophone, and played what records were available. I loved "42nd Street," and "Bye Bye Blackbird." They were fun to dance to and we played them over and over again on the scratchy gramophone.

Usually Rolf and Mary Jo spent time together, but one morning toward the end of August she was sick and stayed in bed. Oh joy. I had Rolf all to myself again. He took me sailing out quite far, almost to the Island, where he had room to navigate without bumping into a junk. He was in a good mood, and began singing a different song.

"I learned this one on vacation in Scotland," he said."It's a song about Bonnie Prince Charlie and the Isle of Skye." I knew the song, so I was able to join him in singing the lyrics:

Speed, bonnie boat, like a bird on the wing
Onward! The sailors cry:
Carry the lad that's born to be King
Over the sea to Skye.

Rolf knew all the verses. We repeated them again and added,
Sail bonnie boat, sail bonnie boat,
Over the sea to Skye
Carry the lad that's born to be King
Over the sea to Skye

We laughed as we stumbled over the words. Every now and then he'd tack and warn me with dire threats that the boat was coming about, and to duck beneath the boom.

During those days of relaxed laughter and innocent games, there was always the undercurrent of concern for what was happening to the Chinese people around us, in addition to the fear for the people of Europe. The Chinese were suffering. No one spoke about hunger or against the Japanese, but we could sense it. We could see it in the gaunt bodies. We could see it in the passive resistance and the inventive ways of circumventing Japan's unwelcome new dictates. We could see it in the absence of chatter and laughter. It got under Mother's skin.

"Do you remember, when we first landed, we felt that something was very wrong here? And I said I'd try to find out what was happening to the Chinese?"

"Of course I do. Do you think you could? Would it be dangerous for you?"

We talked it over for several days, then she determined that she could make a professional undercover survey of Wei Hai Wei under Japanese rule without getting into trouble. It all depended on how it was done. In correspondence with her publisher the project was code-named "*A delightful summer by a China sea.*"

She learned as the weeks passed that the Chinese had very little to laugh about. A "scorched earth policy" had been introduced by the Japanese General Yasuji Okamura in punishment for guerilla resistance against them. People like Lao Lu's sons were fighting from secret mountain hideouts. The punishment was called the "Three Alls Policy": "kill all," "burn all," "loot all."

Mother talked to as many people as she could trust: missionaries, teachers, year-round residents, former officials, shop-keepers; fishermen, farmers and boatmen. Friends like Lao Lu and *Mafu* Jim told others that they could trust her; doors opened to her. I could not be present at these meetings, but they were important to me and to my understanding of what was happening to China. Mother asked me to help type up her notes and gave me permission to quote from them for a school project.

In her outline for her future book, which I here quote with permission from her book *Flight From China*, Mother wrote:

"Before the summer was over, I was to witness Japan's wheels grinding down a self-respecting people – grinding day by day, with calculated cruelty, machinelike thoroughness. Under direction from a realistic Tokyo, they ground without mercy, like the wheels of Hitler's war machine. It was shattering to see a fine people I had known in prosperous independence reduced to slavery – literal slavery; to see their village and countryside suffer under the blight of Nippon.

"As it was in Wei Hai Wei, so it was, in varying degrees, in the thousands of occupied villages. Wei Hai Wei had not been burned or bombed, and in this was more fortunate than countless districts. The occupiers wanted to use this harbor themselves.

"The bitter cry of every Chinese with whom I talked, regardless of position, was that the Japanese had broken his rice bowl... To 'break a man's rice bowl' is one of the worst crimes in China: it is to take away a man's livelihood.

"That is what the Japanese were doing – causing slow starvation in a fertile land where once there had been plenty. The military stationed at the port lived on the country. And the farmers with calculated resistance were growing little. I heard of one district where Japanese soldiers stood over the farmers while they planted the fields. After sunset, when the Japanese were in their barracks, Chinese women slipped out to the fields with hungry field mice hidden in baskets, and there released them. The Japanese could not understand why the spears of green grain did not appear.

"One afternoon while walking in the country we saw Japanese soldiers search a house for bags of grain and peanuts that they believed the farmer had hidden away for the winter. They took up the floor, dug underneath, sounded the walls for caches, poked into the big clay stove, emptied the chests and cupboards. No grain.

"They did not find the false roof that the farmer had built. He would remove the beams to get at the hidden grain, come winter.

"But even when they outwitted the Japanese, the Chinese were hungry. *The North China winter is long and bitter, and I was told of people who had been reduced to eating bark, roots and weeds. Often a Chinese will greet a friend on the road, 'Have you eaten your morning rice?' – that is, 'Have you eaten enough?'*

"*A greeting, meaning not literally rice, for in North China many families customarily eat kaoliang, a kind of grain sorghum. The Chinese in Wei Hai Wei were saying 'Have you eaten your morning bah-bah.'*

"*Bah-bah was a bowl of cornmeal stirred with water, or with peanut oil by those so fortunate as to have it, and steamed. A bowl twice a day with tea was all the food that many would live on during the winter. And they said it grimly but a bit proudly – for a man who ate bah-bah had not sold out to the Japanese, was not serving the military as a puppet. Bah-bah was a symbol of Chinese resistance.*

"*In Wei Hai Wei district, soldiers drove men to their work each dawn, herded them back each night – slaves to the Japanese. In each village the families were divided into tens, and one man was made responsible for the actions of the other nine.*"

"It is a terrible thing for a people when an enemy settles over the land," Mother said to me after writing the above.

A few weeks before we were to leave, Mother decided that Mary Jo and I should have lessons in Mandarin Chinese. This seemed to me a bit curious. Why would we be having lessons in Mandarin Chinese when we were leaving in a few weeks for Shanghai and the Shanghainese dialect? As sneaky and creative as she could be when she wanted something, I decided that the sudden Chinese lessons were a means of getting information on what was happening in the villages through our teacher. And, the teacher could interpret Chinese characters that Mother couldn't read.

With some difficulty she found a teacher willing to risk coming to our house. The elderly man's name in Chinese meant

Golden Bell, so he became Mr. Golden Bell. He came to see us every morning, walking on a little-known path through the hills, coming in at the back door so as not to be seen by the Japanese.

Indeed he was a source of information to Mother about what was going on in town and in the schools. He told her that school children were ordered to write compositions on subjects such as "The Japanese Soldier—Savior of China" and "Japan Will Drive the Foreign Imperialists from China." The students, he said, wrote with double meanings, using classical phrases that the Japanese didn't know.

Mr. Golden Bell taught me a Chinese song about the sun that had a pro-Japanese version. That, he didn't teach me. What I learned was:

Tai yang huang- The sun is yellow太陽黃
Tai yang liang The sun is light太陽亮
Tai yang zao lai The sun rises early 太陽早來
Ming guang guang Very, very bright :明光光

The approved Japanese version also had the words:

"The sun of Japan is very, very bright."

There were several verses extolling the virtues of Japan, but we didn't learn them either.

Mary Jo and I had our lessons in a corner of the verandah with the bamboo blinds drawn so that our teacher wouldn't be seen. Sometimes Japanese soldiers would march up in formation, set up machine guns in the garden, and practice firing at nearby targets.

One day they came up to the doorstep. Mr. Golden Bell, hiding behind the blinds, and we, were hardly able to breathe from fright; my heart beat in erratic knocks. But they just picked all the red flowers framing the stone edge of the terrace, then walked away.

"I guess they were spying on us," Mary Jo decided.

The summer vacation was ending. We held a good-bye party at our house, hanging lanterns around the house, in the garden, and by the gate. A full moon added heartache to the evening.

The next day, Rolf and his mother left for Shanghai."He was just perfect, wasn't he, Patty," Mary Jo sighed. I agreed with her."Do you suppose we'll ever see him again?"

"Probably not, with the war and everything going on," she answered."I know that Dad is sending me back to America in a couple of months. He thinks it's too dangerous now for us to stay in China."

"I hate this war that makes us lose people we really care about."

We spent the rest of the day playing on the raft and talking with other friends, boys who were soon to return to their boarding school, the respected China Inland Mission in Cheefoo (Yantai). Their school, a boy named Owen said, was made up of rambling, ivy-covered buildings built fifty years earlier."It became an English boarding school for children of missionaries like us, and of other foreign residents in Asia. We get a regular English 'public school' education." I had heard about the quality of the school even in Shanghai.

Mother delayed our return to Shanghai and school till the end of August because she wanted to see the Japanese version of the ancient Chinese "Festival for Saving the Souls of Those Drowned During the Year," also called the Seventh Moon Festival. It was one of the Lantern Festivals, an exotically beautiful, somewhat eerie event.

Each past summer in Wei Hai Wei we would all climb the pine-covered cliffs that bordered the bay, and as twilight deepened we would await the festival. Soon a great golden moon would light the hilltops where rose-walled temples nestled, and the rippling ocean became silver lace.

The sound of beating drums and clanging cymbals would grow loud. Chinese children carrying lighted lanterns shaped like lotus blossoms wound through the narrow village streets to the jetty. There, they would join their elders in singing to the lotus flower lamps, asking them to save the soul of a lost one. Chinese women gathered along the shore would set afloat tiny lotus-like boats bearing lighted candles. And suddenly, as the tiny boats floated out to sea, the bay would be sparkling with lights.

I was almost able to sense the ghost *(gui)* of those drowned during the year rushing joyously by, freed from the seas by the guiding lights of the votive lamps. And after the little lights in the bay would have burned out and only the great moon remained, my brother and I went with Amah to a feast given by a farmer friend of hers.

But that was how it was, summer after summer, before the Japanese invasion.

This summer, the Japanese banned the festival a week before the event. In its place the Chinese were "invited" to attend the "Festival for the Japanese Souls Who Had Died Saving China from America."

"Jap man blong one very big damn fool," Amah said angrily. "He take away Chinese-man rice bowl, now he take away he play-play."

The simple country people—fishermen and farmers—were already suffering under heavy new requirements imposed by the Japanese. I heard talk about taxes, about kidnapping men to work in the Japanese labor camps up north, about women having to please men they didn't like. And now they banned this beloved festival.

Mother was invited by a British official stationed at the naval station to attend the new Japanese Festival. She managed to include Mary Jo and me. Amah always accompanied us.

Early that morning we woke to the beating of drums and shouts in Japanese. Then we saw groups of Chinese men, women and children—escorted by Japanese on horseback with drawn bayonets—being lined up the street to watch a Japanese propaganda parade. We were taken to a Chinese temple to watch movies about the glories of Japan, then were excused. Chinese and foreign officials were ordered to go to the ceremony for the Japanese dead.

Japanese flags flew high on every building and pole when our *mafu* and jalopy took us to the port early that afternoon. Still lining the road were the exhausted Chinese who had been forced to stand there in the hot sun since dawn.

'Mom," I complained,"can we stop to give those poor people a drink of water? Or make the Japanese give them a chance to sit down? They're suffering."

Mother answered,"Hush. You know how dangerous it is to offend a Japanese in China. Of course I wish we could help but we would only be thrown in jail or bayoneted like chickens." She added,"And, the Japanese might punish the Chinese for not standing straight enough or something like that. They might punish them for our interference with Japanese orders."

Several of us Westerners joined the crowd of Japanese moving up a wide path toward the Shinto Shrine, where the ceremony would be held. The road was bordered with large four-sided lanterns. We noticed that groups of Japanese soldiers paused before the lanterns, and began laughing uproariously.

"What thing, Missie?" Amah asked.

Mother was the only one of us with enough courage and knowledge of Chinese to go up to the lanterns.

She reported back, her face and voice under careful control. I could see that she was furious.

"Each of the four faces of the lanterns has a drawing ridiculing Americans," she said."On one, a panel shows a U.S. sailor dancing all night, another shows a Marine falling drunk out of a bar. On the third a U.S. soldier is carrying a bag of golf clubs instead of a gun, and in the last one, a pilot is on horseback playing polo.

"In the next lantern they show the U.S. as a frightened, pleading Uncle Sam, writing notes to a big Japanese soldier laughing in his face. Others show Japanese planes bombing our schools and homes."

"My God," Mary Jo said, angry and upset."Is this what they're teaching the Chinese about us?"

A friend translated banners hanging on buildings.

"Japan, Manchuguo, China — three happy brothers — we unite to drive the hated American into the sea."

"That is sickening. The Japs are the ones that should be driven into the sea," I muttered.

Another: "One, two, three, Japan, Manchuguo, China. Three happy brothers, happy brothers together."

We couldn't bear any more of this and decided to leave. But then a drunken Japanese soldier lurched up to us. He was carrying a cheap little American flag, probably made in Japan for sale in the U.S. When he saw us he threw the flag in the dust, laughed and spat on it, then stamped on it. I was so angry that Mother had to restrain me from hitting him. Amah's face blanched; before any of us could stop her she was shaking her fist in his face.

"How fashion you hit my Missie flag!" she shouted. Her voice carried over the crowd."Jap man blong one big damn fool think so he can fight American man. Just now Jap-man have catch head more big he hat, plenty cheeky. Littie-time, American soldier-man help China fight Jap. Jap-fool no got face, my savvy."

My heart filled with love for this woman."Oh, Chiao Kuei, you are so brave! I so proud of you!" I hugged her."I love you!"

Amah didn't hear me. She was shaking, her hands clenched tight. Suddenly she stooped, picked up the wad of red, white and blue, and brushed it off tenderly."American flag good, blong all same my flag."

Mother turned to Amah, quietly put her arms around her. She was crying. She loved Amah; she loved China. This was hurting her.

The Japanese soldier, perhaps stunned by Amah's outburst, disappeared.

We sailed back to Shanghai on September 6th, on the *Shenking*. The three of us and our staff were in a hurry to get home to our familiar safety in the protected International Settlement and away from the Japanese.

I lightly rub my eyes, reflecting. Those days in the beauty of Wei Hai are today as vivid in my memory as if I were still there. A British friend has sent photographs of today's Wei Hai; these show the industrialization of the port, the factories, the heavy construction along what had been the beaches. They also show new residential areas. My friend winters in Shanghai and summers in Wei Hai—just as we had done. Oh where is my magic carpet!

I am now the reverse of that little girl in Shanghai reading the Stevenson poem under the mosquito netting and who wanted to go off on a boat to see the world; I would like to return to see what Shanghai,

Wei Hai, Shanhaiguan and Beijing are like today, seventy years later. I'd like to see a Shanghai without the extreme poverty of the rickshaw coolies, and with its streets all bearing Chinese names rather than those of foreign leaders. There would be Chinese flags in the harbor at The Bund, and no one would speak Pidgin English.

How amazing that would be.

XXI
FAREWELL TO CHINA, NOVEMBER 1940. AGE THIRTEEN

THERE HAS BEEN *too much loved and lost. One home after another. One life after another. The series begins now, in this chapter, in a China become too dreadful.*

I am told that it is God within me that causes me to cry at the altar; that may be so, I don't know. But I am grateful that God balanced me with much, much to be happy about and to be thankful for. I am grateful to have a playful and optimistic nature with which to meet problems. I am grateful for my interesting, attractive children and grandchildren, I am grateful to have good friends to giggle with, and I am grateful for TV programs like Frasier *and* Whose Line is it Anyway *that make me laugh out loud alone at night and* Fox & Friends *to wake me with good cheer every morning.*

That may sound trivial to others, but, well, you haven't lived my life. As Oscar Wilde wrote, "We should treat all the trivial things of life seriously, and all the serious things of life with sincere and studied triviality."

I noticed that Father looked tired and older when, overjoyed at our arrival, he met us at the dock with Ah Ching. Two months alone in the humidity of summer, exacerbated by difficulties created by the Japanese, must have been hard on him. He hugged me twice, patting me on the head.

"You're getting to be a very pretty young lady," he said. I was thrilled to see him again."Oh, Daddy, the Japanese have been just awful! They are starving the Chinese in Shantung. Nobody is laughing except in private and everyone is shabby and thin."

"Is that so?"

"Yes, and *Mafu* Jim looks like a lot of walking bones! Oh I'm so glad to be home." I wrapped my arms around his body, safe at last.

But the next morning, in my familiar bedroom, I met the new Shanghai. The former customary thump-thump thump-thump-thump of the Japanese guns of war had ended. Now, Japanese soldiers playing bugles and drums with forced musical jollity marched by. I angrily slammed my bedroom window shut. Japanese music of any kind did not enchant me. I preferred the sound of the mortars. Johnny wasn't across the hall from me to share thoughts with; I missed him.

After a few days I realized that the unpleasantness of living under the Japanese occupation in Shanghai hadn't abated. Rather, our lives became harder as the Japanese tried to drive us out in order to take all of China. Calamities kept befalling our servants.

Father's bi-monthly accounting with the staff became very difficult. One tragic story of hardship followed another."Mister Potter," intoned Ah Kung soon after we arrived,"Jap-man take Cook boys fight China-man. Cook Mama no got sons for helpee he. What can do Mister?" Of course Father didn't know what to do. Then came Lin Sing."Jap-man takee my sister for play-play. My think so she dead plenty soon. *Ai yah!*" Fo Sun's new buffalo, and now his chickens too, were stolen. Vegetables became scarce, so seeds were cherished.

Our vegetable farm now generated food for our whole staff

and their extended families as well as for ourselves. The greatest problem was that rice was scarce. There were "rice riots" because the price had gone up insufferably high.

Many American businesses, concerned over future operations, moved their headquarters out of China, leaving skeleton staffs.

I was back at the Shanghai American School. The classes were smaller as many students had left. Lessons in algebra or irregular Latin verbs seemed irrelevant.

My route to the school and back passed the bodies of huddled people, the dead and the dying, on the sidewalks and doorways. New groups replaced those who had drifted away. The starving Chinese lacked the energy to wave or call for help; they just sat, staring into space, waiting. Later, some day, they too would be brushed away, like the leaves, like trash. I had to look away from them as we drove through the streets.

In September the Nazis in Shanghai were still celebrating the June fall of Paris. The realization that half of France was now under German rule became real to me only after I heard that there were photographs of Hitler triumphantly entering Paris under the Arch of Triumph. German swastikas now joined the flags of Japan and France flying high all over the French Concession, where the French flags had proudly flown, alone, not subject to any master.

Erika and I discussed what was happening and what the future might be. "Hundreds of French citizens are now staying in their homes," she told me. "They are deeply worried about their families in France. They can't get news, any more than we Austrian Jews can." The French Concession was subdued; the formerly lively restaurants and cafés closed; the detested trio of flags everywhere. One day we drove past the darkened Russian Tea Room, and I wondered about the waiter with the twitching moustache. Was he alive?

It was as though a gray veil had enveloped the French Concession.

I began to think about evil. I felt waves of evil around me so strongly that I began to write an essay on the subject. The Japanese "rising sun" naval flag with rays reaching out, and the official one, the large red fried egg "sun" flag, vied with the German swastika in symbolizing evil. The only difference was that the Japanese flags were everywhere in China. Over every barricade, over every Chinese building. High above us that flag streamed, screamed THIS IS JAPAN!

"To me, what they call the Rising Sun is a like a monster sending out deadly rays to harm us and our Chinese friends and neighbors," I told Erika.

"There's no getting away from them, is there," Erika said. "That flag just flaps in our faces."

There were ever more Japanese soldiers throughout the city except in our safe cocoon. Sand bags, barbed wire barricades, machine guns and soldiers were stationed at every entry into the International Settlement. Gun-bearing soldiers, insulting and arrogant, clunky and coarse, bayonets drawn and gleaming in the sunlight, checked us out with bully's eyes every time we crossed into a formerly Chinese-run part of Shanghai. They still forced Ah Ching to get out and kowtow down almost to the street when leaving or entering the International Settlement.

Worse, to my growing discomfort, they stared at me with unpleasant speculation, now more openly than at the beach, as though I were a goose they were appraising. I asked Mother about it. "Try to stay out of their way, darling, and by all means avoid eye contact," she said. "You aren't a little girl any longer and these Japs like to kidnap pretty young ladies. You must be very, very careful."

Father told us over dinner one night about a lovely surprise that had happened a few days before we returned.

"Tailor approached me one morning with the gift of a set of hand-made handkerchiefs that he had embroidered, with my initials on them." He reached into his pocket."Here is one of them."

"It is exquisite, isn't it," Mother said.

He told us that this was Tailor's present to the family of Glowing Pearl, Sew Sew Amah Mary's daughter, and reported the conversation to us.

"My too muchee wanchee marry Glowing Pearl," Tailor had said."Wanchee he be my wife. But my no got go-between, no can do proper Chinese fashion. Glowing Pearl no got Father, no got brother, all dead. Mother Mary all same me. My family all dead. So my think so you blong Glowing Pearl family, you blong he Father. Can do, Mister? OK marry daughter? My too much likee Glowing Pearl.'

Father had been stunned, and pleased. He replied:

"My talkee Glowing Pearl and Mary, I think so can do, but wait my talkee them."

Tailor smiled broadly."Thank you, Mister. *Zhia zhia noong*," he had said, bowing slightly, his hands together."My not got cash for makee big present, Mary no got cash for present. You takee hankerchief my makee?"

"Handkerchief beautiful," Father replied."I likee very much, you make good wedding present. You go now, I talkee Glowing Pearl."

Father told us that he'd sent Lin Sing to bring Sew Sew Amah Mary and Glowing Pearl to his study. While he saw Sew Sew Amah Mary often, he had never paid much attention to her daughter who came over generally when he was downtown at his office.

Mary, wearing the customary costume of a house servant,

black baggy pants and jacket, ushered in a slender girl of about
18. In order to present her daughter formally, she had dressed
her in a *cheongsam,* the traditional dress of a lady. Glowing Pearl
entered with her eyes cast down as was expected of a well-bred
young woman.

"Mister Potter, *zhia zhia noong,* this blong my girl Glowing
Pearl," Mary introduced her, then stepped back with lowered
eyes.

"Come in, Glowing Pearl," Father welcomed her.

"Good afternoon, Mister Potter."

Her pink silk dress shifted over her slim body as she stepped
forward. She didn't look up at him. "Well, young lady, Tailor says
he want marry you. What you say?"

The girl's cheeks turned a light pink. She then looked up at
Father. Her face came alive as she raised her eyes.

"Oh yes, Mister Potter. My too much likee he." She smiled,
and an unexpected dimple appeared on her left cheek. She is
adorable, Father thought.

"You think so he makee good husband?"

"Yes, please."

"You think he makee good babies?"

Her cheeks colored again, and the dimple reappeared. "My
think so makee number one goodee babies," she said, smiling
shyly.

He called Mary back in.

"Mary, I think marriage good between Tailor and Glowing
Pearl. Two nice people, very pretty."

Mary bowed, her eyes lowered, her hands together, a broad
smile on her face. Father continued, "But we no can do Chinese
fashion, no got go-between. Jap-man makee too muchee problem.
You and Tailor no got cash for give presents. I think so more
better my be family man for Glowing Pearl."

He showed Mary and her daughter the handkerchiefs that Tailor had made."Tailor make this present for me so he can marry Glowing Pearl," he said."Now I give present from Glowing Pearl's family to Tailor." He reached into his desk in the center of the room, drew out some bank notes, folded them, slipped them into an envelope, and gave it to Mary."This is for Tailor from Glowing Pearl family for wedding present. You give to him, can do?"

The two women almost wept with joy.

"Missie come home next week. I talkee her, we talkee Cook, Gardener, Ah Kung, Lin Sing, for Tailor and Glowing Pearl get married. I think so more better here in my house and garden."

With expressions of gratitude and appreciation, the women had left the room.

His recital of the events done, he now grinned at Mother."What do you think, Edna Lee, isn't that a nice surprise?"

The wedding was planned for late in October, a month after our return. This brought great joy to the household; they were an attractive, likeable young pair. The staff became obsessed with preparations for the wedding. Tailor's room in the servants' wing was redecorated for the bride. Mother bought a new bridal bed according to custom. The Chinese kitchen and our kitchen were stocked with foods for the wedding guests. The feast was to be in our courtyard. Strings of red firecrackers had been bought and musicians hired.

Tailor made Glowing Pearl's bright red silk wedding jacket and skirt as well as his own red silk suit for the ceremony. It was harder to find the necessary red shoes so he covered a pair of their regular shoes with the silk.

The joy was contagious and brightened the spirits of all of us. Even amid Japanese oppression love could blossom, and this brought hope to everyone.

Then, two days before the wedding, our world crashed.

I woke to thunder and lightning and wondered what the heavy wind and rain would do to the preparations for the wedding in the courtyard.

The kitchen was silent. I went back up to find Amah crying soundlessly in her room, her face hidden in her folded arms.

"What thing, Chiao Kuei?" I asked, putting my arms around her."Big wind makee too muchee trouble for wedding?"

She shook her head."More better you talkee you Mama, Littie Missie," she said flatly."Too muchee big trouble come."

I found Mother sitting up in her bed, trying to drink a cup of tea without spilling it. Her hand was shaking. Father just sat with his head in his hands.

"Mom, Daddy, what's going on?"

He answered,"There's been a great tragedy in the family," he said quietly."Edna Lee, will you tell her? I can't."

Mother wanted to avoid the task, but couldn't."Patty," she finally said,"The Japanese have harmed Glowing Pearl. There won't be a wedding."

"What?"

"Last night Japanese soldiers prowled through the neighborhood where Sew-Sew Amah Mary lives. They saw Glowing Pearl in the kitchen preparing dinner. They went in after her. She ran screaming and they knocked her down and— and hurt her." Mother stopped to catch her breath, took another sip of tea."When she lay unconscious on the floor one of the soldiers took out his sword, raised it high—" she stopped again, her voice choked."High, then brought it down on her body, chopping her in two . . ."

"Oh, Mama!"

". . . just like a spring chicken."

It was time to leave China. This Japanese China. I could not live in this place any longer. A few evenings later Father presented Mother with two tickets to America on the *Monterey,* a Matson Liner.

"She leaves in four days," he said."The ship is being sent by President Roosevelt to evacuate stranded Pacific-based U.S. citizens — missionaries, teachers, housewives, socialites, artists, children — from all over the Pacific. The ship is to take American refugees back to California with the following mandate: *'Washington urges all American women and children and nonessential males in Japan, Manchukuo, China, Hong Kong, Indo-China, Dutch East Indies to evacuate at once.'*

"I know that this is very sudden but we all know that you have to leave." He glanced over at me.

"We must get you away to safety, my little sweetheart." He gave me a hug. I knew he was thinking about what happened to Glowing Pearl."I don't know when another boat will be available." Father couldn't leave — his American companies were depending on him to look after their interests in Asia, and tickets for the women and children had priority over those for men.

Mother had to agree with Father. If she stayed in China and I went to America to my grandmother's, as she would have preferred, my brother and I might be completely cut off from both parents. She didn't have a choice.

There was neither time nor inclination for goodbye parties. Everyone I knew was in shock and sorrow. My parents notified the school that I would no longer be attending. Then Mother said goodbye to a few friends who were staying in Shanghai. Father took care of providing us with funds for the next few months.

I looked at Teddy Bear House. While I no longer actually played with them, still the bears had been with me all my life; and now — what. What would happen to them? I had to pick out those coming with me to an unknown home in America. Suddenly weak from grief, I sank into my old Mammy Doll's arms again, comforted by her for the last time. I knew there was no room for all my bear family. It was bad enough that I had to leave behind my home, dog, Amah, Erika, our household, most importantly my father. My Daddy! Everything. But I also had to leave behind the bears' house and all of its furnishings, the embroideries that Tailor and I had made for the beds, the rugs and curtains.

I patted the Mammy Doll's smiling face once more, then walked over to Teddy Bear House, opened its front door. I touched the stairs with their carefully fitted tiny runner, fingered the embroidered sheets on the beds; turned the miniature chandelier lights off and on. Gently I placed the left-behind bears onto chairs, tucked some into beds and, tears running down my cheeks, bade them each farewell. What would happen to them? What would the Japanese do to them?

Slowly, slowly, I stuffed the bears coming with me into their own tiny wardrobe trunk. This was the third overseas trip for the little trunk and bears.

I turned off the chandelier lights and shut the front door of Teddy Bear House. Then with aching heart I smoothed one hand along the banister that I'd slid down with so much laughter and naughty pleasure, and, carrying the tiny trunk, walked slowly down the two flights of stairs and out to the car.

The last words of my Shanghai diary, dated October 28th, 1940: "Waiting for the boat to arrive."

Suddenly we were on the tender taking us out to the ship with what clothing and papers we could get together on such short notice for the two month-long boat trip and – what. Where.

Father and Fräulein Erika boarded the *Monterey* with Mother and me to see us off. Erika handed me a lovely two and a half inch brooch of a graceful Chinese lady as a goodbye present. She also tucked my little teddy bear trunk into a corner of our cabin.

Then we heard the "All visitors ashore!" announcement and the first deep sound of the ship's horn. I hugged my Erika and my father as hard as I could, then had to let them each go. For this parting there was no band, there were no bright streamers being tossed across from the boat to the farewell parties. There were hundreds of refugees leaving China, all crying.

Mother and I at the rail watched the tender carry Father and Erika back to the dock. There we saw the rest of our family, our household, the people who had cared for me and taught me right from wrong: my Amah Chiao Kuei, Ah Kung, Lin Sing, Cook, Ah Ching, Fo Sun, Elder Coolie, Tailor, Sew Sew Amah Mary, both Gardeners. All were wearing a bit of white cloth in memory of Glowing Pearl. I was so choked with tears that I couldn't speak, just wave, blow kisses, and look at each face with all the love in my heart.

They couldn't speak either. Tears were running down Amah's face. To these people, we were their family, as they were ours. Their lives too were being tossed into chaos.

Now Lin Sing set off long strings of red firecrackers.

Mother began sobbing.

"The firecrackers wish us fair winds and seas cleared of evil spirits. I can't believe this is happening!" She reached out to hold my hand tightly.

"What will happen to them?"

"Daddy will do the best he can to see that they are safe and nourished, but" — her voice broke — "I don't know what will happen to any of us, including Daddy. I don't know what will happen to him and I'm so frightened for him. I just wish he were with us."

The deep tone of the ship's horn sounded again. The powerful engines turned and groaned As the anchor chain was winched up, the *Monterey* began slowly to get underway, a few inches at a time. Shouts and cries of farewell from the dock faded as we moved further out. Oh! Now I could no longer hear them. Then I couldn't see them. Overwhelmed with sorrow I said a silent prayer for my family.

My next diary began on November 3rd. I wrote: "The tender just left. That means that in two hours we'll start moving out to Manila. This afternoon I had to have a cholera inoculation because we are going there, and it was very painful. My upper leg is quite sore and a bit swollen. I'd better close now."

A year ago, when I was researching material for this book, I dug through old diaries and writings that had survived many journeys. Among them I found some thoughts written after Glowing Pearl was raped and butchered. My last days in China had been shaped by incomprehension and a hurt so profound that it became hard to breathe.

Still, I am very grateful for having China in my essence — having been not just "in," but more, "within" China, plunged within, encompassed by, feeling, smelling, tasting China. Knowing the beauty and strength of the people and the land that I was forced to leave.

From my notes after Glowing Pearl's death:

"I had learned about disease, poverty, war and death. I never knew about Evil until the Japanese occupation, and until my dear German friends became little Nazi monsters.

How can one comprehend evil? How to fathom deliberate cruelty?

I've learned that you have to be personally touched by evil to begin to understand that Evil exists. Evil IS. And it is contagious. Evil has marked generation after generation throughout history. Does this Evil, this apparent Schadenfreude — joy in the pain of others — go back to Adam and Eve? Is it all the fault of that snake? Evil is real but its opposite, Goodness, is also real. And, thank God, it too is contagious."

XXII
USS MONTEREY, 1940. A FLOATING REFUGEE WAREHOUSE. AGE FOURTEEN

I BOUNCE BACK quickly, determined that I will not be conquered by the conquerors, turning off part of my childhood by refusing to acknowledge it. This is my defense against the pain.

Once we were out of the river and into the open ocean I began to feel better. Standing at the railing of the USS *Monterey*, I found that I was enjoying breathing the clean ocean air again. Slowly I began to be grateful to leave behind the smells of death and decay in the city, the filth and pain of war, the uncertainty, the evil that oozed like sweat from the Japanese. I felt that at last nothing would jump out at me to scare or hurt me – there were no Japanese around. A picture of Glowing Pearl's dimpled smile rose suddenly in my mind. She had been innocently stirring the family's dinner over the fire when she was butchered.

I knew I had to stop thinking about that. I told myself that it was behind me and that I had to go forward. The future could not be worse so it would be better. I made myself focus on the present: the ship I was on; the cleanliness and calm; and I began to build the wall, the inner strength, that would protect me from the memories.

We followed the Whang Poo River through Shanghai into the mighty Yangtse River and then turned southeast toward the South China Sea, our destination the Philippines.

The last glimmer of light from China disappeared over the edge of the ocean. I turned away from the horizon to look at the people around me. A school acquaintance was standing nearby.

"Hi, Shirley!" I called. "Want to explore the ship with me?"

Our ship was beginning to move at high speed, propellers churning the water behind us, on her humanitarian mission.

November 7th we reached Manila, docked, and prepared to receive hundreds of refugees. Before disembarking, Mother and I had to line up with some 500 others to see the doctor; he had to OK our cholera shots and smallpox certificates.

She arranged for an interview with General and Mrs. Douglas MacArthur, Field Marshall of the Philippine Army at the time, as she wanted to file a story on the growing Japanese threat to the Philippines, then still an American territory.

On a broad verandah, with luminous Manila Bay spread out before us, the General spoke of the urgency of getting proper arms and training to strengthen the Philippine defenses against the Japanese. Their weapons? Rifles made of wood. How could Washington be so blind to what was happening in the Pacific? His anger and impatience were emphatic.

The discussion was interrupted by white-clad servants with trays of tea and cakes. I took a moment to observe a gecko slithering up the wall. It reminded me of how I loved to feed raw sugar to the geckos at home, and a sudden ache of loss caught me.

After a sip of his tea, Philippine Vice President Sergio Osmeña, also present, spoke up. He warned about strong new Japanese fortifications in the area — in the Marshall Islands, Yap and Palau.

We also learned about a vast atoll, Truk (Chuuk), that could hide the whole Japanese fleet. Tens of thousands of Japanese troops had been transported there, he told us.

"The Japanese," said the Vice President, "claim that the fortifications are defensive. But against whom? There is no aggressor except for Japan herself."

He spoke with bitterness. "What good are wooden guns against the Japanese?" He suggested obliquely that perhaps newspapers could convey the reality of the danger to America. Mother began typing up the story as soon as she got back to our cabin.

After we set sail again the ship snaked her way through the archipelagos in the Coral Sea, en route to Sydney, Australia.

My fellow passengers, some of them teachers from the SAS, had soon organized classrooms for the children who would be missing two months of school on the way to California. Teachers had been selected in the fields of Mathematics, English, and American History.

To my surprise and joy, my American History teacher turned out to be Noel Coward. I loved his plays and music. He was sailing to Australia on a Secret Service assignment for England, at war with Germany for over a year.

With some 200 students of different ages packed into one of the dining rooms, Mr. Coward lectured about the industrial revolution in America. The role of mass production resulting in rows of identical products met with his scorn; however, he emphasized the importance of America's manufacturing the machines of war and getting them to England. He scolded our government for not taking part in the war. He knew about the America First movement sponsored by German-Americans who intended to keep the United States out of the war.

Sydney, Australia, delighted me when we sailed into the

harbor under its great bridge. There we stayed the whole day, sightseeing as the ship took on supplies and more American refugees. Sorry that Mr. Coward was going to disembark, I made a point of thanking him and telling him that I hoped I'd see him again—playing on the words of his lovely song, *I'll See You Again.*

The city was lovely, with its broad tree-lined streets, white bands running down the center and with the smell of eucalyptus in the air. Like Southern California.

Mother was in fine form. She had just cabled her story on the Philippines and added an extra touch of glamor with mention of Noel Coward. We went to see the koala bears and kangaroos unique to Australia. Then she became more adventurous."Would you like to go to the races?" she asked."Wouldn't that be fun!" We bet on horses by the appeal of their names, pretending we knew what we were doing, but we didn't win. It was later than we thought, and we scrambled to get back on the boat in time. The day had been like a vacation.

The departure from Sydney was deeply emotional. A band was playing lively music; I heard *Waltzing Matilda* for the first time. But there was sorrow. Families and friends were being separated for long periods of time, and in most cases, their futures, like ours, were uncertain. Most were crying.

The new refugees crowded the rails, throwing rolls of half-inch wide colored streamers across to the waving relatives and friends on the dock. Sometimes a roll was caught at the other side, the tie between the thrower and the receiver symbolic. I didn't know anyone there, but couldn't resist flinging one of the streamers out high across to the dock.

I considered the streamers crisscrossing each other in the space between the passengers crowding the deck rail and the people on the dock.

"Mom," I said quietly,"The interwoven streamers are creating a sort-of tapestry of love. Don't you agree? It's just beautiful, and tragic, for as our ship begins to pull away, the streamers will begin to break; and the lives and the hearts will also be broken."

"Just like ours," Mother said in a low voice."Just like ours."

With Sydney and Noel Coward behind us, we headed toward the Tasman Sea and Auckland, New Zealand. When the day grew into evening our portholes and windows were shrouded to prevent light from escaping. As I had already had this experience, I didn't complain. Nazi submarines were reported to be prowling this region, as they had been in the China Sea.

The ocean liner sliced invisibly through the calm night. As I stood at the rail admiring the night sky, I became aware that the constellations seemed to be moving rapidly to the left. I realized that we were bearing sharply to the right. Suddenly the ship shuddered, then began to lose momentum. We came to a dead stop.

I was scared; something was clearly wrong. I went to find my mother. She was with a group of friends, also disturbed by the abrupt stop. We began to speculate on the problem, and frightening rumors began to circulate—we were under attack, we had seen a torpedo, we had just missed an obstacle. A mine. Mother reported what we had learned from the meeting with the MacArthurs; that added to the tension.

We heard clanging, scraping, squeaking sounds. Then we saw that a life raft was being lowered. I turned and saw two seamen climbing rapidly down the side of the ship; they disappeared into the night, followed by loud splashing and cries. There was a commotion on board; officers and sailors rushed around, collecting blankets, pots of hot tea, towels. Doctors and their assistants took over one of the salons, bringing in large dining room tables hastily cleared of the breakfast setup.

Finally the Captain broadcast the news to the passengers: our ship had received an SOS from a British freighter torpedoed nearby. The Captain had decided that, regardless of the possible danger to his passengers, he had no choice but to go to the wounded freighter's rescue. He had diverted our ship to its location; one of our lifeboats had been lowered into the dark sea to find and pull the survivors out of the ocean.

They returned with one of the men shaking uncontrollably. Another was wiping blood from his face. There were smells musty from wet burlap, sharp from engine oil, vaguely repellent from dirty water. The injured were moaning; some were crying for their missing shipmates.

As the great engines of the *Monterey* began to turn over again, the ship, now totally blacked out, headed for New Zealand at high speed. The survivors were rushed to the salon that had been prepared for them and were given hot drinks, dry clothes, and supplies from the ship's hospital. The next day in Auckland they were disembarked for medical care.

We picked up more American refugees in Auckland, and continued on our way northeast to Suva, Fiji. A week out I met a group of young Yale University graduate students who had boarded in Sydney. Under the sponsorship of philanthropist Anne Archbold of Washington, D.C., the students were traveling to Suva, where on a diesel-powered reproduction of the 15th-century Chinese junk the *Cheng Ho* (*Zheng He*) they were to cruise in the East Indies and the Pacific, collecting seeds, cuttings, rooted plants, and tubers. With a thousand women to every man on board, they caused a lot of fluttering and twittering among the females.

One of the Yale students, whom I'll call Ken, asked me to a movie being shown on board the ship—my first real date. I was flattered by his attention and asked Mother if I might go.

"Mmmm," she answered. She was preoccupied with writing her new book, *Flight From China,* so I was able get away with making myself look older than the fourteen that I had just become, piling my hair on top of my head and borrowing some of her lipstick. My "date" thought I was around seventeen.

Ken joined me at the railing to watch our dawn arrival into the harbor. He pointed out the *Zheng He* anchored away from the pier, a red fantasy majestically alone in the blue clear ocean, the rising sun catching its gilded spires and rising eaves.

"That's just gorgeous," I whispered.

"It's actually an elaborately fitted research laboratory, awaiting my group's arrival for an expedition to study and document Melanesian shells.

"The junk is named after the Admiral of the Western Seas, Zheng He, on his first voyage in 1405 into the unknown world at the request of the Emperor," Ken explained."Can you imagine, Patty, a fleet of 62 ships, some 600 feet long, accompanied by hundreds of transport and supply ships, arriving in India and even Kenya?"

"What an adventure!"

"The Admiral had a gift for writing." He rummaged around in his notebook, flipping its pages."Here's one of his writings:

" 'We have...beheld in the ocean, huge waves like mountains rising sky-high, and we have set eyes on barbarian regions far away hidden in a blue transparency of light vapors, while our sails, loftily unfurled like clouds, day and night continued their course rapid like that of a star, traversing the savage waves...'"

"That's just beautiful."

"He really was incredible. Can you imagine—he brought home a Somali giraffe."

"What?"

He chuckled."Yep. I was even told that in Somali, the name

for giraffe sounds similar to the Chinese word for 'unicorn.' Maybe this was the legendary animal that was so important in the birth of Confucius."

"How do you happen to know all this?" I asked, bewildered. "I thought that you were an expert on shells. Seems to me that you must have a second Ph.D. in Chinese naval history."

He smiled. "Oh, I just know about shells. Mrs. Archbold required us to learn everything we could about the junk that will be our home for months. Also, of course, this Admiral of the Western Seas interested me, so I looked for information on him."

People were beginning to disembark. Ken shoved his notebook back in its bag, and turned to me.

"Well, time to go. Maybe I'll see you in the States some time."

"I hope so. It's been fun."

The Yale research team disembarked as a group and was propelled by a small launch over to the Archbold junk.

Later, while incoming American refugees boarded the ship, the passengers continuing to the States were allowed to go ashore. The King's Wharf was lively with Fijian dancers and music. Handcraft shops lined the sides of the wooden structures. Here we bought shell necklaces and a fine *tapa* cloth made from the well-beaten bark of mulberry trees.

In American Samoa, our next destination, we picked up refugees by the hundreds.

"We're like a mobile refugee warehouse," I said to Mother. "Is there room for all these new people?"

She laughed. "We might have to stack them on top of each other, you know, like at Zung Kee's go-down!"

The Pago Pago harbor welcomed us with its ring of rich green mountains. In the beautiful deep-water port, many little boats were bearing young Samoans waiting to dive for coins tossed overboard by the passengers. I threw a coin out as far as I could to an especially energetic boy. He dove after it, claimed it with one hand, and turned to give me a wide smile and a wave. I wanted to blow him a kiss, but was too shy.

Samoan dancers met us when we docked, chanting in their melodious language and hoping to attract us to their handcraft shops. Mother and I disembarked, eager to see what they offered, but before we could do any serious shopping the *Monterey's* demanding, sonorous voice signaled us to return to the boat.

We set off for Hawaii. Here, a group of hula dancers met the boat, draping fragrant leis around us. Mother had to stay on the boat to make arrangements about our arrival, so a friend and I spent hours at Waikiki Beach. I was disappointed to find the beach cluttered with seaweed, not like the clean beaches we knew in China. But the Hawaiian music and the fragrance of plumeria entranced us, and we stayed so long that the ship had to send runners out for us; we were delaying its departure. What a satisfying feeling. Mother tried to punish me, but nothing could make me sorry for a few more minutes splashing in the waves.

When we sailed off again, it was to our final destination, America. A new, unfamiliar life was to begin.

Mother had the task during the trip from Shanghai of deciding where we were going to live, and how. After parking me temporarily in a Los Angeles boarding school, Marlborough, she contacted her agent in New York. They worked out a schedule for a lecture series about China that got us city by city from California to New York with the expenses covered and a bit to spare. Friends in New York found a place for us to live.

I loved Manhattan on sight. And so my American life began.

XXIII

...THE LOVE GOES ON...

1941-2014

1941:

<u>New York</u>: After we settled into our one rented room in the 960 Park Avenue apartment of Alice McKay Kelly, a friend of Father's from his Philippine days, I was entered in the posh Spence School.

I felt like a jumping jack. Our departure had been chaotic and my new life as far from normal for me as possible. I had fled our luxurious home with its ten live-in servants, all of whom I had known and loved all my life, to a world where we had to count every penny and I had no friends. My classmates were the daughters of the elite and wealthy Americans; I was learning how to work the office mimeograph machine to help pay for my tuition. Along with schoolwork, I had to learn to cook and clean as mother wouldn't, and how to shop for clothes. But all that was surface. The differences went far deeper.

These nice girls and I had no way of understanding each other. I had grown up seeing people dead from starvation or cholera, or slowly freezing to death, piled up on the streets. Before I was fourteen I had experienced the cruelty of the Nazis and the butchery of the Japanese. But I had also lived in and been embraced and shaped by breathtaking beauty in the kindness and courtesy and intelligence of the Chinese people as well as in their gardens and poetry. I was accustomed to luxuries that my classmates could not imagine.

There was at first a hollowness within me over the loss of my whole life and the people I loved. I couldn't talk to anyone about my real past life, it didn't fit into any conversation, so I began to develop a pretend life without a past.

Nothing had prepared me for how to live in my new world. I knew how to get things done, but not how to do them. I didn't know how to buy clothes. (No French seams. I didn't know how pretentious that sounded.) As silk was needed for parachutes, dresses were made of cotton or rayon, a sleazy new fabric. Eventually mother found an Italian seamstress, Kitty Ladelfa, who made dresses from silk material we had brought from Shanghai.

Money: its absence was not now an adventure, it was a problem. The Japanese froze our assets in China and prevented Father from earning a decent living. We shopped at resale shops (a euphemism for "old used clothes"). Mother's second book wasn't out yet and we lived on royalties from the first book, from the income from her lectures and sales of her articles to magazines, loans from old friends for Johnny's and my schooling, and sales of a dwindling amount of shares of stock.

I accompanied Mother to shops to sell some of her jewelry. She was almost weeping, shocked that it brought so little."John gave me this pin on our anniversary," she told me, her eyes filled with tears. I basted bridal gowns for two summers at Bergdorf Goodman; Johnny worked summers in cranberry bogs on Cape Cod.

Food? I could make popovers, little else. Mother refused to cook, so I scrambled eggs, toasted bread, pulled salads together and made popovers. No frozen foods or microwaves at that time.

I burned the clothes I ironed and the laundry emerged with strange spots. Both of us hated sweeping and washing floors, so we ignored those, waiting around hoping someone else would do them. Finally a distant relative, Ruhe Linn, moved in with us. Not only did she pay a little rent and like to cook, but the floors became her job and she bought our first vacuum cleaner.

What a helpless, hapless, hopeless pair of females we were. I realized, for the first time, how dependent we had been on servants.

Mother, with both of her children on scholarships at excellent schools, wrote her second book, *Flight from China*.

Shanghai: My father was holding things together as well as he could. He made preparations for what he considered would be the eventual Japanese takeover of the international settlements. Mother shared his letters, which had been smuggled out by friends:

My Sweetheart, here is some news from me so very far away from you and the children, far away in every sense. I hope it reaches you.

Lin Sing and I, in the middle of the night, have secretly dug hiding places in the garden in which we have buried some of our precious coin and other valuables to save it from the invaders. I've also made formal accounting of the property we own and of what I manage for others, of our debts and what was owed to us; that will be sent to you for safe-keeping until it is possible for you to return to me."

In his next letter he wrote about our household.

I have closed up our home and moved to the top floor of the Shanghai Club.

You'll be glad to know that I was able to place Ah Kung with a reliable, pleasant Italian family; he should be safe through the war, and perhaps we'll see him again one day, who knows.

Lin Sing remains with me as my personal assistant.

I have pensioned Elder Coolie; he and his wife have gone to his home village with enough money to last them.

Fo Sun was ordered home to the countryside by his old grandmother. Her purpose: to marry him to the daughter of an important family whose sons had been killed in the war. So Fo Sun has become husband and son, and has acquired not only a wife but also farmland and several buffalo – real wealth! Isn't that nice news!

Tailor joined the Chinese guerrilla army to kill Japanese. He died avenging the murder of his lovely Glowing Pearl. I will always sorrow over that butchery. Such a lovely girl.

Ah Ching has gone to West China to fight the Japanese; I've heard that he too was killed on the field of battle. What a fine man he was.

I have been able to find adequate positions for the rest of our staff with good people.

Our beloved Amah Chiao Kuei went to stay with relatives in Soochow (Suzhou) with a good pension. You and the children will be deeply saddened to learn that she died of a stroke a few weeks ago. Oh my sweetheart, how I hate this war.

I couldn't think about these people. It hurt too much. I was safer keeping them in a far-away recess of my mind.

Pearl Harbor, December 6, 1941

A letter after the Japanese attack on Pearl Harbor: *Our house has been commandeered by the Japanese; the legs on our dining room table and chairs have been cut to accommodate their dining habits. All the brass doorknobs are being removed to be used in some way for their war materiel.*

New York: A group of us were sitting in the lounge at school getting a bridge game going when the radio announced that the

Japanese had bombed Pearl Harbor. We all jumped to our feet in shock.

My first thought was for my father. He now had no protection from the Japanese.

"Patty, weren't you in Hawaii last year?" a British friend, Flea, asked excitedly.

Cynthia joined in."Did anyone out there expect any of this? What do you think will happen?"

As the only one who might understand what was happening, I told the girls about Mother's conversation in Manila with General MacArthur and the Philippine vice-president. The teachers asked me to address the school about China, the Philippines, the Japanese, and Hawaii. And as my classmates came to understand a little about my background, life at school became easier.

But there was the ever-present undercurrent of sorrow, a part of the rhythm of my being. It wasn't just about what was happening to China. Not just about the war in Europe with the Nazis and the deaths of soldier friends, not just about the war in Asia and the Pacific with the detested Japanese. It was about our people left behind, and living we didn't know what kind of life. I tried to put the memories and fears aside, but I couldn't. My father was in China somewhere.

Money or no money, war or no war, Mother resolutely set about getting me presented to New York society. Suddenly I found myself a sub-debutante going to sophisticated dances where I knew no boys except when Johnny could come down from St. George's or later Harvard, with his friends as my escorts. I spent a lot of time hiding in the bathroom.

1942:
<u>**Shanghai:**</u>

A horrendous Nazi plot to eliminate the Jews who had escaped to Shanghai was put in motion. It had been conceived by Heinrich Himmler, Chief of the Gestapo, and encouraged by Hitler. Himmler had sent Colonel Josef Meisinger, who had been chief of the Gestapo in Warsaw, Poland, to Japan. His mission: to bring about the "Final Solution" in China — the elimination of the Jewish people who had escaped, and any others they could take. His reputation as the "Butcher of Warsaw" preceded him. Luckily, the plan was not put in motion.

September: I entered my senior year at Spence at age fifteen.

Fall: One night at one of the sub-debutante dances I was dancing with a boy named Hank Luce. The song *Sweet and Lovely* was playing; tall, handsome and warm-eyed, he was singing it to me. But it was my Father's birthday; I was thinking about my father as we danced. My eyes had welled with tears. Of course, Hank asked why. I felt that I could trust him, and told him that my father was in a Japanese prison camp in Shanghai and that my heart was aching for missing him, for fear for his well-being. I had had no knowledge about Hank's family connection to China, nor he about mine. His sweetness to me thereafter endeared him to me. After Hank went off to war my sorrow and worry increased.

1943:

Shanghai:

February 15: Father and other Westerners were forced to march for a mile, four abreast, carrying their belongings in bundles and duffle-bags to The Bund. Tenders took them across the river to Poo Tung. Another march to the Poo Tung Prison Camp followed. They were imprisoned in warehouses that had been condemned years before by the British American Tobacco Co. as unfit for coolies.

Lin Sing joined the Chinese guerillas but continued helping Father. He smuggled some letters out past the Japanese guards; thus we learned that Father was alive and that he had built a secret oven in which he baked bread with flour smuggled in by Chinese friends.

February 18: The Jewish refugees, including Erika Resek and her family, were ordered to move into a ghetto in Hong Kew by May 15th. In America, we knew nothing about this.

May 18: The deadline for my Erika and over 18,000 other Jews from Austria, Germany and Poland to have moved into the ghetto of three-quarters of a square mile, an order imposed by the Commanders of the Imperial Japanese Army and the Imperial Japanese Navy. Already inhabited with 100,000 Chinese and Russians, the population density was twice that of Manhattan. Their lives were very hard. Some 2,000 people died of disease or starvation. The kindness of their Chinese neighbors helped to keep the majority alive.

New York:
June: I graduated from Spence; Mother arranged for my debut at the Junior Assemblies.

I was having a marvelous time in New York despite the on-going war. I loved, and love, New York. There is excitement at every corner, there's always something to walk to see or do. Like London, New York is a magnetic city.

Shanghai:
Lin Sing was captured by the Japanese, he escaped, joined the Chinese Army, and was killed in battle.

New York:
November: I became engaged to Lt. Henry Luce III, USN

Shanghai:
October 10, 1943: Mother received a State Department letter stating: *"Your husband, John S. Potter, is included in the passenger list of persons who embarked on the Japanese exchange vessel to proceed from the Far East to Mormugao in Portuguese India, the port of exchange. From there the persons exchanged will travel to reach New York about December 2..."* Father sailed first on the Japanese *Teia Maru*, transferring at the prisoner exchange center to the Swedish America Line's MS *Gripsholm*.

New York:
November:
I wrote:
   "A POEM TO MY FATHER BEFORE HIS RETURN HOME FROM PRISON CAMP"

My Daddy-John
Yes—that is what I called you.
I trotted down the stairs on baby-chubby legs
Laughing, dimpled, baby-eager.
I peeked around the corner,
Peeked into your room –
My face a funny face of baby-glee.
You played dumb – and read the paper.
My sweet Daddy, so obliging.
I peeked into the room
Sneaked into the room

So-o quietly, stealthily
Then pounced upon your bed
Bounced upon your knee squealing,
"Wake up Daddy-John! This is little birdie!
Tweet, tweet!" Do you remember?

Now I am older, Daddy-John.
Now I am just seventeen, a young lady.
My baby legs are long and shaped
My fatty hands have tapered
For me are earrings – heels – and orchids
Are college weekends – proms -- and balls.
That is the surface,
And that you will expect.
I wonder whether I have changed beneath
Become a better daughter
Or a worse?
Perhaps I am like the sweet and pungent pork,
The pork that is both sweet and pungent,
Good and bad,
All at once.
I hope that I am to your taste,
As is the pork.
I hope that you will like me.

New York:
December 1: My father landed in New York; Mother, Johnny and
I were there to greet him. Some months after his arrival he joined
the Bank of China on Wall Street.

Father had aged greatly during his hard life before and at the
Japanese prison. We were amazed to watch him spoon through
his oatmeal looking for bugs. He saved every scrap of lettuce,

even leaves that were brown. He moved with uncertainty. Later as he gained confidence he became himself again. My feeling of being safe around him never changed; with his arms around me I was OK.

1945: World War II ended.
New York:
February: Mother's second book, *Flight From China*, was published. A half of it was written by my father about his imprisonment and repatriation.

Shanghai:
March: In the Ghetto, Erika and Paul Meier fell in love and married.
August: World War II ended. The Japanese began to flee from China. The Jews in the Shanghai Ghetto were liberated by the US Marines; the Resek family made plans to move to California.
Fall: My father flew back to Shanghai aboard the new Clipper airplane. I had no desire to return and looked forward to my future marriage to Hank, and to future children.

1947:
New York:
June: Hank and I were married. Father flew to New York to walk me down the aisle. After a short visit, he returned to China.

Shanghai:
Mother and Johnny, who had graduated from St. George's School, then Harvard, and had served as a Naval Intelligence Officer in World War II, returned to Shanghai after my wedding, moving into a modern building designed by Hungarian architect Laszlo Hudec.

The marriage united two China families. It is an extraordinary coincidence that my daughter Lila Frances Livingston Luce and my son Henry Christopher Luce are the great-grandchildren of one American family in China, that of the missionary Henry Robinson Luce, while also being the grandchildren of another American family, that of John Stauffer Potter, also living in China at the same time. The families were quite different. The Luces were religious and intellectual leaders and educators, living relatively simply in Shandong Province. The Potters were in business and journalism, living stylishly in cosmopolitan Shanghai. The families did not know each other in China; we met later in New York, when the Luce's grandson Henry Luce III married the Potter's daughter, me.

The families had a major common bond in addition to the Luce-Potter children: a deep, lasting love of the Chinese people. They, in turn, were respected and loved by the Chinese at all levels. The missionary Luces had been in China since 1897 under the Presbyterian Foreign Mission Board sponsored by the Lackawanna Presbytery in Scranton, Pennsylvania. My father arrived in China seventeen years later from the Philippines and Pennsylvania, my mother twenty-one years later from California.

1949:

Shanghai:

January: The Communist army was advancing; the Nationalist government retreating to Formosa. U.S. Consul-General John Cabot asked all Americans to leave as they would not be safe under Communist control. My mother returned to America.

Washington, DC:

February: My daughter Lila Frances Livingston Luce was born in Washington, DC.

Shanghai:
<u>May 25</u>: The Communist government took over Shanghai.

New York:
<u>June:</u> My stepmother-in-law Clare Boothe Luce invited me to lunch at the Colony Restaurant, then the most stylish in Manhattan. Thrilled, I shopped for the right outfit. A hat at Lily Daché, the chicest milliner, was essential, I thought. I was charmed into spending an extravagant $60 — over $600 today—for an adorable little beige straw hat with two heavy straw balls hanging down one side. A beige silk suit, a bright scarf, and I thought I was perfectly presented.

Clare was wearing no hat at all, just a delicate little ribbon tucked into carefully casual blonde waves. Strands of immense pearls embraced her neck. She looked exquisite. And while the heavy straw balls on my hat pulled it to slip down on the left side and I had to keep adjusting it, her little ribbon remained perfectly in place.

The guests arrived. First came Maggie Case, the editor of *Vogue*. Then to my surprise and delight Noel Coward, with a friend of his, sauntered up to our table. He blew kisses at the two other women and nodded to me on introduction, with no memory of having seen me before. The four of them gossiped, tossing famous names back and forth, laughing hilariously at their wit. They didn't stop during the first and second courses. No one spoke to me, and there was no opportunity for me to enter the conversation. Then, as the dessert dishes were being brought, there was a break. I took advantage of it. After all, I was someone too. I knew some people and I'd been a place or two.

"Mr. Coward," I ventured, smiling brightly, "You and I have met before."

"Oh, really? Where?" he asked.

"On board the USS *Monterey*," I replied."I was one of your pupils in the American History class."

Silence. He stared at me, his eyes suddenly widening. Then, his expression changed to shock and despair.

"You—you were one of those children?"

He dropped his head onto his hands, his raised elbows propped on the table. A spoon fell to the floor. He turned back to his hostess, and groaned dramatically.

"Oh, Clare, how I have aged! How I have aged!"

The others murmured sympathetically. I had committed a major *faux pas* by demonstrating that he (and the rest of us) had grown eight years older since that shipboard experience. They returned to their conversation. Harry Hopkins. Ilka Chase. Salvador Dali.

1950:

China:

April 24: Father had to escape from China for the last time, now under threat from the Communists. Chinese friends smuggled him out via Tientsin on the *Empire Glencoe*, heading to New York.

Summer: Johnny boarded the coastal steamer *Cheefoo* for his new life in Hong Kong. He told me that, after the Communists took over, they banned ships from entering the harbor, the radio provided only propaganda, there was no business, and Shanghai was excruciatingly boring.

"And there was a rather compelling reason to get out of town," he said: "Uncertainty about one's personal safety. At any moment, with no provocation, one could be arrested and thrown into solitary confinement or tortured in the notorious Bridge House for an unknown length of time."

USA, 1950:

<u>Summer</u>: My son Henry Christopher Luce (Kit) was born in Cleveland.

My father and mother retired to a lovely home at Lake Agawam in Southampton, New York, called "Pao Hai" — literally "Sea of Waves" but we took the pronunciation of Pao to represent Potter.

Hank's mother had a lovely home on a New Jersey hillside, which she called "Lu Shan", Luce Mountain.

On both sides, China remained alive.

Father, unable to return to Shanghai because China was closed by Mao Zedong, lived at Pao Hai for the rest of his life, relieved by visits to Europe with Mother or to me in Washington DC.

1954: Hank and I had both been so young when we married. Still, we loved each other and our families. I don't know why we quarreled so much, but we did, to the extent of making me quite sick. I know I made him unhappy too. If there had been tranquilizers at that time the marriage might have been saved. But there weren't, and our marriage ended in sorrow on all sides.

1958: I married Hungarian-born architect István Botond AIA, a refugee from Communism, an attraction that grew perhaps partly because of my familiarity with refugees. Well, to be honest he also had green eyes, blond hair, deep knowledge of music and was a gifted architect working with I. M. Pei at the recommendation of Marcel Breuer. He also danced a mean *czardas* and wooed me with the Puccini aria *"E lucevan le stelle."*

1961: Krisztina Lee Botond (Tina) was born in Manhattan.

1963: Andrew Istvan Botond (Sandy) was born in Manhattan.

1970: My father indulged his pleasure in learning, and foxed everyone by reading Pliny the Younger's letters in ancient Latin about the eruption of Mt. Vesuvius, among other tomes including the first six volumes of Will Durant's *The Story of Civilization*. He died at 87 on January 7, 1970, in Southampton.

1972: President Nixon opened up a new US-China relationship.

1973: My son Kit, who continued his family's love of China and was fluent in Mandarin, looked for our old house on a trip to Shanghai. He reported that the place looked run-down and grim; clotheslines ran from window to window with white sheets and underclothing flapping from them. Several families were living there.

1974: My romantic marriage didn't work out; in 1974 a close friend of my brother's in Shanghai, Robert Rosse, introduced me to a true-blue, hilarious, and brilliant attorney, Chauncey Brewster Chapman. I had vowed never to marry again but he talked me into becoming his wife. Through him I inherited three step-children who continue to brighten my days: Chauncey Brewster Chapman III, Rebecca Chapman Booth, and Susan Chapman.

Washington, DC
Mother had her first stroke when she was 60, and had to slow down, still miles ahead of most people. She died in October 1994, aged, according to the census, 101. Now she and my father lie side by side again, under a flowering pear tree in Southampton. His stone reads, at her request: *"Good night sweet prince."* Hers, chosen

by her children: "*And flights of angels sing thee to thy rest.*" Mother recited the stanza before the two of them fell asleep each night.

1980: Washington, D. C.

October 18: I lost my husband Brewster, just six years after we were married, to a heart condition. This was a man I respected and appreciated more every day; and every day he let me know that he thought I was wonderful. His children and I, and my own children, remain close.

2009: California

A phone call from Mill Valley from my darling Erika Resek Meier's daughter Pat, who was named after the little Patty in Shanghai. Amazingly, some years earlier my son Kit, a New Yorker, had been seated beside Pat Meier-Johnson at a luncheon in California. In their conversation the strangers learned that their two mothers had lived in the same home in Shanghai some 70 years earlier. So Erika and I were often on the phone with each other after that, and were able to continue our love for each other across America. This time the news was sad: Pat said, "Mom died a few hours ago."

2013: Christmas

One of my dearest memories is of my father, old and hunched up from the cold, meeting me at the train station in Southampton when I came for Christmas with my children; and then his driving home erratically on the left side of the road in his old dark green Packard. In Shanghai, people drove on the left. The Southampton police were fond of him, knew of his past, and so didn't ticket him. But finally at around age 83 he stopped driving.

And I love the memory of Mother on a ladder hanging silver balls on a pink, yes, pink, Christmas tree in the large entrance hall at Pao Hai, a glass wall behind it reflecting the lights from the tree and also the waters of Lake Agawam; and her exclamations of joy.

This year, for Christmas I gave to Lila a treasure from my past life—the *Fables de la Fontaine* with etchings by Gustave Doré that had been in my parents' library in Shanghai, then given to me for a birthday. It was a curious feeling to think of it there and to see it here. It had been packed away and stored at the Zung Kee warehouse until, during the four-year window after the Japanese and before the Mao Communists, it was shipped to America with other precious family possessions.

January 4, 2014, Martha's Vineyard, Massachusetts

My brother John Stauffer Potter Jr. died at 3:15 a.m. in Martha's Vineyard at age 89. His brave bold heart just stopped working. This was unexpected and is very hard to take. He leaves a wife Joanie, three sons, and grandchildren to keep his legend alive. We all worked on finishing his nearly completed new book *On the Track of the HMS Monmouth's Galleon…and Sunken Treasure!*

Spring 2014, Rockport, Texas

Shanghai and China are being passed on to my next generation. One day this spring I joined my three grandsons playing on the beach near my home in Rockport, Texas. Their parents, Sandy and Lucina Botond, had gone to buy bait. They would soon be joined by Lila Luce and her daughter, my granddaughter Glenis.

The beach was quiet; even the kamikaze seagulls had left to torture people on some other beach. With pails and bright plastic shovels, the boys were building an astonishing fort with moats and crenellated ramparts. I stopped to watch them. One of them was decorating its walls with wet sand squiggles.

"Oh my," I thought, in my mind far, far away. "That's just like Johnny and me on the beach in Wei Hai Wei. We made squiggles just like those."

The oldest, Will, age fourteen, came up to me with a wonderful sandy wet hug.

"Hi, Grandma!"

The two other boys, Henry at twelve and Thomas at eleven, ran up, crushing me most joyously with hugs and wiggly bodies.

"Hi Grandma Lovey!" Henry cried. "*Wo ai ni!* I love you!"

Thomas called out, "Grammy! See what we've made!"

How could I be happier! "Hi, guys. I've just come over for a break from writing my book about how Uncle Johnny and I played on a beach at the other end of the world, in China."

GLOSSARY

Phrase or Name as in the Text	Pinyin (拼音)	漢字	简体字 (if different)	Translation or Description
Amah	ama	阿媽	阿妈	A nanny or nurse, and a favorite of children, including the Potter kids
Ai-yah!	Ai ya!	哎呀!		An exclamation of surprise
Amherst Avenue	Xin Hua Lu	新華路	新华路	The street in Shanghai where the author lived, now known by its Chinese name, which means "New China Road"
An jing	anjing	安静	安静	"Peaceful"
Ang Lee	Li Ang	李昂		The well-known Chinese film director
Bai-Yan-Yu	baiyanyu	白眼魚	白眼鱼	The "White Eye" fish
Bailin Zen Temple	Bailin Chan Si	柏林禪寺	柏林禅寺	The temple near Shanhaiguan
Beihai (Lake)	Bei Hai	北海		The "North Lake" beside the Forbidden City
Beihai Dagoba	Beihai Ta	北海塔		The White tower on Beihai Lake beside the Forbidden City
Bohai (Sea)	Bohai	渤海		A popular seaside location for vacationers

Bu hao	bu hao	不好		"Not good"
Bund, the	wai tan	外灘	外滩	Coming from the Persian word for "embankment," as altered into German, the name for the prominent part of Shanghai which fronts the Huangpu River
Chang Hsueh-liang	Zhang Xueliang	張學良	张学良	The son of the warlord, Zhang Zuolin, who gained brief fame when he kidnapped Chiang Kai-shek, and then spent the rest of his life under house arrest in Taiwan
Chang Shou	chang shou	長壽	长寿	"Long Life!" – a toast for people on their birthday
Chang Tso-lin	Zhang Zuolin	張作霖	张作霖	A famous warlord (1875–1928) in the early 20th century
Chang'an	Chang'an	長安	长安	The former name of Xi'an, when it was the capital of China; it means,"Eternal Peace"
Chang'an Avenue	Chang'an Jie	長安街	长安街	A major thoroughfare in Beijing in front of the Forbidden City, named for the original capital of China
Chapei	Zhabei	閘北	闸北	A northern district in Shanghai which was frequently under attack by the Japanese
Cheefoo	Zhifu (now: Yantai)	芝罘 (烟臺)	烟台	A port in Shandong now known as Yantai, 烟台
Chenghai Pavilion	Chenghai Lou	澄海樓	澄海楼	A popular spot near the water in Shanhaiguan
Cheongsam	changshan	長衫	长衫	A lady's traditional, formal dress

Chiang Kai-shek	Jiang Jieshi	蔣介石	蔣介石	The leader of the Kuomintang (KMT) party in China, until defeat by the Communists forced him to flee to Taiwan
Ch'ien Lung (Emperor)	Qianlong (Huangdi)	乾隆 (皇帝)		The reign of the Qianlong emperor was known for his devotion to the arts
Chingwantao	Qinhuang Dao	秦皇島	秦皇岛	One of the Treaty Ports in the north by the ocean which was frequented by foreigners on vacation. It's name means,"the Island of the Qin Dynasty Emperor"
Chop suey	zasui	雜碎	杂碎	A dish of a mix of vegetables, meat and rice which used to be popular, but is no longer
Coolie	kuli	苦力		A menial laborer: (it means,"bitter strength")
Cumshaw	ganxie	感謝	感谢	A bonus or payment; also used to mean a tip or a bribe
Dashi River	Dashi he	大石河		A river in Shanhaiguan, which means "Large Stone"
"Deh tzao veh"	dan chao fan	蛋炒飯	蛋炒饭	Shanghainese for egg fried rice
Ding hao	ding hao	頂好	頂好	"Very good!"
Dong dee	tongqian	銅錢	铜钱	Shanghai slang for "money"
Double Happiness	shuang xi/ xixi	喜喜		A common expression of happiness for events like marriages
Dowager Empress Cixi	cixi taihou	慈禧太后	慈禧太后	The regent for the young emperor of China in the late 19th and early 20th century
Erhu	er hu	二胡		Two-stringed musical instrument

Eunuch	Taijian	太監	太監	The name of the only males, apart from the emperor, allowed into the Forbidden City
Forbidden City, the	Zijin Cheng	紫禁城		The palace in the center of the capital, Beijing
Front Gate	Qian Men	前門	前门	The southern-most gate of the immense city walls of Beijing
Fu dogs	Fu gou	福狗		Stone sculptures, commonly found in front of each side of a building's entrance, which represented lions in pre-modern China, and thus conveyed protection for those inside
"Gambai!"	"Gan bei!"	乾杯	干杯	"Bottoms up!" (literally, "Dry cup")
Gege	gege	哥哥		"Older Brother"
Gui	gui	鬼		"Ghost"
Go-down	Cangku	倉庫	仓库	In South and East Asia, a warehouse near a wharf; comes from the Malay, "godong"
Golden Bell, Mr.	Jin Zhong Xiansheng	金鐘先生	金钟先生	The name of the children's tutor in Wei Hai Wei
"Golden Lotus" feet	jinlian jiao	金蓮腳	金莲脚	The feudal custom of binding women's feet from childhood, causing them great pain and deforming the feet grotesquely, in order to please men and make them more marriageable
Great Wall	Chang Cheng	長城	长城	The wall, stretching for thousands of miles, built to repel northern tribes from attacking the Chinese peoples which proved to be insufficient, but which is visible from space

Great Western Road	Daxi Lu	大西路		The major thoroughfare through the center of Shanghai
Guilou	Guilao	鬼佬		An epithet for foreigners, which means "foreign devil"
Hakka (people)	Kejia (ren)	客家(人)		A minority peoples in the southeastern coast of the country
Hami	Hami	哈密		The oasis in the Western desert province which is famous for melons, grapes and other fruit
Han mountains	Han Shan	寒山		A mountain range near the intersection of the Pacific Ocean and the Great Wall
Hao	Hao	好		"Good!"
Hong Kew	Hongkou	虹口		A dangerous riverside district in Shanghai, that was filled with Russian and Jewish immigrants, and was occupied by the Japanese army during the war
Hong Kong	Xianggang	香港		The island state which the Qing dynasty ceded to the British for the purpose of trade, and then became an economic power
Hung Jiao	Hongqiao	虹橋	虹桥	A Western district of Shanghai where the Potters lived. The word means,"Rainbow Bridge"
Jade Gate	Yu Men	玉門	玉门	The portal through which travelers on the Silk Route depart Chinese civilization and face the Taklimakan Desert
Jiao dze	Jiaozi	餃子	饺子	Stuffed, boiled dumplings
Jiao mountains	Jiao Shan	角山		A mountain range on which the Great Wall begins its journey from the East to the West

Joss				The word comes from the Portuguese "deos (god) as altered by pidgin English into "joss," and it conveys the idea of "good luck" or of protection from on high
Joss sticks				The incense sticks seen in temples and elsewhere, during special ceremonies and at other times, are lit to get "good joss" and are hence called,"joss sticks"
Kaoliang	Gaoliang	高粱		Red sorghum, a staple crop.
Kowtow	ke tou	磕頭	磕头	The practice of kneeling in front of an emperor to show one's obedience to his rule
Kung shih fat tze!	Gongxi facai!	恭喜發財!	恭喜发财!	"Happy New Year!"
Kuomintang (KMT)	Guo mindang	國民黨	国民党	The dominant political party in the Republic era of China, as well as the party fighting against the Communists, which now rules the province of Taiwan
Kwan Yin	Guanyin	觀音	观音	In Buddhism, the female Bodhisattva of Compassion, a popular deity
Lao Lu	Lao Lu	老櫓		The boatman who transported the family while in Wei Hai Wei
Liaoning (aircraft carrier)	Liaoning (hangkong mujian)	遼寧 (航空母艦)	辽宁 (航空母舰)	China's first aircraft carrier (which still lacks capable aircraft and pilots)
Lin Zexu	Lin Zexu	林則徐	林则徐	The Chinese official whose opposition to the opium trade led to the first Opium War of 1839-42
Liu Gong Island	Liugong Dao	劉公島	刘公岛	The singular island in the bay surrounding the town of Wei Hai Wei

Liuli Chang	Liuli Chang	琉璃廠	琉璃厂	The market street in Beijing famous for shops which made the yellow rooftop tiles of the Forbidden City and also specialized in art supplies and artists' paintings and other kinds of artworks
"Hai-ah, hou-ah"	Hai'a, hou'a	嗨啊,喉阿		A guttural chant made by coolies who pull the boats along the side-paths of the waterways
Hsueh Ren-gui	Xue Rengui	薛仁貴	薛仁贵	A Chinese general (614–683) famous for conquering Korea
"Lu Shan"	Lu Shan	路山		The name of the home of the family, whose son married the author, which had its own extensive history in China
Lunghua	Longhua	龍華	龙华	In the 1940's, the location of a Japanese prison camp in Western Shanghai
Mafu	ma fu	馬夫	马夫	A groom for an exceptional horse
Mao Zedong	Mao Zedong	毛澤東	毛泽东	The charismatic Communist who founded the People's Republic of China in 1949
Marco Polo Bridge (known to Chinese as the Lugou Bridge)	Lugou Qiao	蘆溝橋	卢沟桥	The ancient bridge where the "Seven Seven Incident" took place, which started the Sino-Japanese War of 1937-1945
Mei Lanfang	Mei Lanfang	梅蘭芳	梅兰芳	The famous Peking Opera actor
Meimei	Meimei	妹妹		The word for "younger sister"
Mudong	Matong	馬桶	马桶	Shanghainese for a bucket that is used as a toilet

Nanjing Massacre	Nanjing Da Tusha	南京大屠殺	南京大屠杀	The killing of defenseless Chinese civilians and others by the Japanese Imperial Army in Nanjing
Nanjing Road	Nanjing Lu	南京路		A major East–West avenue from central Shanghai to its Western approaches
Nantao	Nantao	難逃	难逃	Confusion: This place either as to the left or as 南桃. As far as I know, neither place is the old Chinese quarter, which is the Yu Yuan area surrounded by a circular roadway
Ni hao!	Ni hao!	你好!		The common greeting in China
Nine Dragon Screen	Jiulong Pingfeng	九龍屏風	九龙屏风	A large screen sculpted out of stone in the Forbidden City
Noong ze iguh tzu loh!	"Ni shi yi ge chi lao!"	你是一個赤佬	你是一个赤佬	An insulting epithet meaning,"You're a pig!" in Shanghainese dialect
O Me Doh Veh	"a mi tuo fo"	阿彌陀佛		The Chinese pronunciation for the Sanskrit name of the Amitabha Buddha; also meaning "Limitless Buddha" the phrase is chanted by believers seeking relief from their troubles
Old City of Shanghai	Lao Chengxiang	老城厢		The last remaining vestige of the original town of Shanghai, once encircled by a wall, now ringed by a road, and a popular tourist spot
Old Dragon's Head Temple	Lao Longtou Simiao	老龍頭寺廟	老龙头寺庙	So-named because of its resemblance to a dragon, this is where the Great Wall meets the waters of the Pacific. It was thought that Manchus could not swim; therefore, it only extends a short way into the ocean

One-hundred-year-old egg	pi dan	皮蛋		An egg which has been aged by planting it into the ground with other materials intended to age it quickly, which discolors it and makes it smell
Opium	Yapian	鴉片	鸦片	The drug used by the British government to sell to the Chinese in order to balance a large trade imbalance with China due to the British love of the tea it imported from China
Opium Wars	Yapian Zhanzheng	鴉片戰争	鸦片战争	The series of wars in the 1830's and 40's which China launched against the British Empire to avenge its illegal selling of opium to the Chinese
"Pao Hai"	"Pao Hai"	泡海		Chinese transliteration of the home the family lived in when they returned to America
Pearl River	Zhu Jiang	珠江		The dominant river, which flowed through Canton (Guangzhou) and which was a major treaty port with the British government
Pei Ta Ho	Beidaihe	北戴河		A famous beach resort on the Pacific Ocean frequented by foreigners as well as Chinese
Peking	Beijing	北京		The northern capital of China, one of many in its history, which used to be called Dadu and other names
Peng Liyuan	Peng Liyuan	彭麗媛	彭丽媛	The wife of China's current leader, Xi Jinping

Pidgin (English)	Yangjingbin (yingyu)	洋涇濱 （英語）	洋泾滨 （英语）	The means of communication between people of different races for the purpose of trading and business. It derives from a mixture of several languages, and is the dialect many Chinese met by the author spoke
Poo Tung	Pudong	浦東	浦东	The eastern bank of the Huangpu river, which was created by the Huangpu river's deposits of mud, unlike the Puxi region to its west which was built on granite
Pukow	Pukou	浦口		A small port on the Yangtze River near Nanjing
Rickshaw	renli che	人力車	人力车	A two-wheeled cart usually for a single passenger and pulled by one runner. It comes from the Japanese pronunciation of the Chinese characters,"jin riki sha," which was shortened to "rik-sha"
Sampan	shan ban	舢舨		A shallow river craft used to transport cargo, and often inhabited by the owner's family. From the homophone "三板" meaning "3 planks," it was made very simply of one plank for the bottom and two for the sides
Sea God Pavilion	Hai Shen Miao	海神廟	海神庙	An ancient temple located where the Great Wall emerges from the sea in Shanhaiguan
"Seven Seven" Incident	Qi Qi Shibian	七七事變	七七事变	The July 7th Incident, which is said to have started the Sino-Japanese War of 1937-1945
Shanhaiguan	Shanhaiguan	山海關	山海关	The place where the Great Wall meets the Pacific Ocean

Shantung	Shandong	山東	山东	The peninsular province which hosted more than thirty foreign religious groups who spread the Christian gospel and built and ran schools and hospitals, as well as churches
Siccawei	Xujiahui	徐家匯	徐家汇	A region of Shanghai to its southwest
Soochow	Suzhou	蘇州	苏州	The town to the northwest of Shanghai which generated fame for it lovely and intricate gardens
Soochow Creek	Suzhou He	蘇州河	苏州河	The small stream which flows through Shanghai's northern region
Soong Mei-ling	Song Meiling	宋美齡	宋美龄	The wife of Chiang Kai-shek
Sun Yat-sen	Sun Zhongshan	孫中山		A leader of China, called the "Father of the Nation," (1866–1925), who founded the Republic in 1912, after two millennia of imperial rule
Tael	Liang	兩 or 倆		A unit of weight for silver which was used in transactions, like a coin, although shaped like a shoe
Tang hulu	tang hulu	糖葫蘆	糖葫芦	A winter treat for children, made of jujubes and other kinds of fruit, which were then glazed with sugar
Tianxia Diyi Guan	Tianxia Diyi Guan	天下第一關	天下第一关	The legend, composed by Xiao Xian (583–621), which was inscribed on a stone edifice in Shanhaiguan, which means, "The First Pass Under Heaven"
Tianshan	Tian Shan	天山		The Heavenly Mountains, a mountain range in the far west of the country

Tian An Men Square	Tian'anmen Guangchang	天安門廣場	天安门广场	The immense central square in Beijing, just south of the Forbidden City
Tientsin	Tianjin	天津		An important city in China's north, as it was the nearest port for Beijing
Tongren Fuyuan Tang	Tongren Fuyuan Tang	同人扶元堂		The true Samaritans in Shanghai in the 1930's, this benevolent society fed and sheltered the poor and homeless, and removed the dead from the city's streets
Tsingtao	Qingdao	青島	青岛	A city in peninsular Shandong province on the Pacific Ocean, famous for German beer, spring water and its beaches, where many foreigners spent summer vacations
Waah, noong sa ning, ah ?	wei, ni shi shei ren, a?	唯，你是誰人,啊?	唯，你是谁人，阿?	The common telephone greeting, in Shanghai dialect, which means,"Hello, who are you?"
Waitan	wai'tan	外灘	外滩	The Chinese name for The Bund—the stretch of shoreline in central Shanghai along the Huangpu River, where many important buildings were located
Wanping Town	Wanping Cheng	宛平城		Town near Beijing which was used by the Japanese army while preparing to attack the Chinese armies in the south
Wei Hai Wei	Wei Hai Wei	威海衛	威海卫	The seaside vacation spot for British and Americans, on the tip of Shandong, surrounded by the ocean, which was an important bastion for the British Navy

Weihsien	Weixian	威縣	威县	An important town at the end of the rail system in peninsular Shandong province, which was used by the Japanese army as its headquarters
Whang Poo River	Huangpu He	黃浦河		The most prominent river running through Shanghai and past The Bund
White Tiger of the West	Xifang Baihu	西方白虎 (星化)		Because of his many victories in battle, a famous legend had it that Xue Rengui was the reincarnation of General White Tiger of the Celestial Army. (White Tiger is one of the four constellations in Chinese astrology)
Wing On (Department Store)	Yong An (Baihuo Shangdian)	永安 (百貨 商店)	永安 (百货 商店)	A famous department store, founded in Shanghai and now located in Hong Kong, whose name means "Eternal Peace"
Wu Peifu	Wu Peifu	吳佩孚		A famous warlord (1874–1939) who battled the government and other warlords from 1916 until 1927, and whose wife became a friend of the author's mother, Edna Lee Potter
Xiao Xian	Xiao Xian	簫銑	簫铣	A legendary ruler of the Liang Dynasty, Xiao Xian (583–621) defeated the Sui Dynasty's army, but was captured and executed by the emperor of the new Tang Dynasty
Xuan Zang	Xuan Zang	玄奘		A Buddhist monk who lived in the 7th century and is said to have introduced China to Indian Buddhism
Xiexie!	Xiexie!	謝謝!	谢谢!	"Thank you!" in Mandarin

Yanhuang Chunqiu (magazine)	Yan Huang Chun Qiu (zazhi)	炎黄春秋 (雜志)	炎黄春秋 (杂志)	A prominent and unusually outspoken magazine of political and cultural matters in China
Yangtze River	Chang Jiang	長江	长江	China's greatest river, which flows from Tibet and empties into the Pacific Ocean near Shanghai
Yongding River	Yongding he	永定河		The river which flows under the Marco Polo (or Lugou) Bridge
Yongle (Emperor)	Yongle (Huangdi)	永樂 (皇帝)	永乐 (皇帝)	A Manchu, born as Zhu Di, who was renamed Yong Le ("Eternal Joy") when he became emperor and whose important reign dated from 1360–1424
Yuan Ming Yuan	Yuan Ming Yuan	圓明園	圆明园	The Emperor's "Summer Palace" outside of Beijing
Yuloh	Yaolu	搖擼	摇橹	A scull, the paddle used at the stern, which sways back and forth to propel the boat
Yangtze River	Chang Jiang Yangzi	長江 洋子	长江	The longest river in Asia, its name in Chinese means "long river." Its Western name, "Yangtze," meaning "son of the ocean," — a misunderstanding by Marco Polo and all later cartographers
Zheng He	Zheng He	鄭和	郑和	Living from 1371-1433, he was the greatest mariner in Chinese history. A Hui Muslim, he was a eunuch in the Ming Dynasty court, and led many extensive voyages throughout Asia and as far as the east coast of Africa
"Zhia zhia Noong!"	"Xiexie Nin!"	"謝謝, 您!"	"谢谢 您!"	"Thank you!" in Shanghai dialect
Zhu Di	Zhu Di	朱帝		The name of the Manchu before he ascended to the throne, becoming the Yongle Emperor

Sources

- Angulo, Diana Hutchins. Peking Sun Shanghai Moon. Hong Kong: Old China Hand Press, 2008
- Bacon, Ursula. Shanghai Diary. Dark Horse Books 2004
- Ballard, J. G. Empire of the Sun. New York: Simon and Schuster, 1984
- Blumenthal, W. Michael. The Invisible Wall. Counterpoint 1998. From Exile to Washington. Overlook 2013
- Booker, Edna Lee.News is my Job. New York: The Macmillan Co., 1940 Flight From China. New York: The Macmillan Co., 1945
- Bull, Bartle. Shanghai Station. Carroll & Graf 2004
- Clark, Kenneth G. The Boxer Uprisingo 1899 - 1900. Russo-Japanese War Research Society
- Cobden, Richard. China and the Attack on Canton. Given to the House of Commons, 26 February 1857.
- Coward, Noel. The Letters of Noel Coward. Edited by Barry Day. Vintage Books 2009. Cranley, Tay, Johnston, Movius, Savadove, Hewitt. Still More Shanghai Walks. Old China Hand Press, 2011
- de la Vaissière. Journal Asiatique.Vol. 298, 1. (2010), pp. 157-16. Note sur la chronologie du voyage de Xuanzang."
- Earnshaw, Graham. Tales of Old Shanghai. 2008. Earnshaw Books
- Esherick, Joseph. The origins of the Boxer Uprising. University of California Press. 1988
- Fay, Peter Ward. The Opium War 1840-1842. Chapel Hill: University of North Carolina Press, 1975
- Fairbank, John King. Trade and Diplomacy on the China Coast: The Opening of the Treaty Ports, 1842-1854. 2 vols. Cambridge, MA:

Harvard University Press, 1953.

- Fleming, Peter. The Siege at Peking: The Boxer Rebellion New York: Dorset Press, 1959

- French, Paul. Midnight in Peking. Penguin Books, 2012

- Garside; B: A: One Increasing Purpose: Mei Ya Publications. 1967.

- Gavin, Philip The Rise of Adolf Hitler. The History Place.

- Gilkey, Langdon. Shantung Compound. Harper, 1975.

- Grossman, Rosdy, Sukowa, Tausig. The Port of Last Resort. Documentary, 1999.

- H. Peter. Nazi Shanghai, Bundesarhiv website, 17 Dec. 2008.

- Hadingham, Evan. Ancient Chinese Explorers, 01.16.01, NOVA.

- Harris, David. Van Slyke, Lyman P. [2000] (2000): Of Battle and Beauty: Felice Beato's Photographs of China. University of California Press. ISBN 0-89951-100-7

- Heppner, Ernest G. Shanghai Refuge. U. Of Nebraska Press, 1995.

- Highland, Monica. 110 Shanghai Road. New York: McGraw-Hill Book Co., 1987.

- Hopkirk, Peter. Foreign Devils on the Silk Road. Amherst: University of Massachusetts Press 1980.

- Hsu, Immanuel C. Y. The Rise of Modern China, 6th ed., Oxford University Press, 2000.

- Ignatius, Adi. The Asian Voyage: In the Wake of the Admiral. TIME magazine Aug 20, 2001.

- Ivory, James. The White Countess. Movie, 2006.

- Janklowicz-Mann, Dana and Mann, Amir. Shanghai Ghetto. Rebel Child Productions 2002, New Vudeo Group, Inc. 2004

- Kranzler, Dr. David. Japanese, Nazis, and Jews. Yeshiva University Press 1976.

- Kuo, Ping Chia. "Caleb Cushing and the Treaty of Wanghia, 1844." The Journal of Modern History 5, no. 1 (1933).

- Kaufmann, Fritz. Transcript of his talk at the N.Y. Tiffin Club, Dec. 2, 1963. The Jews in Shanghai in World War Two, Memories of a Meeting

of the Directors of the Jewish Community. Bulletin 7i3/1986 of the Leo Baeck Institute.
- Kutcher, Norman. "China's Palace of Memory," The Wilson Quarterly (Winter 2003).
- Lane, Charles. Shanghaied. Green Bag, 2004.
- Latourette, Kenneth Scott. A History of Christian Missions in China: Gorgias Press 2009.
- Lethbridge, H. J. All About Shanghai, A Standard Guidebook. Shanghai: University Press, 1934-5 and Hong Kong: Oxford University Press, 1983
- Lin Yutang. Famous Chinese Short Stories. The Pocket Library, 1954. Lin Zexu: Letter to Queen Victoria.: Suyu Teng and John Fairbank, China's Response to the West, (Cambridge MA: Harvard University Press, 1954), repr. in Mark A. Kishlansky, ed., Sources of World History, Volume II, (New York: HarperCollins College Publishers, 1995), pp. 266-69
- M'Ghee, Robert James Leslie. (1862). How we got to Pekin: A Narrative of the Campaign in China of 1860. London: Richard Bentley
- Meier, Erika Resek. Autobiography, unpublished
- Meier, Ryan. Biography of his Grandmother Erika Resek Meier, unpublished
- Naquin, Susan. [2000] (2000). Peking: Temples and City Life, 1400-1900. University of California Press. ISBN 0-520-21991-0
- Novitch Miriam,.Le génocide des Tziganes sous le régime nazi (Genocide of Gypsies by the Nazi Regime), Paris, AMIF, 1968.: ZYKLON GAS: Proester, Emil; Vraždeni čs. cikanu v Buchenwaldu (The murder of Czech Gypsies in Buchenwald). Document No. UV CSPB K-135 on deposit in the Archives of the Museum of the Fighters Against Nazism, Prague. 1940.
- Pan Guang, Ph.D. Jews in China: Legends, History and New Perspectives with Wang Jian, Shanghai Jews since 1840, Beijing, 2002 Shanghai as a Haven for Holocaust Victims Discussion Paper

- Potter, John Stauffer, Jr. The Treasure Diver's Guide, Florida Classics. My First Nine Lives, 2013
- Power, Desmond. Little Foreign Devil. Hignell Printing Ltd., Manitoba, Canada, 1996
- Preston, Diana. The Boxer Rebellion. New York: Berkley Books, 1999
- Pringle, Henry F. Bridge House Survivor. Earnshaw Books. 2010
- Purcell, Victor, The Boxer Uprising. NewYork: Cambridge University Press 1963.
- Ristaino, Marcia Reynders. Port of Last Resort. Stanford University Press 2001.
- See, Lisa. Snow Flower and the Secret : Bloomsbury Publishing Co., 2005
- Spence, Jonathan D. In Search of Modern China. New York: Norton, 1990.
- Swisher, Earl, ed. China's Management of the American Barbarians; a Study of Sino-American Relations, 1841–1861, with Documents. New Haven, CT: Published for the Far Eastern Association by Far Eastern Publications, Yale University, 1953.
- Têng Ssu-yü. Chang Hsi and the Treaty of Nanking, 1842. Chicago: University of Chicago Press, 1944.
  "The Church in China". Catholic Encyclopedia. New York: Robert Appleton Co. 1913.
- Thompson, Larry Clinton. William Scott Ament and the Boxer Rebellion: Heroism, Hubris, and the Ideal Missionary. Jefferson, NC: McFarland, 2009.
- Tokayer, Marvin and Swartz, Mary, The Fugu Plan, The Untold Story of the Japanese and Jews during World War II. Weatherhill, 1996.
- Vámos, Dr. Péter."Home Afar": The Life of Central European Jewish Refugees in Shanghai During World War II. 2001.
- Van Gulik, Robert. The Chinese Bell Murders. University of Chicago Press 1977.

- Viviano, Frank. China's Great Armada, National Geographic.
- Wagenstein, Angel. Farewell Shanghai. Other Press 2007.
- Walsh, Billie K. The German Military Mission in China, 1928-38, The Journal of Modern History, Vol. 46. The University of Chicago Press 1974).
- White, Theodore H. and Jacoby, Annalee. Thunder Out Of China. William Sloane Assoc. Inc. 1946..
- Wood, R. Derek. 'The Treaty of Nanking: Form and the Foreign Office, 1842-1843', Journal of Imperial and Commonwealth History (London) 24 (May 1996).
- Yen-p'ing Hao, Assoc. Prof of history, U of Tennessee, Knoxville, TN: "New Class in China's Treaty Ports: The Rise of the Comprador-Merchants. The Business History Review, 1970.
- Zhufeng Luo, Chu-feng Lo, Luo Zhufeng. Religion Under Socialism in China, 1991.